AND WE
CAME
OUTSIDE
AND
SAW THE
STARS
AGAIN

AND WE CAME OUTSIDE AND SAW THE STARS AGAIN

Edited by
Ilan Stavans

Writers from Around the World
on the COVID-19 Pandemic

RESTLESS BOOKS

BROOKLYN, NEW YORK

First Restless Books paperback edition August 2020
Paperback ISBN: 9781632063021
eBook ISBN: 9781632063014

Library of Congress Control Number: 2020940658

Cover design by Jonathan Yamakami
Set in Garibaldi by Tetragon, London

Portions of this book appeared previously in other publications. See
the Acknowledgments section for details.

3 5 7 9 10 8 6 4 2

Restless Books, Inc.
232 3rd Street, Suite A101
Brooklyn, NY 11215

www.restlessbooks.org
publisher@restlessbooks.org

Printed in Canada

"To show you how the world begins again:
One word at a time.
One woman to another."

EAVAN BOLAND,
"ODE TO GRACE MURRAY HOPPER" (2001)

Contents

PART II: THE PATH TO PARADISE BEGINS IN HELL

Introduction

UNPRECEDENTED was the ubiquitous term first used to describe the COVID-19 pandemic that swept the world in 2020, as if the event were unlike any other. The truth is that it has been rather routine in its procedure, part of the eternal cycles of nature. Even in the Bible, similar disasters—earthquakes, deluges, famines, plagues of insects, pestilence of livestock, boils, thunderstorms of hail and fire—are recurrent visitors in the theater of human affairs. Which doesn't mean, of course, that new calamities such as this one aren't extraordinary.

It isn't surprising that the official approach to the pandemic was initially forensic, with an insistence on numbers: how many deaths and infections per day in a given hospital of a given city in a given country, how long a possible vaccine could take to bring us all out of purgatory, and so on, as if suffering could be quantified, ignoring that each and every person lost was unique and irreplaceable. The *Talmud* says that death is a kind of sleep and that one person's sleep is unknowable to others.

Although the misfortune arrived at a time when the essential tenets of globalism were being questioned—tariffs imposed, borders closed, immigrants seen with suspicion—the pandemic was planetary, hitting wherever people did what people do. It preyed with distinct fury on the poor and vulnerable, as natural catastrophes always do, especially in countries ruled by tyrants responding with disdain and hubris.

Inevitably, the lockdown also forced a new method to everything everywhere. The sound of the kitchen clock suddenly felt new, the warmth of a handshake, the taste of fresh soup. As an antidote to numbers, it was once again left to writers to notice those changes, to chronicle them by interweaving words. That's what literature does well: it champions nuance while resisting the easy tricks of generalization. This international anthology includes over fifty of those writers representing thirty-five countries and arriving in about a dozen languages. Cumulatively, their accounts are proof of the degree to which COVID-19 brought about the collapse of a hierarchy of principles we had all embraced until then. Call it the end of an era.

Shenaz Patel, from Mauritius, for instance, realizes that "suddenly, like an octopus disturbed in its sleep, everything kept hidden under the placid surface latched onto us with its many arms and spit its ink into our faces." She adds: "We are faced with a true 'civil war' of speech, echoing through radios and social media, between those who respect the lockdown and those who don't; those who understand and the '*cocovids*,' the empty heads who go out anyway; between the 'true patriots' and the selfish few who knowingly put others in danger." Patel continues: "Trying to disguise the fact that the lockdown will be experienced differently by all, depending on whether one lives in a spacious house with a garden and pool, or with a family of six in a ramshackle shack and a bank account that doesn't need a pandemic to see its curve flatten. Deaf to the screaming paradox that we create by demanding that those whom our neoliberalist policies have exploited and crushed for years help us save our own skin."

For Maxim Osipov, from Tarusa, Russia, the concern over the elderly masks other fears. He writes of a man who began telling anyone who would listen that he was worried about his mother. "What else would he be worried about? No sense in thinking of the children (they weren't vulnerable), his wife was eleven years younger than him, and, needless to say, he wasn't concerned about himself. Do the math: what were the chances of him croaking? One percent, maybe one point five. A real man doesn't lose his head over trifles. *If I die in a combat zone, box me up and ship me home* . . . Oh, speaking of, he'd prefer to be cremated—everyone clear on that? People had always told him he had a pleasant voice, and now he was growing convinced of it. He kept singing and singing—vigorous, patriotic songs. He'd have loved to sing democratic ones, but there just weren't any. A nervous reaction? Maybe. . . . But it was his mother he was worried about, not himself."

The need to recalibrate, to use the pandemic as a new beginning, or at least to try to, is clear to Francine Prose, from New York. "I always hope that crises will make me more compassionate and less irritable," she posits, "but it's rarely the case. I suppose it would help if I stopped watching the evening news. It can't be healthy to yell at the TV for the entire White House press conference. And how can the newscasters keep telling us that 'We're all in this together,' when, in so many important ways, we have never been more alone?"

Jhumpa Lahiri, in a letter to Italy, a country—and its language—she has adopted as her own, feels heartbroken by what she sees in the news. Arshia Sattar, from India, believes that her generation "inherited every capacity—wealth, education, potential solidarity—to make the world a better and brighter place. But now we are faced with dysfunctional political and economic systems, a planet in deep distress, the disappearance of plant and animal species, perhaps the death of life as we know it." Gazing at her old books in her mother's house, she remarks, "The young woman who stands beside me at the bookcase remains eternally poised on the cusp of a radiant tomorrow, but thirty-five years later, I stand on the verge of crippling despair. The books that she read as paranoid dystopias (Orwell, Kafka, Huxley, Zamyatin), have become the gross and brutal reality of my time."

In a misfortune that knows no boundaries, it ultimately comes down to the fear of death. That's what moves Mario Vargas Llosa, the Peruvian Nobel Laureate, who writes from Spain: "What will never pass is our fear of death, of the afterlife, which is at the heart of a collective dread like the fear of the plague. . . . It is difficult for us to accept that all of life's beauty, all the adventures life has to offer, belong ultimately to death, and that at any moment it may all come to an end. It's difficult to acknowledge, too, that if death did not exist, life would be infinitely boring, without adventure or mystery, a cacophonous repetition of the most banal and unpleasant experiences ad nauseam. It's thanks to death that we have love, desire, fantasy, art, science, books, and culture—all the things that make life unpredictable, exciting, and bearable. Reason explains all this, but the turmoil that lies within us stops us from accepting it. Fear of the plague is, quite simply, fear of death, which accompanies us through our lives like a shadow."

Majed Abusalama, from Palestine, looks back at the intifada imposed by Israel as a forced quarantine. Rivka Galchen, writing from New York, follows a doctor through his daily routine of confronting the inevitable. Jon Lee Anderson, writing from West Dorset, England, is concerned about the difference between the haves and have-nots: "I have Brazilian friends who are self-isolating despite their absurd, irresponsible president Bolsonaro, who is actively encouraging them to do the opposite, for his own inexplicable reasons, and against the advice of his own health minister. Brazilians, then, must contend with a double measure of foreboding—not only of the pandemic itself, which is still just beginning to spread in that country, but for the day of reckoning they must face with the imbecile they chose to lead them. Clearly, they must get rid of him, sooner rather than later—one way or another. It's a very analogous predicament to that faced by Americans with Trump, who happens to be Bolsonaro's role model."

Looking to the future, Juan Villoro, from Mexico, prophesizes that the wreckage caused by COVID-19 will be turned into art, despite its relegation to the bottom of the priority list: "Churchill claimed that Britain won the war because they decided not to close theaters. A people that puts on *Hamlet* during the bombardments is one that cannot be defeated. . . . What is the point of emerging from lockdown into countries with no theaters, bookstores, or concert venues? Artists do not seem to be a priority in times of emergency. Support is taken away from them, overlooking the fact that people need aesthetic gratification. In times devoid of greatness, nobody is taking to the parliamentary rostrum with Churchill's spirit, or even his rhetoric." Villoro continues: "And yet imagination is what is getting us through the crisis. To escape mental imprisonment, some share memes, GIFs, or tweets, while others recite poems, dress up, sing, talk on the phone or skype, dream, listen to the dreams of others. Thousands of artists have given away their plays, films, books, and concerts online. The species persists through forms of representation of reality (eliminated from public budgets as the most expendable part of reality)."

Andrés Neuman, writing from Spain, reconfigures the sprawling images of Genesis through the lens of COVID-19. For Wu Ming-Yi, from Taiwan, the quarantine is an occasion to reflect on the passion a father and daughter share for raising monk crabs. And Giacomo Sartori, an Italian novelist and soil scientist in Paris, is thankful for the chance to spend more time with animals: "If there aren't any pretty girls there are loads of animals to make up for them, and I have an instinctive bond with animals. They don't bother me, they amaze me and they move me. Outside the window of my study, it looks like an aviary; I've never seen such a coming and going of birds. A multitude of cats have appeared on the streets, and the rats dart between your legs, and on the canal not far from home, a pair of swans have built their enormous nest right beside the street, and they take turns sitting on it. The fish in the canal are jumping like dolphins, so pleased that nobody's giving them a hard time."

Conversely, Carlos Fonseca from Costa Rica reflects on how the lockdown reveals the ways in which we had already been walling ourselves off: "The paradox behind this pandemic is that it has made evident the world in which we were already living: a world of isolation, of frontiers and walls, a world where the elderly are secluded and forgotten, a xenophobic world, where death is something invisible that happens always behind closed doors and against which we prove incapable of mourning. A world that mixes the possibilities of technological globalization—Zoom, Skype, FaceTime—with the tightening of borders and the rise of contemporary nationalisms."

These are only a few examples of the wealth of observation and witness contained within *And We Came Outside and Saw the Stars Again*. Inspired by the last line of Dante's *Inferno*, in which the poet and Virgil emerge from their journey through hell to once again view the beauty of the heavens, our invitation to notice went out. The response was overwhelming: from almost every corner of Earth, dispatches poured in. But there were also regrets. And endorsements of silence as the best possible response. One writer said he had "utterly freaked out," to the point of being unsure he could even come up with anything other than the banal. Another put it more bluntly, arguing that only numbness was suitable to the circumstances. Two very close members of her immediate family had just been carried away by the virus, the first two weeks before (no funeral, no *shiva*) and the nearest and dearest one of all had died at eleven o'clock that morning in the ER. "Beyond this, I have nothing to say."

A handful responded with the opposite of silence. "I'm eager to be part of the symphony of voices. Yet my piece should be about anything but the disaster," one replied. "That's why I write: to escape. I couldn't contribute with a grim, desperate essay. That would be too easy. I want to allow readers to see other things, to reach out. Isn't that what the stars are about? We look at them as alternative universes." Others, among them Chris Abani, Sayed Kashua, and Matthew Zapruder, asked to participate with a text they had already written. "I'm not sure it will fit in," another writer stated, "but if I had to write about this now, I would do it exactly as I did when I wrote my poem." And Hubert Haddad, a French-Tunisian poet writing from Paris, collected and reassembled a few months' worth of "false starts, drafts, approximations, broken-off openings." The result, he writes, "might well serve as the ghostly diary of a novelist on the lookout, suspended in his fictive desire." Veering into science fiction, "The Hieroglyphs of COVID-19" grapples with how to make art about a catastrophe unfolding in real time: "I've aspired with all my being to freedom. It's only a matter of getting past an unlikely impasse. Perpetual seclusion can only be a figment of the imagination. But what is the imagination if not a blind specter standing in for some original flaw in the living world, the universe?"

Translators, naturally, are the conduits here. Twenty-three of them have made these ruminations at home in English. It goes without saying that their renditions were made under adverse conditions as well.

Other lines from the *Divine Comedy* serve as the titles of the five parts into which the fifty-two contributions are divided, albeit loosely: Part I, "A Mighty Flame Follows a Tiny Spark," focuses on the eruption of the plague; Part II, "The Path to Paradise Begins in Hell," on the need for a road map; Part III, "I'm Not Alone in Misery," on empathy; Part IV, "Faith Is the Substance of Things Hoped for," on hope; and Part V, "Love Insists the Loved Loves Back," is the door through which we might come outside again and see the stars.

The anthology is dedicated to three women who fell victim to COVID-19, directly or otherwise: in her New York apartment, Madeline Kripke kept 20,000 books, the majority of them dictionaries from as early as the sixteenth century; Eavan Boland, a magnificent poet who died in Ireland, was finishing her semester with her Stanford students online; and Frederika Randall, a superb translator, completed both a translation for this anthology as well as her own contribution, "Augury," a week before succumbing to a prior illness.

What makes all these appreciations unprecedented, I suppose, is their capacity to make tragedy feel new again while also placing it in context, as if saying that other disasters will come and go yet this one—yes, this calamity!—is ours and these considerations are a record of how we lived through it.

ILAN STAVANS
AMHERST, JUNE 19, 2020

Lo duca e io per quel cammino ascoso
    intrammo a ritornar nel chiaro mondo;
    e sanza cura aver d'alcun riposo,
salimmo sù, el primo e io secondo,
    tanto ch'i' vidi de le cose belle
    che porta 'l ciel, per un pertugio tondo.
E quindi uscimmo a riveder le stelle.

DANTE, INFERNO (1320)

The Guide and I into that hidden road
    Now entered, to return to the bright world;
    And without care of having any rest
We mounted up, he first and I the second,
    Till I beheld through a round aperture
    Some of the beauteous things that Heaven doth bear;
Thence we came forth to rebehold the stars.

TRANS. HENRY WADSWORTH LONGFELLOW (1867)

AND WE
CAME
OUTSIDE
AND
SAW THE
STARS
AGAIN

PART I

A Mighty Flame Follows a Tiny Spark

Our Lives as Birds

SHENAZ PATEL

Translated from the French by Lisa Ducasse

Journalist and writer Shenaz Patel (Beau Bassin-Rose Hill, Mauritius, 1966) is the author of novels, plays, short stories, and children's books in French and Mauritian Creole. She was awarded the Grand Literary Prize of the Indian and Pacific Ocean (Paris) in 2007 for Le silence des Chagos, published as Silence of the Chagos by Restless Books in 2019. Patel was an International Writing Program Honorary Fellow at the University of Iowa in 2016 and a fellow at the W. E. B. Du Bois Research Institute at the Hutchins Center at Harvard University in 2018.

ISLANDS BELIEVE they are blessed by the gods. There lies their vanity.

On March 15, while Italy was entering its second week of lockdown, while France was beginning its first, while the death count for COVID-19 was rising in Iran and elsewhere, the island of Mauritius kept baiting tourists, seducing them with half-priced plane tickets, offering the privilege to buy three bottles of whiskey at the duty-free store upon arrival instead of the customarily approved two. . . . No, coronavirus wasn't coming for us. It was merely something worrying the rest of the world, far away, something we could even—who knows—profit from, crowned as we are with sun and sea. Despite being swept by all the winds of tourism, we were floating above all this, on the proud wings of the *paille-en-queue*, the beautiful endemic bird adorning the flanks of our national airline's planes.

Then the *paille-en-queue*, out of the blue, had its wings clipped.

The dumbfounded look of our prime minister as he reported the island's first three registered cases of COVID-19 on March 18 signaled the beginning of a nosedive. Lockdown was instigated two days later, followed by a round-the-clock curfew, and, in a flash, the closing of all supermarkets, bakeries, and other food-related facilities.

The proud island was confronted, with the violence of a slap in the face—one of those faces no one is allowed to touch anymore—to the meaning of its own name: island, from the Latin *insula*, *insulae*, from which also springs the word *isolation*.

How to describe an isolated island in the midst of a world closing in on itself like a carnivorous plant?

Imagine a sky emptied of all planes. An ocean on which countless cruise ships aimlessly carry about the new *boat-people*, those whose money no longer guarantees them hospitality in every port. Four-star hotels turned into quarantine centers. Stray dogs have taken possession of the few public beaches spared by the waves of touristic development that have overtaken the island's shores—that is, those stray dogs that haven't yet been picked up by the pound, where hundreds have died from going unfed through the lockdown. Cows munch on seaweed brought to shore by the sea, a sea into which chill-wary Mauritians would have liked to jump one last time before the advent of our southern winter.

An island locked in on itself like a closed fist.

Suddenly, like an octopus disturbed in its sleep, everything kept hidden under the placid surface latched onto us with its many arms and spit its ink into our faces. We are faced with a true "civil war" of speech, echoing through radios and social media, between those who respect the lockdown and those who don't; those who understand and the "*cocov-ids*," the empty heads who go out anyway; between the "true patriots" and the selfish few who knowingly put others in danger. Trying to disguise the fact that the lockdown will be experienced differently by all, depending on whether one lives in a spacious house with a garden and pool, or with a family of six in a ramshackle shack and a bank account that doesn't need a pandemic to see its curve flatten. Deaf to the screaming paradox that we create by demanding that those whom our neoliberalist policies have exploited and crushed for years help us save our own skin.

To die is one thing—it's not like we have much say in the matter. But to die alone, without the comfort of a familiar hand to soothe away the pain, is simply unimaginable. Everything we'd learned and interiorized about human contact and its physical expression has been turned inside out like a dirty glove one throws in the trash. Now, to even get close to another human makes potential criminals out of all of us.

So, to fill the time, the self-imposed stillness and latent anxiety, to convince ourselves that we are capable of transcending this kind of social distancing, which is, after all, merely physical, we exhibit our insides on the Web. Never have we seen so much of other people's interiors—be it their kitchen or their living room, their childhood pictures, their fear or their bitterness, all coated in humor and half-believed reassurances. We rejoice over examples of triggered solidarity. But solidarity is often the currency of those whose only wealth is that of the heart. Meanwhile, in the (finally) reopened supermarkets, the price of a tin of sardines in oil now makes it akin to some kind of local caviar, while masks and other basic protection devices are sold at criminally inflated prices.

While some despair of the precariousness of their situation, others are keen to broadcast their ability to turn the lockdown into an art. To serenely explore the depths of their own being. To reinvent their family life. To prepare healthy meals. To be sensitive to the return of the birds.

Where do birds go in a cyclone, when the winds behead the trees and wrench their bodies from the earth?

Closed in so the birds can be free. Locked down so the earth can breathe. Are we then sentenced to the unbearable Manichaeism of a world forever condemned to be either red or green?

The dodo island doubts. Between those who claim that the emblematic bird disappeared because it was too heavy (or too stupid) to fly, and those who blame its extinction on the gluttony of its exterminators, we continue to live out our lives as birds. Small, fragile, stubborn, hopeful, nest-weaving, breeze-seeking, soaring in bright and fleeting swarms.

MAURITIUS
APRIL 9, 2020

Letter to Italy

JHUMPA LAHIRI

Translated from the Italian by Alta L. Price

Jhumpa Lahiri (London, United Kingdom, 1967) received the Pulitzer Prize in 2000 for Interpreter of Maladies, *her debut story collection. She is also the author of* The Namesake (2003), Unaccustomed Earth (2008) *and* The Lowland (2013), *a finalist for both the Man Booker prize and the National Book Award for fiction. She has written three books in Italian, including* In altre parole (2015) *and the novel* Dove mi trovo (2018). *Editor of* The Penguin Book of Italian Short Stories (2019), *she divides her time between Rome and Princeton.* Il quaderno di Nerina, *her first collection of poems in Italian, will be published in 2021, as will* Whereabouts, *the English version of* Dove mi trovo, *translated by the author.*

DEAR ITALY, yesterday I should have landed in Rome to reunite with my son, who goes to school there. I should have returned home and headed out to the piazza to shop for food. I would have undoubtedly run into a few neighbors and friends on the streets. I'd have said hello, and they'd have said, "welcome back."

It's just that my son, along with millions of kids throughout Italy and elsewhere, doesn't go to school anymore. A few days ago he unexpectedly and urgently returned to America, and shortly thereafter Trump banned travel from Europe, a scornful and already pointless gesture. On the one hand I'm truly relieved my son is back, and that both my children are under the same roof during this time of deep uncertainty. And yet not returning to Rome this morning, not setting out for the market, even at the height of this crisis, pains me. It's the same distress a daughter would feel at not being able to run to her gravely ill parent and lend a hand, because she feels compelled to, because she can do no less.

For a week now I've done nothing but follow the news in Italy and reach out to Italian friends, both in Italy and in the United States. My friends in Italy tell me things aren't looking too good. They send me photos of empty streets all shuttered up. They tell me that the market stalls in Piazza San Cosimato have thinned out, and that supermarkets have signs asking people to stay a meter away from one another. I can picture all of this, more or less. They tell me they're afraid, that they're stunned, that the situation is brutally serious. And up until a few days ago, when I was still planning to board that plane, many told me, "Jhumpa, don't come."

I absorb their fear and feel equally stunned. At the same time, I absorb their courage, their patience, and their determination to battle and defeat this invisible enemy. Amid it all I laugh like mad, right along with them, when they share the hilarious memes spreading on social media. This is why Italy alone—which has already taught me so much—is now showing me how to face the coronavirus: with chin up, discipline, a touch of irony, and a healthy dose of optimism. And I'm gladly infected by their attitude.

Here in America alarmism is on the rise and friends are telling me: thank god your son got out! They have a point, sure—it's better the family can be together in times like this, otherwise things would have been even harder. And yet I'm nettled by such remarks.

Italy remains my point of arrival. For me, Italy is still a balm. A week ago, when I advised my son to come back, I told him Italy needs fewer people out and about right now, that we need to stand back and give the country the time and space it needs to recover. What I don't understand is the attitude some people are displaying toward Italy now that it's on lockdown, struck by an unprecedented crisis. It fills many with fear, even dread. Incomprehensibly, compassion is scarce—the US president expresses none whatsoever. I'm ashamed of it.

I still feel protected by Italy—even an Italy on its knees, bowed by such utter isolation. It's precisely now that I feel Italy standing by my side, sharing—despite the ocean between us, despite Trump's travel ban—its strength and dignity. It continues sharing its affection and advice, guiding and protecting me and my family. Yesterday, for example, my publisher, a gentleman from Milan who loves to stroll his city's streets but is now cooped up at home, wrote me a serene email reassuring me that my next book would be released there in a few months. I had dropped him a line just to say, "I'm thinking of you all," hoping to offer some solace. And yet he was the one who, with remarkable elegance and composure, replied "this, too, shall pass."

And so, in my own world, and in its own way, the coronavirus has already healed a wound—or rather, cured a condition that has afflicted me for five years now: the condition of feeling sadly separated, exiled from Italy when I'm away, always eager to return. Even a few days ago when, at the very last minute, I gave up on the idea of returning to Rome for the time being, I cried for some time. But today, here in Princeton, where I'm following live news reports as if I were in my living room in Rome, I finally realize that there is no distance between me and Italy. And I'm astonished by the fact that Italy—even in such a critical, compromised state—is nevertheless right here with me, lending a hand. The closure of Italy's borders makes those outside of them feel somehow protected, but they aren't. Over the last few days we've all inevitably become Italian, and what is happening there is starting to happen everywhere. The coronavirus temporarily separating us has demolished all borders, destroyed all distance. Today will be the last day of class for my daughter, who goes to school in America. I'm relieved; according to my friends in Italy, they should have canceled in-person classes even earlier. Every morning I call friends in Italy so we can face the new day together. I follow their advice, and listen to them. When they say "don't come," I understand, and consciously keep my distance. Soon, I hope, I'll return to Rome and find a city back on its feet, a country transformed, forever marked.

Dear Italians, although I'm not on my way there today to lend a hand, please know that it's not because I want to protect myself from you, but to protect you from me. I'll never be afraid to stand by your side—only to fall out of touch with you.

I send, from afar, my deepest solidarity and affection. With these words, in the language we now share, I send you my heartfelt thanks for the gift of perspective you continue giving: an example of what to do, how to be, and how to get through this.

Together.

PRINCETON, NJ
MARCH 17, 2020

12

A Return to the Middle Ages?

MARIO VARGAS LLOSA

Translated from the Spanish by Samuel Rutter

Peruvian writer, politician, journalist, and essayist Mario Vargas Llosa (Arequipa, Peru, 1936), is part of the generation of Latin American writers known as "El Boom" that achieved international attention in the sixties. He received the Nobel Prize in Literature in 2010 "for his cartography of structures of power and his trenchant images of the individual's resistance, revolt, and defeat." His novels, translated into numerous languages and adapted into film, TV, theater, and radio, include The Time of the Hero *(1963)*, Aunt Julia and the Scriptwriter *(1977)*, The War of the End of the World *(1981)*, The Feast of the Goat *(2000)*, and* The Bad Girl *(2006)*. He writes a regular column in Spain's* El País.

THE CORONAVIRUS is beginning to wreak havoc upon Spain. Or, more precisely, the fear caused by this virus that originated in China now fills the pages of every newspaper and is the subject of every bulletin on TV and the radio. Schools and colleges are closing, along with libraries and theaters. The traditional Falles festivities in Valencia have been postponed, legislative assemblies have simply stopped meeting, and sporting events are taking place without spectators. Despite the fact that suppliers insist there will be enough merchandise, the shelves in supermarkets are half-empty, indicating that people are stockpiling essentials for what they understand will be a long lockdown. Of course, in private conversation, it's all we can talk about.

All of this, in practical terms, seems quite overblown, but there's nothing to be done: Spain is afraid, and the governments (of the nation and the autonomous regions) are facing up to this terrifying illness with ever-stricter measures that, in general, the Spanish people support. In fact, many are demanding stricter and broader measures. Thankfully, official statistics provide a number of positive indications. In the period up to March 11, there have been only forty-seven deaths caused by the pandemic, and the regular flu is in fact much deadlier than coronavirus, because it causes at least six hundred deaths a year. The number of people who recover from coronavirus is much higher than those who die from it, and Spain has one of the best health systems in the world—far better than the average in Europe. The work being done by doctors and health-care workers is efficient and up to the scale of the task, etc.

But statistics have never been able to calm a society overwhelmed with panic, and the present situation is no exception. In today's civilized times, the Middle Ages have returned, meaning that while some things may have changed, many others have not, like the fear of the plague. Literature also experiences an inevitable renaissance in these times of collective fear: when we cannot understand what is happening around us, as a society we turn to books to see if they offer any answers. Albert Camus' worst novel, *The*

Plague, has been suddenly reborn. In Spain and France alike, it has been republished in new editions, turning a mediocre book into a bestseller.

No one seems to realize that this wouldn't be happening all around the world if the People's Republic of China were a free and democratic country and not a dictatorship. At least one eminent doctor, and perhaps several, detected this virus with plenty of forewarning, and instead of taking the corresponding measures, the Chinese government tried to cover it up, silencing those voices of reason in order to stop the word getting out, the way all dictatorships do. Just like Chernobyl, a lot of time was lost before the search for a remedy began. The existence of this plague was acknowledged only once it had already spread far and wide. It's a good thing that this is happening now, so that the whole world realizes that true progress can never be made without freedom. Will the fools who still believe that China—a free market in a political dictatorship—is a feasible model for the third world, finally wake up to this fact? The coronavirus ought to open their eyes to it.

Throughout history, the plague has been one of humanity's worst nightmares, and this was especially so in the Middle Ages. It drove our oldest ancestors mad with despair. Locked away behind the sturdy walls they built for their cities, encircled by moats filled with poisoned water and drawbridges, they weren't so afraid of visible enemies they could fight off on equal footing, facing up to them with swords, spears, and daggers. But the plague wasn't human, it was the work of the devil, a punishment from God visited upon the masses and which struck down the innocent along with the sinners. There was nothing they could do to fight it, except pray and repent for the sins they had committed. Almighty death was a constant presence, and after that came the eternal flames of Hell. Ignorance reigned and there were cities that tried to quell the infernal plague by offering human sacrifices of witches, infidels, unrepentant sinners, and agitators. At the time when Flaubert traveled to Egypt, he was still able to see lepers wandering the streets who rang bells to warn people to get out of the way as they passed, lest they see (or become infected by) their pustular sores.

15

But plagues almost never appear in chivalric romances, which are a different, more positive product of the Middle Ages. Those novels are filled with extraordinary physical feats, like Tirant lo Blanc defeating massive armies all on his own. But the enemies of a knight errant are human beings, not devils, and devils are what medieval man feared most, the kind hidden in the heart of epidemics that kill the guilty and the innocent indiscriminately.

This historical fear hasn't quite disappeared today, despite all the advances of civilization. Everybody knows that just like with AIDS or Ebola, coronavirus will be a passing pandemic, that scientists from the most advanced nations will soon discover a vaccine to defend us against it and that all this will come to an end. With time, the coronavirus will be no more than an old news story that people barely remember.

What will never pass is our fear of death, of the afterlife, which is at the heart of a collective dread like the fear of the plague. Religion can soothe this fear, but never fully banish it. There's a disquiet deep inside all believers that sometimes flares up and turns into panic, the fear of not knowing what will be there once we cross the threshold of life into the great beyond. Is it total oblivion, forever? Or, like religion tells us, is there a mythical divide between heaven for the good and hell for the bad, with our final destination decided by a whimsical god? Perhaps there is a different kind of afterlife altogether, one that remains undiscovered by philosophers, theologists, and scientists? The plague brings these questions to the fore, which in normal times are confined to the depths of the human psyche, making them essential to the present moment. Mankind must respond to them and acknowledge the fleeting nature of existence. It is difficult for us to accept that all of life's beauty, all the adventures life has to offer, belong ultimately to death, and that at any moment it may all come to an end. It's difficult to acknowledge, too, that if death did not exist, life would be infinitely boring, without adventure or mystery, a cacophonous repetition of the most banal and unpleasant experiences ad nauseam. It's thanks to death that we have love, desire, fantasy, art, science, books, and culture—all the things that make life unpredictable, exciting, and bearable. Reason explains all this, but the turmoil that lies within us stops us from accepting it. Fear of the plague is, quite simply, fear of death, which accompanies us through our lives like a shadow.

MADRID
MARCH 15, 2020

Pandemania

DANIEL HALPERN

Daniel Halpern (Syracuse, New York, 1945) is the founder and longtime editor of the influential literary magazine Antaeus. Halpern is the president and publisher of Ecco, an imprint of HarperCollins Publishers. The author of many books of poetry, including Something Shining: Poems (1999), Foreign Neon (1991), Tango (1987), and Traveling on Credit (1972), his honors include fellowships from the Guggenheim Foundation and the National Endowment for the Arts. He also received the Maxwell Perkins Award. He has taught at Columbia, Princeton, and The New School. Halpern lives in New York City.

There are fewer introductions
In plague years,
Hands held back, jocularity
No longer bellicose,
Even among men.
Breathing's generally wary,
Labored, as they say, when
The end is at hand.
But this is the everyday intake
Of the imperceptible life force,
Willed now, slow—
Well, just cautious
In inhabited air.
As for ongoing dialogue,
No longer an exuberant plosive
To make a point,
But a new squirreling of air space,
A new sense of boundary.
Genghis Khan said the hand
Is the first thing one man gives
To another. Not in this war.
A gesture of limited distance
Now suffices, a nod,
A minor smile or a hand
Slightly raised,
Not in search of its counterpart,
Just a warning within
The acknowledgment to stand back.
Each beautiful stranger a barbarian
Breathing on the other side of the gate.

MARCH, 2013

The Hieroglyphs of COVID-19; or Lockdown

HUBERT HADDAD

Translated from the French by Jeffrey Zuckerman

Hubert Haddad (Tunis, Tunisia, 1947) is a French prize-winning poet, playwright, and writer. Four of his novels have been translated into English: Palestine *(2014), which won the Prix des cinq continents de la Francophonie;* Opium Poppy *(2015);* Rochester Knockings: A Novel of the Fox Sisters *(2015); and* Desirable Body *(2018). A pioneer of creative writing workshops since the 1970s, he taught in high schools, universities, prisons, and community centers. Since 2016 he has been chief editor of the literary magazine* Apulée, *which gathers French-speaking authors from all over the world as well international authors and poets. His latest novel published in French is* Un monstre et un chaos *(2019).*

The decisive moment in human evolution is perpetual. That is why the *revolutionary spiritual movements* that declare all former things worthless are in the right, for nothing has yet happened.

FRANZ KAFKA,
THE BLUE OCTAVO NOTEBOOKS
TRANSLATED BY ERNST KAISER AND EITHNE WILKINS

WHEN THE FOREIGN BODY slips in and indiscriminately, even-handedly puts each one of us to the test, it's not odd at all to preemptively feel some sort of survivor's guilt. So violently confronted with this mystery of what is close and what is far, now we can assess our shred of reality in light of the leaden, all-too-palpable presence of the outside world incomprehensibly materializing.

Imagine a novelist living in Paris, a veritable connoisseur of the railroads, usually burdened with a thousand obligations, meetings, workshops, signings across France and abroad, and keen to finally pick up his pen again, to get back to his work in reciprocal solitude. On January 8, on yet another train to a bookstore event, it was with some inattention that he read a brief article buried deep in a recent issue of a French newspaper:

"Since December 12, nearly 60 people in Wuhan, central China, have been infected by a mysterious virus. As this number continues to rise, local authorities and virology experts are still working to identify the origins of this illness. . . ."

Two months later, in early March, headed to Antwerp and then Nantes to talk about the Lodz ghetto, the topic of his latest novel, *A Monster and a Chaos*, the same author, now fully aware of the virus's pandemic nature, is only vaguely astonished by the close-knit, good-natured friendliness unperturbed by even the occasional mask. An unprecedented event of

21

global scope that might be unfettered by the fluctuating cause-and-effect of history is fundamentally unthinkable. A war, even a world war, would still be imaginable. The Chernobyl and Fukushima disasters are direct results of human industry, a hellish enterprise undone by its own mechanisms. But suddenly, in the middle of March 2020, in our old Europe, entropy overflows and muddles all prospects. A good half of humanity will soon be hemmed in by lockdown. Among these billions of his ilk, sent to a common fate, the novelist of which we speak finds himself sentenced overnight to total solitude in his abode in the heights of Ménilmontant. Paris, stunned and dazed, is empty. A few days earlier, a canny subsection of Paris had swiftly undertaken a lavish exodus of sorts. Never before had this city, even while panic's shocks and aftershocks radiated across media and social networks, seemed so tranquil.

Might it not finally be time to write? All meetings have been canceled. It's too perfect an opportunity: entire weeks, months no doubt, a long shorefront of time stretches out invitingly as far as the eye can see. But each morning, lying in wait for words after a dream-wracked night, nothing really comes. Hazy starts, incoherent lines, stillborn snippets of fiction, rudiments of description, muffled echoes and slippages dredged up from abysses. It wasn't so long ago that the blank page was shorthand for a fear of the void. Staring at the screen, all he feels now is hazy driftlessness, unraveling, bottomless stupor: how could anyone write a novel when a fiction of supreme reality has crept in, has taken the world hostage? As a virus, a simple DNA fragment wrapped in a few protein molecules, rises out of once-inert, now-viral magma (a mass three times greater than all humanity), our daydreams go further astray than ever before, far from mere ghosts and fleeting shadows.

In bedrooms and parlor rooms, ideologues are inclined toward conjecture, or even divination, as metaphysicians or pious strategists. An immense mill churning out diatribes and orations promises us, in equal measures, the apocalypse or a new golden age. Never have we seen such an intellectual anthill so thoroughly shaken by a pangolin's snout. Might this be some way of counteracting worldwide lockdown, the detention of every honest citizen? As voluntary prisoners, we're all our own jailers. Guilty of nothing, we have to hand down our sentences ourselves. And our indictment has to mirror the immeasurable extent of this foreign body. Writing a novel even as one sees oneself contaminated by the inhuman fiction of a reality undergoing rapid upheaval feels closer than ever before to something impossible.

For all that, it's likely that, when pieced together without overthinking it, the repeated attempts, all these incipits, false starts, drafts, approximations, broken-off openings, might well serve as the ghostly diary of a novelist on the lookout, suspended in his fictive desire . . .

*

Imagine that you wake up one fall morning in the year 2027. Little has changed in your immediate surroundings: the cotton sheets crinkle with dunes around your eyelids, below your sand-filled eyes. You retain the vague memory of having drunk heavily the night before, owing to your candidate's defeat in the dictatorial elections: white wine and single-malt scotch. A hangover that could uproot a forest only barely allows you not to feel dizziness as you recall the harsh jolts of a dream, gravity's sudden acceleration, the troposphere's thrust faults. But little by little, with an almost hallucinatory specificity, sleep's images cleave to pure reality as if it all were absolutely true in this world, starting with the clouds, the clouds drifting by back there, back there, the appalling clouds.

*

I am a wounded man, I died alongside so many in the last generation that asked so little of this world. If there is another world, a Garden of Eden where eternity could be savored, an Islamic Jannah with doors so immense that it would take forty years to walk from one panel to the other, it would be my turn to experience the downy hell of this land. Human gullibilities, luckily, have no hold on me now and one day I'll disappear from this

23

land like a terrible wound that's finally scarred over. Any look backward, however, will open up gulfs: a bridge suspended between two dark shores that collapses behind your heels with every step is the past, is yesteryear, is what we had once presumed was an ineradicable tree. Memories, in turn, won't hold together after one or two lives. Everything swirls together with time, marbled and misty.

*

The hotel. The room of metamorphoses: always identical, but each guest brings his or her own story.

*

A mutiny among the elderly barred from immortality flared up in less than a week across all the surrounding hospices and nursing homes. It was well known that these establishments were doomed to be shut down in the not-too-distant future. In Paris and elsewhere, ISD elective serum therapy resulted in mutations that weren't observable, phenotypically, but still upended the geography of those urban spaces.

*

Dropping anchor in the lake at Cumae and then awaiting the end of the world.

*

Say that civilization had arisen out of children's games, treating distinct natural elements (pebbles, branches, seashells, bones . . .) as toys, as things charged with meaning; over time, formerly uncultivated adults would have had to realize, by analogy, their practical uses as tools, and, by mental leaps and jumps, for educating.

*

All is a secret code for attaining the truth—an unfamiliar song, a painting depicting Shelley's death, a silhouette dancing this way and that, a particular one-armed statue in the middle of a public square.

*

I was young and in love. Life seemed to smile eternally. After a terrified childhood with a crazy mother and years of withdrawal within the stunted realms of drugs, my encounter with the Foreign Body reopened all ways forward. I felt confident once again. My research in some domain I couldn't really name, somewhere in the area of biochemistry and neuroscience, fascinated me thoroughly. And then came this string of planetary catastrophes, the inexorable pandemic out of China, civil wars more or less everywhere, upheavals of all kinds. Authoritarian powers locked down the last democracies in Europe and elsewhere. Of course, there were protest movements, student revolts, petitions. As always happens when institutional safeguards waver, the repression underscored the scope of the disaster. Thousands of youths and intellectuals, union members, and plain old stubborn citizens were all jailed.

*

I myself was put away for "ideologically aiding and abetting the rebellion," in the words of a discretionary arrest report. In indefinite detention without any legal recourse, I was sure I would go mad within the four walls of a maximum-security, zero-tolerance prison. I was deported in a police van with other men to a jail out east. The memory of electric wire-mesh doors closing shut behind your back on a succession of concrete-block corridors, after the procedures stripping you of your identity, will remain within me as the preparations for an execution. When nothing, at first glance, ought to have brought you there, the ordeal that is prison is indescribable, a sort of drawn-out, interminable exsanguination reinforced by a methodical degradation of all humanity, which I had to undergo each second of the days and years that followed.

*

Writing a novel that fuses with life at the moment of its writing.

*

Trapped within the paralysis of sleep, that fundamentally benign condition one naturally emerges from after a few seconds of total terror, I found myself physically and mentally walled up, this time indefinitely, which only compounded my fear of being buried alive. No assistance would allay my distress given the emptiness of moorless time detached from all life, bereft of beloved faces, open skies, landscapes. I didn't, strictly speaking, have any right to anything in this cloistered limbo, not even some dreary task that would have rooted me in reality. Visits were prohibited. And besides, who would have been able to find me in this non-place even more anonymous than an unknown soldier's grave? No information ever came from outside. I didn't even have the name of this massive coffin in the middle of nowhere, dreamed up by architects that the prison administration had hired. In my solitary cell, it was almost impossible to communicate with the other detainees. Ordinary activities—games, the library, group study—were forbidden. Twice a week, a tight-lipped warden took me to the shower; I washed with cold water the rest of the time. The sink tap was programmed to work two or three minutes an hour. Some mornings, at random, I was allowed a walk at the bottom of a well, its opening covered with barbed-wire fencing where trapped starlings' corpses had been caught. I don't think that it's possible to reduce the human spirit to an information-processing system, a sort of algorithm of mental states rooted in our gray matter, but what other freedom of movement is granted to a man torn away from his sentient self and the thousands of action potentials of his living memory? I was stripped of everything. There would be no other possible outcome if not for the prospect, however uncertain, of still being loved and recognized somewhere. But I could find no certain reality on this earth. All the flesh of my bones had been flensed along with my foreign body. Often I forgot that name, it opened up an abyss of pleas and whispers. Muted voices murmured around me. The only human beings I interacted with, for a few minutes a day, were even less warm than robots of steel or collared dogs with no known owner.

*

In nights of insomnia, so as not to lose all reason, I struggled to flesh out various outlines of my past life, to imagine how it went on without me.

*

As an engineer in fundamental physics, I was involved in developing a new generation of microprocessors designed for an intelligent molecule. The experiments I'd carried out in a high-security lab no longer seemed credible to me, somewhat like the absolute truth beheld in a dream that, upon waking, boiled down to a hand-drawn circle on a blank sheet. This secret laboratory ultimately slipped past my vigilant defenses. Sapped by an excess of disheartening loneliness, I grew overwhelmed and the dream work, freed from the cycle of sleep, that gatherer of illusions, overpowered my mental states again and again.

*

I don't know how many years went by like this, steeped in a pool of stagnant violence where days liquefied. One morning or one night, paralyzed in the inchoate eternity of my cell, I wanted to die, to give myself over body and soul to the bitter, intestinal night. An intermittent fever crept into me. I stopped eating. It was my yearning that went on strike, not my hunger. From that moment on, I foreswore all food, and was met with indifference; the wardens soon stopped changing my cold bowl of soup.

"When that's empty," the attendant said, "you can have hot soup."

But I barely heard his words. After a week or two of total fasting, my hunger unraveled in the twisting of my organs. My mouth's propensity for doughy, revolting organic matter gave way to a sort of nebulous relief. It was possible to breathe a purer air before starvation and death, as if I were now free. Greek physicians, in hopeless cases, were in the habit of sending their patients to a deserted island for a month with an earthenware jar of drinkable water. Many regained their health by slowly dying.

*

A novel in the shape of remnants, the preserved scraps of a manuscript, consisting of textual fragments, lonely sentences, the occasional line of dialogue: these shreds were found after a disaster without any real idea of the author. Like a banged-up black box in the wake of a crash.

*

Le Palace Univers. Nothing more than a shady, shabby hotel in a crumbling neighborhood on the outskirts. But within is, truly, the universe.

*

We know almost nothing about eclipses of the mind. Losing all connections and bearings, what we call *comatose*, when the functions of wakefulness slip away one by one and the senses cease to respond to external irritations, may open us up to the secrets of the universe, where known and unknown measures coincide in maddeningly incomprehensible ways. But I won't say more on that topic before I've shed light on my story (which is more or less identical to that of all mortals). I was taken to the fortress prison's infirmary, likely a hospital facility with an operating theater and intensive-care unit. Owing to circumstances that remain unclear to me and a reason I've never understood, I've been kept alive. How long was I gone in this tropical greenhouse of organs estranged from senses? Weeks or months, probably; all that should have ended in clinical death within the long sleep of prison. With respiratory assistance, and the steady drip of an IV, I feel mysterious impulses gathering within. They converge in a cluster of impressions and affects in which some sort of profound feeling reemerges and enables me to get my bearings, the "I" of some singularity. In layman's terms: I regained consciousness. This sponge of emptiness, the brain, suddenly disgorged a welter of shadows and the word set the world to rights again.

*

A shaky light illuminated the iron bed and the walls. Opening my eyes again, I was struck by a harsh feeling of déjà vu. This preliminary, inherently neutral image surged from one time, one life, into another, without even catching my memory. The nurse present right then, a very young blonde woman with a rigid smile, seemed to start moving again at that very second, as if called back to her role.

"What's happened to me?" I said, inexplicably seized by the memory of dead birds caught on the grille covering a small walled-in yard.

"You've undergone a severe loss of consciousness," she said. "Luckily, it was temporary."

Her long, very white hands were performing oddly synchronized movements all around me: grabbing a linen to smooth out the creases, moving around flasks and other implements on a metallic table. Her old-fashioned smock and nurse's hat pinned to her short hair struck me as an elaborate costume.

"How long have I been here?" I asked.

She didn't answer as she kept on tidying up around my bed.

"I don't see any bars on the window," I declared, feeling buoyant, though my body seemed heavier and more pain-stricken than ever. "Why was I taken out of prison?"

She seemed unsurprised as she cocked her head as sharply as a bird.

"I wasn't told that."

"We're not inside a prison, are we?"

"That's a question above my pay grade."

Those were practically the only responses I could pry out of the young nurse, who proved to be fastidious about fluffing my pillows, washing my face, and swapping the saline bags of my IV. Even as my limbs were freed and the extreme pain of post-coma ankylosis subsided, I imagined all sorts of explanations for why I was in this clinic or hospital room despite the bothersome lack of clarity.

*

Sensory disconnection. Visits are obviously prohibited. Do they want to convince me that I'm a criminal? (There's no music, nor enthusiasm, like the ocean in my eyes.)

*

Outside, a river of liquid plaster or quicklime bears away the ever-changing statues of nudes, Titans, and Cyclopes with this immaterial slowness reminiscent of eternity. I almost recall that I have nothing, no roof over my head, no bank account, and that my ability to love has foundered along with my vain hopes as an artist. Can I set to writing and painting anew without first having scrubbed away these black marks? Shapelessness and insignificance have dragged me down the slippery slope of fraud. And how will I eke out a living now? Life isn't a matter of style. I own nothing, apart from a nightmarish museum as vast as a city overrun ad nauseam by the most legendary masterpieces.

*

I've aspired with all my being to freedom. It's only a matter of getting past an unlikely impasse. Perpetual seclusion can only be a figment of the imagination. But what is the imagination if not a blind specter standing in for some original flaw in the living world, the universe?

*

Locked in his childhood bedroom, he's five years old. Weeks, months, years go by. His furniture doesn't change, his stuffed animals still clutter his room, he's fed in the same way. His mother, surprisingly, huddles further and further out of the way, his father (he'll take his clothes when he's dead) looks away from him while crying. Now that he's an adult, nothing moves, his temples are graying. Now he's old and alone. He doesn't change anything. His little bed, his toys.

*

Prison. Outside. Omens. Heaven. We're on the brink of the secret, we approach it, the reality barrier is about to be broken. The decohering effect of our unequivocal universe can be interrupted. I maintain that psychic activity brings into step the flow of subatomic waves entangled on a quantum level with all possible universes.

*

Story. An ordinary, divorced man of no profession—he suddenly joins the resistance.

*

He says: "Last year, at this time, I was a free man."

31

*

On occasion, time, this fighter against chaos, allows us the time to come face-to-face with this lightning that, once unleashed, permanently strips us of all superfluity: of everything, apart from the thunderclap of being where the universe dies. But I'm speaking to you of an old experience that left me practically dead and remains the deepest solitude I have endured.

On the most heavily populated island, everyone dreams of returning to the deserted continent. Each one of us is one Crusoe too many.

PARIS
APRIL 30, 2020

The Life of a Virus

JAVIER SINAY

Translated from the Spanish by Robert Croll

Journalist Javier Sinay (Buenos Aires, Argentina, 1980) is the author of The Crimes of Moisés Ville: A Story of Gauchos and Jews, *forthcoming in English from Restless Books (2022),* Sangre joven (2009), *winner of the Premio Rodolfo Walsh de la Semana Negra de Gijón, and* Camino al Este (2019). *In 2015, he won the Gabriel Garcia Marquez Journalism Prize for Best Text for his chronicle "Fast. Furious. Dead.," published in* Rolling Stone. *He writes for Redaccion.com.ar and was a correspondent in South America for* El Universal *(Mexico) and was the editor of* Rolling Stone *(Argentina). He lives in Buenos Aires.*

IT IS REPLETE WITH SPINES, and that is probably its most striking feature. Spikes without edges or points that completely cover the round, almost bloated body of this virus. Because of these spines, which a group of English scientists saw for the first time in 1967 through an electronic microscope, the viruses in this family were given the name coronavirus. The scientists said that their figure resembled that of the sun with its luminous corona, but the virus doesn't look like a sun so much as a stray asteroid, perhaps, accelerating out of control. There are many members of the coronavirus family because of their ability to mutate, but these viruses only became famous after one of them caused an aggressive outbreak of pneumonia that affected thousands of people around the world and then dissipated as mysteriously as it had surged. Now, seventeen years later, the pneumonia has returned. It isn't exactly the same, but neither is the coronavirus itself. It is tremendously worse.

It is called SARS-CoV-2 and measures around one hundred nanometers across. An army of ten thousand of these coronavirus particles, placed side by side, would reach a length of one millimeter (and still need another fifty thousand soldiers to equal the size of a flea). The spines that give them their name are actually a kind of protein, called the Spike protein. Once inside the human organism, they bind to other proteins that project from some of our cells. In this way, the bodies of the virus and cell fuse together. Through the encounter, the virus releases some of its ribonucleic acid. The RNA is a molecule (in biology textbooks it appears pictured like a strand of DNA, though not a double but a single strand) that carries the coronavirus's package of genes: its simple genome or, put another way, a manual of instructions one hundred thousand times shorter than that of a human being (thirty thousand units versus three billion; fifteen genes versus thirty thousand).

The human cell acts according to the instructions of this foreign RNA and begins to work without the immune system noticing (it will do so fifteen days later). All viruses do the same thing: hijacking, parasitizing,

34

confiscating the cells of a host. This is how they reproduce. As a result, only half of scientists consider them to be living beings; for the other half, viruses are merely genetic residue. What is disputed, in fact, isn't the definition of a virus but that of life itself, and that's a difficult discussion. After one day, a single coronavirus particle, using a cell, can generate between ten thousand and one hundred thousand copies of itself. These will take over other cells and repeat the process. Later, each of the captured cells will be annihilated, and that, on the surface, is manifested as the symptoms of COVID-19: fever, cough, sore throat, pneumonia. A virus is a ravenous zombie.

And even though a coronavirus particle is seventeen million times smaller than a human being, in the war of the species, for a moment already too prolonged, it has been able to corral all of humanity with its spikes.

*

The world colonized by SARS-CoV-2 offers us a collection of scenes in which we encounter a new life, replete with perplexity. The virus has overturned everything in its path. It has exposed the ties of solidarity that can flourish among strangers, the fragility of certain power structures, and the dismal position of the elderly in society. Even words and names have changed. A boy and a girl, fraternal twins born in India on March 27, were named Corona and Covid. "We wanted the names to be memorable and unique," said Preeti Verma, the mother. In the Philippines, another baby was given the name Covid Bryant: an homage to the recently deceased basketball star Kobe Bryant. And one, born on April 15 in the small city of Ceres, in Argentina, was named Ciro Covid. "This is how it is documented in the hospital, but we don't know if in the Civil Registry they will make it official," said a doctor. Adapting to the new world isn't easy.

My son turned one not long ago. He's a smiling and bold little boy who goes running and stumbling all through the house, saying to us with his eyes and his syllables: Hey, what are you doing there, let's play! It was a first year filled with emotions, as any father and mother will know from personal experience, and Higashi, my wife, said that our son deserved a good party because in her family—which is of Japanese origin—first birthdays are something special. And so we had already begun putting together a long guest list five months in advance, and a few weeks later her mother started baking *pastelitos* and packing them in the freezer. And then March arrived, the coronavirus arrived, and Argentina shut down into total quarantine. To put a long story short: the birthday party was an afternoon on Zoom, the now famous video call app. We set a cake on the table, at home, and connected with two phones. The guests? Only his grandparents, excited, and a few of our friends breaking up the tedium of their confinement. Of that party we are left with a few screenshots, which in this new world occupy the place once held by photographs.

We weren't the only ones to celebrate a birthday over Zoom in the last few weeks: the app has become the digital stream through which everyday life now flows. Zoom also works for distance learning and remote work, and every morning, in fact, I have a video meeting with my colleagues from the newsroom, and Higashi teaches classes to high school students who log on with sleepy faces. Other people use the app to take tango lessons or share a coffee with their friends. Boris Johnson, the British prime minister, was using it for his cabinet meetings before he became infected.

Eugenia hasn't adapted to doing group therapy via Zoom. She tried it, of course, but what kind of result can a session have if she has to connect while shut away in her bedroom, on her phone? She's a woman in her forties, with two children, a husband, and a job to attend to from her home in a suburb of Buenos Aires. And it isn't for lack of experience: she's been going to analysis since age sixteen (in Argentina, psychotherapy is a very popular activity). She's had phone sessions before, yes, but while sitting on a bench in the plaza, not like now.

"We talked a bit about what was happening to us in quarantine, about our fears," she tells me of her first group session: half of the patients were in the consulting room with the psychologist, the other half on their phones. Eugenia managed to connect, first struggling with her Mac and then with a little tripod, chasing after her cat, finally holding up the phone in her hand. "It was distracting, I couldn't concentrate," she tells me. After another, equally bad session, she now thinks she will abandon the group.

*

In this new world, in which the majority of us have been left as perplexed losers, there is one definitive winner: Eric Yuan. He is the Chinese engineer who, in 2011, created Zoom. As a teenager, he would routinely travel ten hours by train to see his girlfriend and fantasized about a future device that would let him click a button to see her and talk to her. Over the years, he created one himself, and, amid the self-isolation measures around the world, Zoom emerged over other video call services to reach a value of thirty-five billion dollars on Wall Street: higher than the total of the five main airlines in the United States, held in check by the crisis. Eric Yuan, according to Bloomberg, now occupies the 192nd place among the 500 richest people in the world. Before the coronavirus, he wasn't even on the list.

*

Today, which is Monday, April 27, the first patient samples arrived at the COVID-19 testing lab at the National University of Quilmes. Ten scientists were waiting for them there at 8:30 in the morning, but it was not until 11:40 that thirty-eight test samples turned up in an ambulance; and at 4:00 in the afternoon, another eleven. And so, a bit anxiously, the scientists spent the morning labeling some three hundred tubes and waiting. Each test arrived inside three containers. They had to be extracted carefully: a few were spilled while opening the pot that contained the swab and touching the material could mean contagion.

They had set up the laboratory in three weeks, when the government decided to multiply the number of tests. "We did it at a sprint," the head of the team, biotechnician Hernán Farina, tells me. He's an energetic man, evidently passionate. To put together the site, he had to do things that, as a scientist, he wasn't accustomed to: dismantling some laboratories in order to set up another, creating new installations, connecting cables, disassembling things. And bringing in the QuantStudio, a real time thermal cycler. It is a white and shiny machine, the size of a CPU, which can read genetic material. The process isn't too complicated: someone extracts what arrived on the swab, submitting it to a biochemical treatment in which the RNA of the supposed virus (single strand) is converted to DNA (double strand); then the test is submitted to an amplification reaction inside the machine. This means that the temperature is raised in cycles from sixty-five to ninety-five degrees, and the double strand is separated into two. Then, using chemicals, the single strand is duplicated. In this way, we now have two single strands. And these form a new double strand. The duplication continues in this way until the DNA becomes visible to the machine, which will give its verdict after three hours: the virus is present, the virus is not present.

"If I'd stayed in doubt, thinking that we had all we needed to do the tests but weren't doing them out of fear, or because it required a lot of preparation, or because it was easier to stay at home, I don't think I would have liked it very much," Farina tells me. These are days that become unforgettable; today, the first session of testing, he made it home at night. He left his shoes outside, sprayed alcohol on the soles, undressed in the laundry room, placed all of his clothing inside a trash bag, put alcohol on his wallet, his watch, his car keys, and his phone, ran naked into the bathroom, and took a shower: he disinfected himself. Only then did he greet his wife and two children. It was time to rest.

*

For up to fourteen days inside a freezer, coronavirus can remain active. Or alive. That's twice the lifespan of a mosquito, yet some would say that a virus isn't alive. Viruses reproduce, they have DNA or RNA and can evolve, but they lack autonomy and metabolism, and they can go through periods of stasis. The boundaries of life and death sometimes become gray. Is a virus alive? Or just a thing?

Biology has a definition for life. So do medicine, cosmology, physics, psychology, genetics, and religions. But to return to biology, all known life on this planet is based on carbon polymers: nucleic acids, proteins, and polysaccharides; non-living chemicals that long ago combined in random ways and gave rise to a competition of microorganisms that sought to survive and reproduce. But on another planet, life could take another form and still be life. Is a virus alive? To respond to that question, it is first necessary to know exactly what it means to be alive, and perhaps we aren't yet able to understand that completely.

*

How to describe all that is taking place is more or less clear. We must seek out stories, extract them from reality, and bring them to the paper (or the screen). How to write is not so simple. If it is already difficult in itself to sit down at the computer and recount something in words, doing so while lying in wait for the virus is like running an obstacle course. I live in an apartment with Higashi and our son. We haven't watched any series, except for the brief *Unorthodox*, the story of a girl who escapes from an ultra-Orthodox Jewish community, which touched me to the point that it led me, a few days later, to attend a reading of *Megillat Hashoah*, a symbol of Jewish solidarity in times of crisis. It was on Zoom, and, since the rabbi was reading in Hebrew (and I don't speak Hebrew), I left before long. We haven't watched any movies either; we don't have the time, and perhaps we don't have the energy. I haven't even been able to read more than four pages of a book since all of this began; I get caught up in the social networks, which present the pandemic as a biothriller, told in fragments. Around here, we each do our own things. Even our little son does his own things: he plays, he runs, he falls, he laughs, he cries, he eats, he gets excited when he hears a dog bark, he wants to touch the wall outlets and break the windows. He is pure desire and instinct, and, little by little, he is becoming something more. He delights us at every instant even as he plunges the house into a new era of chaos and anarchy. Higashi does her own things: she leads a group for *chadō*, the Japanese tea ceremony, she gives classes. And I do my own as well, and here I am, writing where I can manage to settle in, while in the distance I hear videos with baby songs in Japanese and the wind gusting on this sunny day. In a while, after my work meeting on Zoom, we'll have lunch together.

However, it is dawn, not morning, that is the best moment for writing. There are no distractions, no rush; it's as if the tea doesn't get cold in the cup. There is a different time. As is known to nuns in the cloister, or prisoners, or scientists in Antarctica, living all day within four walls alters your perception. But quarantine makes it so that even that experience becomes specific and distinct. Many people are easily losing their notion of what day it is, from one day to the next. Google searches for "what day is today" have increased considerably in the United States, almost doubling the figure at the end of February. Time has gone soft.

In the last few days, Higashi has returned to *Hōjōki*, the classic of Japanese literature written by Kamo no Chōmei, a monk who lived as a recluse in a small hut. Today, *Hōjōki* takes the form of a short and powerful book describing a series of disasters that befell Kyoto in the thirteenth century: earthquakes, fires, famines, and epidemics. It has become indispensable among Buddhist treatises on impermanence. The monk wrote: "And so the question, / where should we live? / And how? // Where to find / a place to rest a while? // And how to bring / even short-lived peace / to our hearts?" Higashi said, after reading it to me on her iPhone: "More contemporary than that, impossible."

*

A week before mandatory quarantine in Argentina began, Natalia met Daniel at a bar. She went in, greeted a table, and saw him. Since she was a regular, she also went up to the bar to say hello to the owner and the cook, and she sensed that someone was watching her. Daniel approached and spoke first. He broke the ice, saying in a Madrileño accent (he was a Spanish diplomat posted in Buenos Aires) that he was there on a trip, and she responded that she'd been dreaming of traveling for a long time. They took out their phones, followed each other on Instagram, and he went back to his friends at the table. The first match had concluded.

He left a while later, but not too late. "Lovely to meet you," he wrote, when he got home. "Maybe we can get a drink sometime." And they saw each other again that very night. "We were walking down the street, with no direction in mind, kissing," she tells me now. "In barrio de Palermo, just walking around and kissing."

The next day, which was Saturday, everyone knew that the shutdown was imminent. Daniel asked her out on a date, but Natalia preferred to get dinner with her friends one last time. He persisted: Monday, at a hotel? She, who was actually ending things with someone else, told him no.

But on Thursday, once that other person was out of the picture, Natalia was on her own with a Malbec, and she wrote to Daniel. Quarantine began at midnight; they decided the date would be a video call on WhatsApp. "After several days in pajamas and slippers," she tells me, "I put on my makeup again and uncorked the wine." The emergency had purified their feelings: they chatted, watching each other through the screen, often falling silent, just looking at each other. "I imagine those are the spaces that would be filled with kisses," she tells me.

After Cupid's arrow struck, they spoke every morning and every night. Sometimes during the day as well. Yes, they considered breaking quarantine and seeing each other, but it was impossible because he lived in a residence with guards outside the door. He could only go out for work; he couldn't receive lovers. So they sent each other poems and photos: some erotic, of course.

A passionate kiss that lasts ten seconds can transmit, in addition to the coronavirus, eighty million bacteria, according to the Netherlands Organization for Applied Scientific Research (TNO). Mononucleosis, herpes, group A streptococcus, cytomegalovirus: being in love was never a simple activity. Today, the cold safety of an unshared bed is a symbol that, as in the 1980s, has been imposed once more. Self-pleasure is recommended by the New York City government in a guide to sexual practice during the pandemic, and in Buenos Aires a Ministry of Health specialist discusses "virtual sex." "But in the end, our connection is one based on words," Natalia tells me. "We can't hug or kiss, and that creates a bit of desperation. . . . I don't even know if I should call it a 'relationship.'"

Later, little by little, Daniel started to withdraw. He said he had a lot of work. One day, he informed her that he was leaving. That he had to leave. That there were only a few Spanish citizens left to be repatriated and he was flying on the last plane with them. They were sending him to France first, then Madrid. It was a hard blow, but not unexpected. She made a Spotify playlist for him to take on the plane: the titles, placed one after the other in sequence, formed a message of love. "Motivos," by Mery Granados and Juani Bernal, was the first track. But he didn't even notice.

*

Every night at nine, people come out to applaud on the balconies of Buenos Aires. It's a bit dismal now, but when it began, on March 19, it was a sensation. Our applause was born from the example of the people clapping and singing in Italy and Spain. The sound of palms became a new global language. But it's one thing to applaud in the countries where the virus is taking the most dramatic toll and quite another to do so in Argentina, where, on that March 19 when the applause began, there were twenty-four deaths in total (that very day, Italy became the country with the highest number of fatalities: 11,591). Perhaps that's the reason why the applause is dying down. I still go out to the balcony all the same (my son comes with me, and I carry him in my arms: he loves to clap).

Behavioral specialists contend that any form of applause satisfies the human need for self-expression. It's something that no one teaches you. Children and monkeys applaud when they become excited. In the theater, applause allows the audience to participate. Although one theorist of applause, the theater director Jan Lauwers, says that the clapping of palms is a way of releasing what each spectator could carry in silence (like taking photographs on trips, a mechanism of substitution for lived experience), another, Peter Sellars, disagrees: applause is a post-religious form of prayer.

Laura Echezarreta, who works in the City Legislature, continues to applaud with enthusiasm. Sometimes, she even plays the national anthem for her neighborhood on a little speaker. In the beginning, people applauded her as well; now only two or three neighbors do it. It doesn't matter. She believes that her mission has been accomplished: she wanted to bring the people together and thinks she succeeded. Because, when all of this began, President Alberto Fernández's detractors were trading insults with his devotees in a war of balconies.

She's divorced and has two teenage children. Laura is in the home stretch of her forties. Before the pandemic, she used to play tennis, work out at the gym, and go sailing. Now she does push-ups and smokes. And she claps for the medical personnel, for the delivery people, for those who collect the trash . . . but more than anything she claps for herself and her own. Her community is the group of neighbors in the building where she lives. They all know each other. One woman and her daughter came back from Italy and isolated themselves in order to comply with the fourteen days of quarantine (before it was mandatory for everyone), and three days later the woman had a birthday and the neighbors all sang "Happy Birthday" to her from behind their doors. At the end of the week, the daughter came down with a fever. Masked paramedics, covered in white, came for her, and the neighbors turned out once again to anxiously say goodbye to her from their balconies. For a few days, they thought the coronavirus might be in the building, yet, far from putting up signs in the elevator with threats to teach the mother a lesson (as happened in other cases), they all participated in the disinfection. "When she left, and when she came back with a negative result," Laura tells me, "we shed tears for her, for ourselves, for everyone." Even the most routine thing, your interaction with your neighbors, is restructured in this new world.

*

The coronavirus SARS-CoV-2 was far away, on the other side of the planet. That's how we first saw it: its form was the emptiness it had left in the streets of Wuhan. Then we had it among ourselves. Although the virus took hold of the cities and paralyzed them, the strongest hypothesis is that it originated in a natural habitat: in bats from the family *Rhinolophus affinis*. They are small animals with beady black eyes, misshapen noses, and pointed teeth. The genome of SARS-CoV-2 shares 96.2% of its sequence with that of a virus that lives in them. Not much more is known; all bats have a formidable resistance to the viruses that they carry and spread.

Of the first forty-one Chinese patients, twenty-seven had been to the animal market in Wuhan. By this stage, everyone will have heard that some people consume bat soup in Wuhan, but this doesn't seem sufficient to explain how the virus jumped from bats to humans. Could it have been transmitted, instead, through a bite? Or through an intermediate animal? There is talk of the pangolin: a scaly mammal in danger of extinction, highly sought-after, which eats ants and lives inside hollow trees. One pangolin coronavirus resembles ours in certain proteins. Some scientists believe there was a recombination of viruses, but we can only shrug our shoulders . . . who knows? The moral is that humanity invades wild habitats and nature gives it back what it deserves.

Other scientists are inclined toward the artificial fabrication of the coronavirus. In a hectic world, a good story is like a balm. The United States accused China, and China the United States, but the most original hypothesis is that of Luc Montagnier, the French virologist who won the Nobel Prize for discovering HIV, and who explained in a TV interview that SARS-CoV-2 was created in a lab where DNA sequences of HIV were being inserted into a coronavirus, perhaps with the objective of discovering a vaccine to combat AIDS. "It's the work of professionals, of molecular biologists," said Montagnier. "A very meticulous work."

*

I wonder how much of all this my son will remember. How much will remain stored in his unconscious, to awaken, perhaps, many years later. I wonder if we will have been good enough parents to steer him through the pandemic without casting our fears onto him. Suddenly he no longer goes into the street and never sees his grandparents except on video calls: how can he feel about that? He isn't talking yet. If he could talk, would he be able to communicate it? Coming and going from the house in our surgical masks and latex gloves, using alcohol to disinfect the packaging of the food we buy, touching doorknobs and the buttons on the ATM with apprehension: in what way has all of this touched us in turn?

There are some escapes. One Friday night, a delivery came to us from 878, our favorite bar. It's a place with dim lights, with tables and tall chairs along the bar. They serve drinks and very good food. It was there that Higashi and I had our first date; it was there that we celebrated our marriage three years later with many friends, invading the bar one Wednesday until it closed in the early hours of the morning. It isn't the typical place that one would expect to do delivery, but, in this economy of confinement, everyone is adapting. And so we received a few small plates from 878, and, in two bottles, a Torrontés punch and a pear gimlet. We brought out a few glasses of ice, and each bottle held enough for two rounds. We toasted. The alcohol was just right.

In Spanish, we don't have the distinction between words like "loneliness" and "solitude." We use *soledad* for both. *Soledad* can feel overburdened with stigma and be a word that no one wants to be identified with. Or it can refer to being with oneself, on a journey within, with no other people around. Quarantine aggrandizes these matters, and I'm one of the hermits, like the monk Kamo no Chōmei. And so I wonder, sometimes, how confinement would have touched me if I'd been alone, really alone. How much I might have suffered. How much I might have enjoyed it.

There's a party that became a quarantine sensation in Buenos Aires: it's called Bresh, and it goes live on Instagram at midnight on Saturdays, lasts for several hours, and brings together thousands of people. It's like being at a rave, but all of the people are dancing in their own houses, watching

DJ Bröder and his girlfriend, Ruidito, two energetic young people who spin reggaeton in a living room decorated to look like a club. One night I stayed up, enchanted by the spell of their movements and the music they were playing: Don Omar, Bad Bunny, Daddy Yankee, and, of course, J Balvin. Alone in the living room, I spent the time flowing with the *dembow* and sensed that I was in the presence of something both addictive and slightly mysterious. Thousands of comments were crossing the screen, most of them from fairly young kids who desperately needed to go out and party. And I remembered.

I remembered many nights, some years ago, when I was one of those kids. I remembered the time when I went to a warehouse to hear a techno duo, Audio Bullys, because I wanted to be there even though no one came with me. Or the festival where I saw M.I.A. in a tent with the lights turned up, packed with frenzied and joyous people all shoving in. Or the time that, after an Erick Morillo show when one of us scored some pills, we went home in a taxi that sped too fast down an avenue, and the driver spoke to us, twisting around to stare us in our faces, telling us that he also worked at a funeral home. I don't know why we didn't crash. When we got out, we were still alive, still young and magnificent, though no longer quite as high. All the same, we couldn't stop laughing.

I carry all of those nights with me, though I'm not quite sure where.

The day after the Bresh party I woke up late, still tasting the noise of another time, and found that Higashi and our son had already eaten breakfast and were playing on the floor with a few action figures. I drank some tea and slowly entered the day. My after-party came a while later, with more dembow, dancing with my son held up in my arms, while he laughed because he loves music. Next Saturday, I told myself, I'll go out partying again.

*

While I am reaching the end of this text (but not of this story), at least thirty-five pharmaceutical companies and fourteen countries are searching for a vaccine against the coronavirus SARS-CoV-2. The problem is that no one knew, at the beginning, how to defeat a new virus. And so they had to start from zero, turning to other vaccines and combining different methods. The race to find a cure is moving at a rapid pace never before seen in medicine, but even so, they tell us that the process will require between twelve and eighteen months (provided we are lucky). Although that seems like a great deal of time, it really isn't much when compared to the ten years that the process of research and production for a vaccine usually takes. At the same time, other researchers are testing treatments for hospitalized patients using antiviral medications like remdesivir, which is also used against Ebola; favipiravir, which they use to treat influenza in Japan; and chloroquine, which can work against malaria, lupus, and rheumatoid arthritis. But, for now, COVID-19 is slipping away from the scientists like sand between their fingers.

When an unknown element presents itself in the human body, it is recognized as something foreign and attacked. The body must learn to produce antibodies, and it makes itself vulnerable in the process. Vaccines are nothing more than a bit of virus without the capacity to make a person ill. Some contain a live (or active) virus so that the disease can infect without developing. Others have a dead (or inactive) virus. And others still, only part of a virus. Many of the trials for coronavirus vaccines feature the Spike protein, those spines that bind to cells and allow the virus to enter. These vaccines try to make the body recognize this protein and prevent it from linking with the cell receptors. One Chinese trial utilizes the purified Spike protein along with adjuvants taken from an influenza vaccine. Another trial, from the United States, introduces an RNA into the body that causes the cells to synthesize that same protein. In one way or another, each seeks to create antibodies against the Spike protein.

And, sooner or later, they will manage it. The scientific community swears to it. Humanity needs it, and humanity isn't just an abstract thing. It is also people like Eugenia, Laura Echezarreta, Hernán Farina, Natalia and Daniel, DJ Bröder and Ruidito, Eric Yuan, Luc Montagnier; people like you and me. Once the coronavirus has been defeated, we will return to the streets and the parks. We will go out to breathe a diaphanous air with lungs no longer held under the weight of a threat. Will it be a new world? Will it be a new era? I read the opinions of the most varied experts, who say that everything will improve. But it's impossible to know what will come after all of this, and if, at the end of the road, we will have learned anything. Or if, at least, we will be able to decide how we want to live. The history of life on this planet is a history of the joint evolution of parasites and hosts, one which involves many different forms of cooperation. And here we are, perplexed, living through a milestone in the history of life on this planet . . . almost without noticing.

BUENOS AIRES
APRIL 30, 2020

An Area of Critical Concern

RAJIV MOHABIR

Rajiv Mohabir (London, United Kingdom, 1981) is the author of The Cowherd's Son (2017), winner of the Kundiman Poetry Prize, and The Taxidermist's Cut (2016), a finalist for the 2017 Lambda Literary Award for Gay Poetry. He is the translator of I Even Regret Night: Holi Songs of Demerara (2019), which was supported by a PEN/Heim Translation Fund Grant. His memoir Antiman, winner of the 2019 Restless Books Prize for New Immigrant Writing, is forthcoming from Restless Books (2021). He is an assistant professor of poetry at Emerson College.

SLATE CLOUD COVER. Hanging high the sun is a silver smear casting gray light. The water in Rumney Marsh is low or the reeds and grasses on its banks hang low.

Red-winged blackbirds call out from the banks,
          conk-la-ree—

I know it's not a crow from its song.

I remember the bridge over the St. Johns river in Sanford, how crossing over it was like watching a sleeping dragon. Econlockhatchee, ēkvnvlikehvcce in Mvskoke, is a little big snake. One bright day, it will open its water-eyes and swallow the flat land.

*

*

ēkvnvlikehvcce

 Big snake, stream sitting on earth
black serpent

  The Timucua echoes
   noronoromota
   do it with devotion

 How when my mouth
is stone

    alligator scales blinding me

do I claim you
when under your black skirt

a pool of ghosts?

*

*

But here the marsh is tidal, drawn to sea in the odd hours that I'm starting to keep too.

A neighbor on the gravel path through Saugus comments that the streets are empty like they were after the bombing in 2013.

A peregrine fans its tail above us, falconing a corvid low on the branches, now still. I can see clearly the rock face along the path covered in emerald moss.

He gave me a half bottle of wine I drank too quickly two nights before. The birches are waking up.

Red buds. But all around only crows.

I pass the soft buds to my lips. Mourning doves. Sparrows. Red-winged blackbirds warble as though some life shifts under these fallen leaves, some life that I cannot see as yet, if there was a promise of something, some sleeping spark waiting.

*

A squirrel skull gleams
white against fur. A femur.
Pelvis. Yellow incisors
that never stop
growing. Ribs.
Vertebrae.

*

*

From the Rumney Marsh-Adele H. Toro Commonwealth Interpretive Sign

In 1607 the Pawtucket Confederation of Indian Tribes cared for this land. They fished, mollusked, and grew corn along the coast of North Massachusetts. Their cultural area spanned from Winnisemet, Saugus, Swampscott, Naumkeag, Agawam, Pentucket, Pisataqua, and Accominta, through alliance wrought and lived.

The Great Sachem, Nanepashemet, ruled Saugus, Lynn, and Marblehead. His sons Wonohaquaham, Montowampate, and Wenepoykin—also known as Sagamore John, James, and George Rumney Marsh. It was Wenepoykin who fought with Metacomet in King Philip's War and was sold as a slave in 1676 to Barbados, as was his wife Wootonekanuske, and one of her sons.

*

It took three years after the English settled for smallpox to claim its Imperial toll.

Nanepashemet died in 1619, The Moon God or New Moon, and was succeeded by his wife Squaw Sachem of Mistick—her name was unknown but what passed into white history books was her blood quantum and her deeding Cambridge and Watertown to the colonists. The logic of elimination (Patrick Wolfe) holds that the power of the settler necessitates that the indigenous people create the land's narrative and that they be erased by colonial logic. This is why she is known as "Squaw Sachem."

I have also been trained by the settler state to imagine that forced migration was only ever one way. There has been a conversation between Massachusetts and the Caribbean since racialized enslavement and the settler colonial project.

*

*

Boughs of pine, oak, ash,
birch, in their crooks,
joints of limb, abandoned
nests woven of sticks,
leaves, napkins, plastic.

*

August 22, 1988—Massachusetts protects 2,800 acres of estuary for its
"biological significance." Adam tells me not to fish the waters up here in
any of the estuaries. Centuries of runoff from factories, and contemporary
earth-stripping projects deposit toxic waste into the water. *The Boston
Globe* reported in 2016: "As much as ninety percent of ground water in
Massachusetts may be corrosive."

My own Caribbean community survives on fish. In fact, my father's family lived on the river; my mother's by the sea. I've been craving fish and have some cumin seeds saved from my mother's repurposed cookie tin.

*

I text Katie after a long silence. *Nineteen crows!* I keep saying *nineteen crows*. There is no emoji, so she sends me nineteen black hearts.

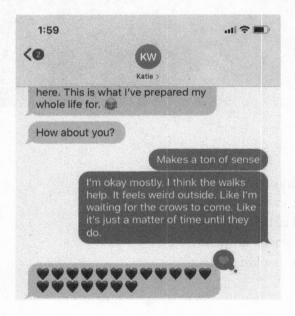

*

Right now, the public-school system makes my mother work in an office where she is at risk of being exposed to the virus. She had a cardiac event last year. She doesn't have money to be able to take a break. White policies put my brown, immigrant, working-class mother at risk. They put my mixed-race nephews and niece at risk.

*

Eastern cottontail corpse.
Eyes eaten out. Bones
protrude ticked fur. Ears
fray. Underbelly and tail: white.

*

*

The Pennacook people: Pawtucket and Merrimack spoke Algonquian languages and were related to the Abenaki, who named them "Penakuk," meaning "at the bottom of the hill."

*

A hairy woodpecker throws
his head into the tree.

I turn my face up,
consider the black
wings flecked white.

I know it's male
for the flicker of red
behind its head.

Foragers, they pick
bark in search of European corn
borers.

How did corn get to Europe?
What magic keeps
his skull in one piece
as he pecks and hammers?

*

*

We drove north on the US 1, deeper into Saugus, to get some groceries, since Jordan had started to panic that we were low on peanut butter. We'd not had real peanut butter for some time.

In the market things were slim. Shelves empty. People crowding. Severe looks bordering on anger. The store imposed a limit of only two purchases of each item per customer.

We got two pouches of skipjack and two cans of tinned fish in oil.

Is this the last time I'm ever going to buy tuna or peanut butter? Has this kind of hunting/gathering, as unsustainable as it is, finally pulled its own number?

We live in a land where resources are scarce to us if we don't own the means of production. Even with the raw resources, we need America to distribute and market. What is it about trade? Either by fin or by wing?

It's enslavement and exploitation of the natural world that kills us, whether through zoonotic virus or by poisoning by harsh chemicals.

Once upon a time fish lived under fluorescent lighting, deboned and tinned. Flowery music piped into the room where they sat in neat pyramidal displays.

Once upon a time the rivers and marshes in Malden were not already poisoned.

*

From underneath,
a rust-colored fan
and wings barred
in black and brown,
breast marbled white.

Three circle.

*

In the midst of the pandemic the United States with 100,00 confirmed cases of COVID-19 acts as a murder of nineteen hungry crows. The Secretary of the Department of the Interior moves to disestablish the Mashpee Wampanoag Tribe's reservation.

*

*

From Patch.com, "These 13 Nasty Pollutants in Massachusetts Drinking Water Put Your Health at Risk," July 26, 2017:

Total trihalomethanes (TTHMs)
Chloroform
Bromodichloromethane
Radium-226
Radium-228
Dibromochloromethane
Dichloroacetic acid
Trichloroacetic acid
Chromium (hexavalent)
Manganese

These contaminants were detected above legal guidelines:

Antimony
Haloacetic acids
Trihalomethanes

Legal does not mean safe. Ask whose law. Ask who protects the law. Ask who protects the water. Ask who protects the land. These are not the same horses.

*

*

At low tide Rumney Marsh wetland becomes a severe mudflat; rivulets and drying reeds tell a water-marked tale.

Bivalve mollusks I imagine as ghosts. I want to see the land as it was.

The red-tailed hawks circle above. Red-brown fanned tails color against the blue sky.

Buteo jamaicensis found from North America to the West Indies. I see Jamaica hiding in plain view. The Eastern red-tail race migrates from south Maine to Florida, drawn to the Gulf Coast and by the Gulf Stream. When did the races of hawks diverge, migrating to the Caribbean?

I imagine Puerto Rico, Jamaica as its name suggests, and the West Indies. Migration routes north and south from the West Indies to Massachusetts. Only this time, free.

Maybe I'm searching for a connection, for my body that represents the settler state, an "arrivant" to the Caribbean, having an ethical way of being here.

*

*

A tawny body dashes
across the gravel path.
Short black tipped mammalian tail.

A stoat?

*

Shona N. Jackson wrote a book called *Creole Indigeneity: Between Myth and Nation in the Caribbean* that charts the ways in which the Creole society in Guyana has absorbed the logic of elimination and have remade themselves the "natives" of the area.

Jackson, attuned to the fraught ethnic divides in Guyana, says, "Creole may be a noun used primarily to refer to blacks, and an adjective when applied to Indians in the post-Indenture twentieth century. I use the term to indicate the way in which both their identities are now collectively woven through with state power" (Jackson, 47). For her the nuances and contestations of the category "Creole" (Indo-Creole for descendants of Indian indentured labor in Guyana) are mobilized to show the settler/native colonial remnant philosophy as a settler colonial paradigm.

Jackson shows this transformation as a five-part process in order to show various developments and subjectivities of the "Creole." The first is a geographical shift from Africa to the Caribbean, the second is the shift from being enslaved as an African to being a Creole, the third the shift from Creole/enslaved to Creole/free and the distinction between the Creole and the Indian indentured laborer, fourth a new creolization for indentured people, and, finally, fifth, the shift from Creole/colonial to Creole/postcolonial and native subject (51).

Ninety percent of Guyana's population lives on the coast. Indo-Creole is a kind of *arrivant* who has the *right blood* and therefore inherits the state.

The "International Year of Indigenous Languages" launched in Guyana brings attention to the languages that survived Creolization and missionization. These languages are: Patamona, Akawaio, Wapichan, Makushi, Wai Wai, Warrus, Carib, Arecuna and Arawak (Loko).

Moses Nagamootoo said, "Hold on to your languages. Promote them. Protect them. You should be proud of your languages. . . ." as though the state is not responsible for genocide through its desire for "social integration."

"Social integration" sounds like attempted erasure to me.

*

*

65

From the Mashpee Wampanoag Tribe's website:

https://mashpeewampanoagtribe-nsn.gov/news/2020/3/27/message-from-the-chairman-we-will-take-action-to-prevent-the-loss-of-our-land

March 27, 2020

Message from the Chairman: We Will Take Action to Prevent the Loss of Our Land

. . . on the very day that the United States has reached a record 100,000 confirmed cases of the coronavirus and our Tribe is desperately struggling with responding to this devastating pandemic—the Bureau of Indian Affairs informed me that the Secretary of the Interior has ordered that our reservation be disestablished and that our land be taken out of trust. Not since the termination era of the mid-twentieth century has a Secretary taken action to disestablish a reservation. . . .

. . . we the People of the First Light have lived here since before there was a Secretary of the Interior, since before there was a State of Massachusetts, since before the Pilgrims arrived 400 years ago. We have survived, we will continue to survive. These are *our* lands, these are the lands of our ancestors, and these will be the lands of our grandchildren. This Administration has come and it will go. But we will be here, always. And we will not rest until we are treated equally with other federally recognized tribes and the status of our reservation is confirmed. . . .

Kutâputunumuw;

Chairman Cedric Cromwell
Qaqeemasq (Running Bear)

*

Trade by wing.

When I was seventeen, I went to Guyana for the first time. We took a boat down from Skeldon into the Corentyne River, deeper into the jungle's heart.

My Aja used to trade tinned goods from Corriverton to Orealla.

Where he purchased these initially, with start-up from selling rum and tailoring shirts, I am not certain. He traded with people in Native villages along the route, bringing a new idea of commodity, goods, and scarcity like a slug trail. Bringing settler logic into the Interior.

When we disembarked in Orealla, up in the trees were massive cages. In these cages were scarlet macaws and blue and gold macaws to be traded north to the United States for breeding and selling. The north economy, devastating local communities, is the opposite of sustainable.

On our voyage back to Skeldon our boat ran out of gas, and the boatman did not have any oars.

The night sky bright with stars. I had never seen anything as clearly as the Milky Way that night.

I wrote about it obscurely in a poem once that David Dabydeen read. He said "You're a real poet."

We drifted with the current upstream to Skeldon.

*

*

Red-Winged Blackbird

As a child in Florida, they perched on reeds and plants bound by roots to the water. I carry the Central Florida waterways inside me. The St. Johns. The Econlockhatchee. Lake Jesup. The Homosassa.

*

Black and blue iridescent
in the first light
the trill

I hear them first, a staccato cry
and then I look up
to the night with a red
sun halved for each wing

I am in a chorus

MALDEN, MASSACHUSETTS
MARCH 14–30, 2020

Obstacle

MONA KAREEM

Born in Kuwait in 1987, Mona Kareem is a scholar and poet who was exiled to the United States in 2011. She is the author of three poetry collections and, most recently, the trilingual chapbook Femme Ghosts *(2019). Her selected translations of Iraqi poet Ra'ad Abdul Qader's work will appear in 2021.*

Laying dead on bricks broken
by little plants

laying dead between two
plastic summer chairs

laying dead on the shore
of an unwanted ocean

laying dead on stairways
which are the sisters of ladders

laying dead in a dream
right before it mares

laying dead in someone's world

laying dead six feet away

laying dead after work

laying dead in the warm company
of autumn trees

laying dead at your mom's kitchen

laying dead vertically, horizontally,
and to the left

laying dead small

laying dead close

laying dead falling from a swing

I want a swing in the living room

OBSTACLE

laying dead between bed and tv and window

laying dead by the only window

laying dead at a Greek theater

laying dead while exiting the abyss

laying dead next to my shadow

laying dead as an obstacle to people,

to ways, roads, bridges, markets

pools, steps, sand, concrete, forests,

down, dead, right on the face

BINGHAMTON, NY
MAY 2020

PART II

The Path to Paradise Begins in Hell

Journal of the Kairos

FILIP SPRINGER

Translated from the Polish by Sean Gasper Bye

Filip Springer (Poznań, Poland, 1982) is a self-taught, award-winning journalist and photographer. His nonfiction debut, History of a Disappearance: The Forgotten Story of a Polish Town, *published by Restless Books in 2017, was shortlisted for the Ryszard Kapuściński Literary Reportage Prize and was nominated for the Gdynia Literary Prize and the Nike Literary Prize.*

Journal of the Kairos

1

THE SLEEPING PROBLEMS began on October 8, 2018 at 8:17 a.m. He was drinking his morning coffee. He picked up his phone and tapped his thumb on the icon for the *New York Times*.

"The Intergovernmental Panel on Climate Change has released a report," reads Kajetan Rost. "By 2030 we must reduce emissions of greenhouse gases by 45%, and by 2050 we must eliminate them. If we do not, the climate will fall into a sequence of changes we will not be able to halt. In many places on earth, life will become impossible for billions of people."

Further down, an expert explained: "We will not only lack food, but also the possibility of a dignified burial for victims. All this can happen within the twenty-first century."

Kajetan tosses and turns in bed, only getting to sleep in the middle of the night, and even then he sometimes has terrible nightmares.

His dreams are disaster movies with the characters running through streets he knows.

Being awake isn't much better. Kajetan, sitting in a café over his daily paper, has started catching himself making cynical calculations. Will the Catastrophe strike him and his wife? Their son? Or maybe only their grandchildren? Rost is thirty-seven, he's never thought about grandchildren before; after all, he's just recently become a father. Will his son decide to bring children into the world, already knowing what that world is going through? (Kajetan realizes how self-serving this reflection is—since, after all, it's easier for him to believe he didn't read about any of this until October 8, 2018 over his morning coffee. But that's nonsense, isn't it? It had just taken him that long to open his eyes.)

Sometimes Rost manages to get his mind off things for a moment. But then he'll get hung up on a single sentence, word, or image. Like one evening when they were getting to bed, and he was reading to his son about the new adventures of Winnie-the-Pooh. There was a section about a drizzly fall. Kajetan's mind thrashed with fear that in ten or twenty years, "drizzly" would be a concept consigned to the past.

"Dad, keep reading," whispered the little boy.

He read to the end. The boy fell asleep. But Kajetan was wide awake.

This awareness of approaching disaster led Rost to decide to change his life.

He stopped eating meat. That was no trouble.

He didn't take planes anymore.

He refused to use plastic bags and disposable coffee cups.

He bought a cotton tote bag, a thermos, and a bottle for tap water.

The next day, he read that the production of cotton tote bags, thermoses, and bottles for tap water was hastening the destruction of the planet. So were avocados.

One day, as Rost was walking past a bookstore, a poster caught his eye: "Chronos, Kairos, Aion—the Greek Understanding of Time." He stepped inside. A bearded philosopher was explaining:

"Kairos is 'this very moment' or 'the proper time,' the right moment to act, created by opportunity and unique, transient circumstances. Kairos therefore designates a critical, decisive moment, the one moment among many, the perfect moment, when, in the blink of an eye, circumstances, fate, and the readiness to act all coincide."

Kairos—Kajetan smiled to himself. That had been his nickname in high school. Except, of course, when because of his skin problems he was just "Crusty."

He bought the book. He read it at home, underlining dozens of quotes. One he marked in red: "Wars break out, the planet warms, species go extinct. Yet this is like many wars in that its extent and which species we manage to save depends on whether we take action. The future is swathed in darkness, the darkness both of the womb and the grave."

Kajetan took out a black notebook and jotted down the quote. Underneath he added:

"For the moment, nothing is happening that I—an affluent resident of a large European city—couldn't cope with. None of these calamities affects me directly. Our household budget will have no trouble standing up to high food prices, and could likely also cope with a hike in the electric bill, for now. Barring a completely out-of-control market collapse, hyperinflation, or similar disturbances in the coming years, my family's existence does not seem to be at risk. We have savings. We live in stability and comfort. . . ."

(As he was writing this, Kajetan Rost did not realize he was starting to compose a journal. A few months later, when the Disaster was picking up speed and strength, Kajetan would add a title to the first page of the notebook: *Journal of the Kairos*.)

"Today, the highest price I am paying for the disaster is only that when I look at my sleeping son, I feel paralyzing fear. I could stop leaning over his bed, turn away, and it would still be there. The evil that lurks in the relentlessly advancing future. Tangible, within arm's reach.

"On a global scale, I am in a very comfortable situation—by only feeling that fear."

2

He started to focus on the little things, he almost completely cut himself off from news services, he bought an old cell phone with no internet access. He got up earlier, learning to enjoy early mornings. Especially this time of year, when the wind rustling the tops of the trees heralded the final end of summer, when he had to get his rain jacket out of the closet, and every trip out to the playground with his son was delayed by a frantic search for the boy's hat, which they always found somewhere different than either had expected.

One such early morning, he was standing by the window with a cup of coffee, with no intention of going anywhere. He simply couldn't sleep anymore. The view of their side street was still shrouded in darkness. The dim gray of predawn was only broken by the rhythmic explosions of hazard lights on a van delivering bread. Rost could see the driver rushing back and forth with boxes of rolls. In the corner of the man's mouth he could make out the glow of a cigarette. At a certain moment the man stopped his hustling and looked up.

Rost lifted his gaze from the man up to the trees. The tall poplars standing in the street were swaying under the pressure of the wind. He had recently caught himself stopping more and more by them, staring at them. There were times, amid the crush of everyday business, when Rost found himself marveling at their mere existence. They were living smack in the middle of a country that hated trees. Every day his media bubble was bursting with depressing news about more and more trees being cut down. In Kajetan's country, they were resources to be taken advantage of. Most weren't allowed to live to a mature age. When Rost realized this one day—that most of the trees in his country weren't allowed to grow to their full size—he couldn't shake the feeling that it was just like slaughtering dairy calves. After all, their flesh was the most tender. That had made him shudder even when he still ate meat.

This budding inner sensitivity toward trees was a little alarming, since he associated it with those weird people who dressed in linen gowns and hugged birches. He didn't know a single person like that; honestly, he'd never even seen one. Still, he found that sort of behavior extremely pretentious. So Kajetan viewed the transition taking place inside him with caution. But the trees moved him. There was no helping it. It moved him to have them here with him.

In time, he absorbed a few scientific facts.

Plants have lived on Earth for around seven hundred million years.

They make up ninety percent of the biomass on our planet.

Most species can survive damage on a large scale.

In the case of plants, removing parts of their bodies does not lead to death. They can reorganize themselves, divide, grow more, and multiply.

Humans have never mastered any of these arts.

If perpetuating the species and reproductive success was the basic goal for the existence of living beings on this earth, thought Rost, it was hard to shake the feeling that humans were doing markedly worse in the race than plants—that they were the rulers, not us.

Though humans obviously thought otherwise.

"But what do the trees think?" he wondered as he sipped his coffee, then suddenly realized the absurdity of this reflection. Linen-clad tree-huggers were swiftly encroaching on the horizon of his imagination, sporting triumphant grins. He drove them away.

In asking himself what the trees think, Rost saw the fully manifested danger of the ground slipping away beneath his feet. The foundation on which his world stood. Because individually, maybe trees didn't think anything. But what about a forest? Or a park? Scientists already knew trees could warn one another of danger, sense fear, and share resources—water and microelements. Such exchanges also took place between species.

"Sentience or intelligence isn't a thing, you can't find it in, or analyze it out from, the cells of the brain," read Rost, from a story by his favorite author, Ursula K. Le Guin. Her books, published in the nineties with night-marishly hideous covers, had sat neglected on his bookshelves. Recently he'd found himself returning to them more and more often. In her story, "Vaster than Empires and More Slow," he was surprised to find his own underlining from years ago. "Now let's just suppose, most improbably," said one of the characters in the story, "that you knew nothing of animal brain-structure. And you were given one axon, or one detached glial cell, to examine. Would you be likely to discover what it was? Would you see that the cell was capable of sentience?"

It was a rhetorical question. Rost smiled to himself. It was liberating, even, to realize the insignificance of his own species. Humans had the power to cut off certain evolutionary paths by wiping out entire ecosystems. They had mastered the technologies to do so. But why should that ability, of all things, indicate some superiority over other species?

Looking at the poplars rustling in the first autumn wind, Rost realized we were one of evolution's dead ends, rather than its most perfect achievement. And the end of the world that he feared so terribly would be only the end of humankind. The world would do better without us.

3

"Come on, kiddo," he said one day, "we're going on a ride to the river." Though by "we" he mostly meant himself.

The day before he'd gotten on a city bus. The two women sitting in front of him had gone on at length for a few stops about how beautiful the weather was this fall. Kajetan had to get off. He knew by the next stop he'd be transformed into one of those nuts who suddenly, out of nowhere, started berating strangers with incoherent sermons.

It was October; for ten days the temperature hadn't dropped below fifteen degrees Celsius. The sun was shining and there was no rain. This wasn't normal. Kajetan even started leaving for work a bit earlier than usual, to enjoy the cool of the early morning. At 6 a.m. it still felt roughly like fall should: chilly, gray, and damp. Yet he knew doing this was only maintaining his delusion. Because then the sun would come out, and even before he'd had his morning coffee he'd have to toss his warm jacket over his shoulder.

That's why he thought a trip to the riverside would be a good idea. He wanted to go back to where things were still relatively normal. Yes, he realized there was no pure nature anymore. But he still believed he could get close to what was left of it. In the city it was easy to overlook the remnants of it. They would find a pleasant spot, he thought, gather up some kindling, light a little campfire, and roast potatoes. They got together a pocketknife, food supplies, and a garden trowel, and they set off. They wanted to take one of the ferries to the right bank of the river, to give their trip a flavor of adventure, but the ferries hadn't been running for some time. The reason was the low water level and the risk of running aground. Hadn't they themselves one day watched from the boulevards as a small, private riverboat had gotten caught on a sandbank and been unable to break free? The party taking place on its upper deck had kept going as the captain raced from stem to stern and back, trying to get the boat unstuck. He'd had no luck until a police motorboat with strong engines arrived.

Kajetan hadn't been able to shake the feeling that the people partying on the deck didn't even realize what was going on. Though of course he couldn't be sure—he'd been watching from very far away.

The other side of the river was overgrown. Rost headed for a northbound path that ran through the trees. He rode his bike fast, only avoiding the deeper potholes so the seat his son was strapped into wouldn't jostle too strongly.

Finally, they found the right spot, a small clearing hidden in the undergrowth not far from one of the bridges and the sandy beach. Rost scraped the turf away with his shoe, then started digging a small firepit with the trowel. Here, the gray gravel and riverside sand was mixed with shards of glass, beer bottle tops, cigarette butts, and bits of plastic. Rost thought he'd just had the bad luck of picking a spot where someone had buried some trash. So they moved a dozen or so meters in another direction, found another break in the undergrowth, and set up another campground. Rost started digging again.

And again he found the same. Gravel, glass, bottle tops, trash, cigarette butts.

Yet again they changed places and with even more passion, he drove the trowel into the ground.

The same.

"Dad? Aren't we gonna have a fire?" He heard the familiar little voice behind him and knew exactly what expression he'd see if he turned his head in that direction.

"We will, kiddo. We're gonna have everything," he said. "Come on, let's find some sticks."

They went into the trees to hunt down some dried branches and twigs. They walked around with their eyes glued to the ground, but only found empty bottles and pieces of machines dumped by the river at some point—washers and televisions. Everywhere he looked, Kajetan could see violently broken-off branches. They were most likely from people who'd run out of patience looking for kindling on the ground. Some of the branches were dangling sadly—their tormentors couldn't defeat them, so they had abandoned their work midway through.

Rost clenched his fists. He wanted to get out of here, but he knew that was out of the question. He couldn't disappoint his son. Finally, they found some brittle, dusty sticks in a dry wall by the river. They arranged them in a miniature pile and set them alight. A strip of gray smoke made its way straight up into the blue sky. It smelled like the smoke of all the campfires Rost had sat beside in his youth, somewhere out in the woods, actually far from civilization.

At moments like that, he occasionally imagined he was the last person on earth who didn't know the world had just ended.

Now he saw that person in his son, who was munching without a care on a roasted potato.

4

The freeze-frame was unclear. He could make out stormy seas, a large border patrol boat and a dinghy attached to its hull, full of people. Their figures were difficult to distinguish, much less their faces. Kajetan Rost peered closer at the monitor. His finger tapped and the picture moved. Rocked by the waves, the boats were knocking against one another, the human figures in the dinghy were wobbling uncertainly and trying to clutch the ropes running along its side. Rost had seen videos like this before. They were recorded on the Mediterranean Sea, where every week coast guard boats were pulling from the water refugees trying to make it to Europe.

But this film was different.

Rost clicked again and saw a man appear on the deck of the large boat—now he could see clearly it belonged to the Greeks—holding a long stick. Yet instead of giving it to the people in the rubber boat he went to the side and started bashing them with it on their heads.

Rost paused the video again. The sea, the boats, the people, the stick hanging in the air.

The people in the raft attempted to defend themselves, raising their hands to shield themselves from the blows. Finally, from somewhere astern, a round, green object appeared over their heads. They passed it forward until it reached those who were most endangered by blows from the stick. They shielded themselves with it for a good while. Then the boats moved apart. The Greek boat retreated a short distance, only to head toward the refugees a moment later at full speed, passing close by them and causing a broad wave. The cameraman filming the whole incident zoomed out. Now two Greek boats were clearly visible, circling around the dinghy, making aggressive maneuvers, most likely attempting to force it to change course.

But it was that green shape that gave Kajetan no peace.

He rewound the recording a little and once again moved his face closer to the display. What was it? A tarp, a blanket? He clicked the film along frame-by-frame, second-by-second. But it was no use.

The whole situation had taken place a few days earlier on the coast of the Greek island of Lesbos. Rost typed the basic information about it into a search engine box. After a few seconds, the algorithm spat him out the complete results. They included a link to one of the Italian photo agencies. Their photographer must have watched the whole scene unfold from the same boat as the camera operator. His shots were almost exact copies of the recording, only sharper.

They showed Rost, in full detailed precision, terrified women hugging their children and men at the bow of the boat trying to grab the long boat hook the Greek border guard was clutching. In one picture, he saw the men holding over their heads an inflatable ball you would play with at the pool or the shore. It was green and looked like a smiling dragon.

A happy green dragon.

Rost froze. He couldn't take his eyes off the picture. The refugees in the dinghy were probably people fleeing the war in Syria. He knew this was a conflict that experts referred to as a climate war, though for the moment, few people thought of it that way. After all, it was more comfortable to view it as some bloody, localized turmoil with the greatest global powers trying to use the opportunity to win something or other. Yet he knew that year after year, these wars would multiply. They would take place over access to water and food. Conditions would get increasingly difficult in the regions suffering most from global warming. And they would finally become impossible. Rost wanted to believe that such a scenario wouldn't affect either the country or the region where he and his family lived. And right there, on the threshold of that belief, he plunged into an abyss he had no way of climbing out of.

Because the more wars there were, the more refugees would be storming the gates of Europe. Which meant more border guards, more motorboats, more boat hooks. And ultimately, they would have to ram the boats, shoot at the people.

"And how will we explain this to ourselves? That we need to kill women and children at the gates of our fortress?" he wrote in his journal. "For now we're just telling them to die somewhere else, keeping our hands clean—someone else can pull the trigger. But what does it make us once we decide to start shooting? What will it mean then to publish books, make movies, write, and read poetry? How will we be able to sit down to dinner together and look one another in the eye? Since, after all, we'll have to keep our eyes closed all the time."

5

"Cmd dot exe," the man said with a bitter smile. These words jolted Rost out of his reverie. They'd called for help half an hour before, but the dispatcher had informed them they weren't going to send a helicopter for a simple sprain. "The rescue patrol will come on an ATV," Kajetan heard through the receiver. "Please stay with the injured person."

Rost wasn't going anywhere. They exchanged a few courteous remarks, then they sat in silence amid of the mountain solitude.

"Pardon?" asked Rost.

"Cmd dot exe," repeated the man. "Did you have comp sci in school?"

"With a notebook." Kajetan remembered peering at the screen of the only computer in the classroom while their teacher dictated to them the operations for starting up a text editor.

"I teach in a tech school," explained the man. "Cmd dot exe is a program that opens the text control window. You know, the black screen where you can enter different commands in Windows. The real face of the system, which is usually hidden behind those aesthetic windows and icons. Whenever I show it to students for the first time they're disappointed, some are even frightened."

"Frightened? Of what?" Rost didn't really understand.

"Suddenly it turns out the reality they were living in," replies the man, "is not only virtual, it's nothing but a colorful overlay for something so . . . prosaic."

Rost knew he'd be sitting here a little while yet. He was familiar with this trail. He'd come here for the first time back in childhood, with his father. In the morning he'd left his wife sunning herself in the autumn sun on the terrace of the hostel (they had an agreement: she would never set foot on a mountain trail, nor he on a dance floor). The weather report called for sun all day. In fact, the whole of September had been like this. Kajetan couldn't actually remember the last genuine rain, a solid fall downpour. As a matter of fact, he'd even considered not putting a rain jacket in his backpack.

The first thing that surprised him was the sizeable area of cleared land that began just beyond the outermost structures of the town. Rost was sure that three years before, the last time he'd been there, a forest had stood on this spot. Now trees arranged in even cords were already waiting to be transported out, while the ground had been torn up by the huge harvesters. The cleared land revealed a new panorama, but Kajetan was incapable of enjoying it. He felt something had been taken away from him here. He kept his eyes glued to the ground and walked straight on.

The first climb took an hour. Kajetan took a break every twenty minutes to calm his struggling heart. He knew this was the most difficult section of the trail, and the least picturesque. Once he reached the right elevation, the paved forest path took a sharp turn eastward via a traverse, and the trail led Rost upward into towering spruce trees. In the air he could sense pricks of cold, completely unnoticeable down below. There was no one around. Rost walked briskly, climbing quickly. He knew he had another two hours of hiking before the nearest shelter. There, he planned to allow himself a one-time dispensation for meat and eat a pork cutlet. Like the ones he'd eaten back in the day with his father. They'd been as large as oars and the staff had to put the potatoes on top of them, not next to them, or else they wouldn't fit on the plates.

At this elevation, he was already encountering clusters of dwarf mountain pines. Now the trail was running along a ragged, stony path framed with crowberries. It occurred to Rost that this was the moment when he was furthest from any human outpost, in a way that could only be possible on that day. And that was when he saw him. The man was lying in the grass, right by a small footbridge meant to stop tourists from trampling a peat bog. He was propped up on his elbows and his face was twisted in a grimace of pain. For a moment they eyed each other uncertainly.

"You all right there?" asked Rost.

The man hoisted himself up on his elbows. He was older than Kajetan, probably by twenty years.

"Afraid not." He glanced at his ankle. "I think this has finished me off for today."

Rost took off his backpack, took out a bottle of water, and offered it to the man.

"Do you have a phone? Mine can't get reception up here."

Kajetan's phone was picking up a Czech signal. They could call.

After three-quarters of an hour, from somewhere in the distance and down below them, they heard the growl of a motor.

They realized this was the volunteer mountain rescuers they had been waiting for.

"Text control window?" asked Rost, because he still didn't understand what the man was talking about.

The man nodded.

"That's right, the delusions evaporate, the masks slip," he said, peering in the direction of the arriving help, "and you and I are here for the sake of relaxation, rest, reset, a few moments for us to breathe. Call it what you will, anyway. In any event we came here to be enchanted, because someone drummed it into our heads that we live in culture and only occasionally return to nature. And we return on our own terms."

He gently patted his twisted ankle.

"But all it takes is a trifle like this in a wilderness that, after all, I entirely consented to, and I feel panicked anxiety. That no one will find me, that I'll freeze and die. In one moment everything I came here for—these rocks, the trees, the sky, the view of a distant landscape—I started to treat like enemies who wanted to annihilate me. But after all, that's nothing other than life laid bare. Truly sobering, don't you think?"

6

And then the pandemic broke out. After a week stuck at home, Kajetan reached for his journal.

"Kairos is 'this very moment' or 'the proper time,' the right moment to act, created by opportunity and unique, transient circumstances. Kairos therefore designates a critical, decisive moment, the one moment among many, the perfect moment, when, in the blink of an eye, circumstances, fate, and the readiness to act all coincide."

Rost smiled to himself. Then he wrote:

"I'm standing on the balcony and looking at my housing complex. Every window really does have a light shining in it. I don't think it's ever been like that here. It's 7 p.m. and they're all home. We're spending less, we've stopped dreaming of vacations by the warm sea, we're not flying. Empty planes are still flying, but they'll stop soon. We're reining in our needs, economizing. We're doing what we should have done long ago to save ourselves. The virus has forced us to. We would never have done it ourselves."

Day nine:

"The peak of the Matterhorn is lit up with optimistic slogans. They've installed some space technology there, enormous projectors, I have no idea. And they're shining visualizations on the mountainsides.

"Humans won't back off from anything that would prevent us from making constant chit-chat. Human yammering knows no limits. It can taint anything. Right now we're living through a scenario where nature is forcibly reminding us of our own existence and that we are only a small, fragile part of that nature itself. And what do we do? Instead of being in this, instead of accepting this with even a shadow of humility—we jabber. As if it were the silence and quiet that were going to kill us, not the virus."

Day ten:

"So far I have thought that mistrust of one's own country is more like a sign of common sense. I'm sure I've thought so because I didn't especially need this country's government for anything. I've scorned it. But how can you not scorn an administration that in the first week of a crisis was playing political games instead of tackling the problem?

"Now I can see that, during a crisis, my almost total lack of interest in having anything to do with this government translates into my concrete emotions and actions. Because when the state introduces prohibitions and limits, one after the other, my immediate instinct is not to trust that they're well-intentioned. When it proposes that I download an app that will track my contacts and meetings out of fear of spreading the virus, my first instinct is suspicion of the state. It's never done a good job, why should it do one now? This whole crisis is showing me that as soon as it's possible, I need to do whatever I can to free myself from this government. To move where the state can be more functional because its citizens trust it, because I trust it."

On day twenty of the pandemic, Rost decided to go for a walk. After walking for a quarter of an hour he found himself in an urban sacred spot, a fragment of damp meadow surrounded by housing developments. This area had only lasted so long because the ground was too soft to be profitable for some developer to put something up here. There were nooks and crannies in this place where Rost could feel like he was in the truest untamed wilderness. On this bright, crisp morning a thin layer of transparent ice sliced across the surface of the marshy ground. Last year's yellowing grass was weighted down with coral beads of hoarfrost. Rost walked along a barely visible path, watching carefully where he stepped. This took him across the whole swampy field and he emerged not far from one of the newer developments on the other side. He was just approaching the car-filled parking lot when something startled in a nearby clump of bushes. In a moment, a pheasant flew out. With vigorous movements of its short wings, it flapped up to a low altitude. Thrilled, Rost followed its flight until the bird's silhouette vanished against the blinding orb of the sun. Then he closed his eyes for a moment and heard a dull thud. When he opened his eyes again there was no trace of the pheasant. Yet a young woman in a nightshirt was standing in the balcony door of an apartment on the second floor of the nearest building. She was staring through the closed glass door at the dead bird lying at her feet.

That day Rost wrote in his journal:

"I feel a little like that pheasant. I'm afraid for myself and my family. I see lines in stores and people quarreling over basic goods at the cash registers. I see an administration that's taking advantage of the opportunity and dismantling democracy even further. And big companies, untouchable in all this, who will soon be able to make all of us even more dependent on them. I see borders closing, the police using excessive force, and cruel looks from people on the streets. I hear about a smartphone app that's supposed to track my every move and contact. All for the sake of my safety.

"I don't see any future, there's none today that I can think about seriously.

"I knew this would all come, I was afraid of it, it wouldn't let me sleep. But I was betting that none of it would arrive until twenty, thirty years from now, because of a different catastrophe. I thought we still had a little time. A little more flying, ungracefully but freely, just above the hard ground."

POLAND
SEPTEMBER 2019

A Cowardly New World

TERESA SOLANA

Translated from the Spanish by Peter Bush

Teresa Solana (Barcelona, Spain, 1962) is the former director of Spain's National Translation Centre. A Not So Perfect Crime *(2009), her first novel, won the Brigada 21 Prize, and A* Shortcut to Paradise *(2011), her second, was shortlisted for the Salambó Prize. Solana lives in Oxford with her husband and translator Peter Bush and their daughter.*

THE LAST TIME I boarded an airplane was at the beginning of March this year. I was off to visit my elderly mother, who, for the last three years after my father's death, has been living in Girona, a small, beautiful city some sixty miles from Barcelona where one of my brothers lives as well. I was born in Barcelona, the city where my family comes from, and where I have spent most of my life, although I now live in the UK, my husband's country of birth. When we floated the possibility of moving to Oxford six years ago, the knowledge that I would be able to travel to Barcelona frequently was key in reaching such an important decision as changing my country of residence. I am delighted to live in England, but remain closely connected to Barcelona, which I often visit thanks to low-cost airlines.

Traveling has been part of my life since I was appointed director of the Spanish Translators House in 1998 and began to participate in international meetings with directors of the other national centers dedicated to literary translation and partly funded by the European Union. My role was to promote literary translation through grants for residencies and enable contact between translators and writers from different countries, at a time when we still dreamed of a Citizens' Europe and the European Union aspired to be more than a mere club of states. Subsequently, as a writer, I have been fortunate to see my books translated into several languages—including English—and that has allowed me to participate in literary festivals in different parts of the world. Over recent months, the promotion of my novels has taken me to Toronto, Istanbul, and, coincidentally, to Barcelona, where every year, at the beginning of February, Barcelona Negra is held, one of the most popular international festivals for fans of noir.

I had just returned to Oxford after participating in the last edition of this festival when news that my mother had been taken into hospital with a hepatic complaint forced me to get back on an airplane. I landed in Barcelona on February 25, worried about my mother's delicate state of health but not at all concerned about the coronavirus. And, naturally, never imagining that a few days later I would be hurrying to buy a return ticket to England out of a fear that borders would be closed.

At the end of February, despite the spectacular lockdown suffered by the population of the Chinese city of Wuhan, the WHO had yet to declare the coronavirus as a world pandemic—such a declaration would come on March 11—and epidemiologists were still saying that COVID-19 wasn't a very dangerous virus and had a much lower death rate than influenza.

At that time, despite the usual conspiracy theories already circulating on the internet, most of us didn't question the opinion of those experts who assured us that there was nothing to worry about. After all, there seemed to be a unanimous consensus in the international scientific community as to the scant lethal nature of the virus. Conversely, we had learned from our experience with type A flu in 2009 when alarmist predictions and the pressure of the pharmaceutical industry led governments to spend vast amounts of money on millions of vaccinations that in the end weren't required.

While I was in Girona, staying in my brother's apartment, the news coming out of Italy about the level of infections and deaths began to make me anxious. There had been a few cases of coronavirus in Spain, but with rare exceptions most experts were still stating there was no reason to be alarmed, supporting the continued organization of the World Mobile Congress in Barcelona, and assured us that there was no need to cancel the mass feminist demonstrations planned for March 8. However, for the first time, I began to feel seriously concerned. My husband and teenage daughter were alone in Oxford, and the fear that a health crisis would erupt and governments would decide to shut down airports precipitated my return to the United Kingdom the moment my mother's health began to improve.

A few days after arriving back in Oxford, on March 16, a state of emergency was declared in Spain and an enforced lockdown of the population began.

*

The lockdown started a week later in the UK than in Spain. As I write these pages, I have been shut up at home for over a month, though in much less stringent conditions than if the lockdown had trapped me in Catalonia. In the UK, we are allowed out of our homes for an hour a day to exercise, alone or accompanied by the people we live with, and children are allowed out for a walk, accompanied by their parents; moreover, when we do go out into the street, we don't feel the police breathing down our necks, or fear we will be landed with a huge fine if some policeman arbitrarily decides that our presence in the street isn't duly justified.

The measures adopted by different governments to combat coronavirus vary hugely from one country to another. At one extreme we find Switzerland, where citizens have self-confined responsibly and the Swiss government has felt no need to impose coercive measures. Spain is at the other extreme and is a country where it has been decided to treat the population as if it were collectively underage and where, in the best tradition of its legislative system—based on the elaborate Napoleonic code—common sense has been replaced by an immense, absurd set of norms that attempt to regulate what you can and cannot do during lockdown: you can't exercise in the street, but you can take your pets out to do what they have to do (though strictly only the minimum time needed); very young children can only go out in the street to avoid being left alone at home (with the exception of children suffering from a learning disability, who, like similarly disabled adults, are allowed out for a stroll); you can only buy essential items; some localities have imposed a thirty-euro minimum for purchases to stop people leaving their homes more than once a day; you can't go out with the people cohabiting with you, unless it's a disabled person who needs a helper. . . . And the nonsense has increased over the last few days, when there is discussion of letting kids under fourteen go out for an hour a day, with norms aimed at limiting the time outside according to age groups, and even the toys children can take with them. Norms that determine the number of minors who can go out with an adult, the maximum distance they can journey away from home (a radius of half a mile). . . . There is even a norm stipulating that no adult can use a child as

94

an excuse for going out, leaving it to the discretion of the police to decide if an adult is taking the child for a walk or if the child is taking an adult for a stroll. . . . Predictably, the absurdity of such hyperregulation has inspired picaresque responses. "Law passed, ploy in place," as a famous Spanish proverb has it. Thus, we have seen individuals taking their goldfish and toy poodles for a stroll, or disguising themselves as deliverers of food in order to stretch their legs for a bit. You must be really desperate to have recourse to such gimmicks.

Generally, in all this time, and except for the occasional outrageous act, most Spaniards have respected the spirit of the lockdown, which is all about maintaining social distancing in order to avoid infection. Nevertheless, the authoritarian manner of tackling the health crisis—based on prohibitions and economic sanctions rather than appealing to individual responsibility—has encouraged the police and the army to take over the streets and spend their time pursuing, fining, and, in some cases, arresting the population in an arbitrary fashion. On social media, we have seen police beating defenseless citizens, often motivated by racism. And we have witnessed actions verging on paranoia, like the policeman who fined an individual who had left their receipt of purchases in the shop, arguing that it could be a purchase made the previous day and used as an excuse to evade lockdown.

Right from the start, the Spanish government has opted to approach the coronavirus as a war, establishing a military scenario and using bellicose language with patriotic resonances. It was decided to apply a law known as the "gagging law," passed by the previous conservative government, theoretically in order to fight Islamist terrorism but which in practice has been used to suppress political dissidence and freedom of expression. There is a daily televised press conference in which three uniformed, medallioned military leaders appear who employ military rhetoric and patriotic slogans as they give their "dispatches from the front": "Today is Monday, not Saturday, because weekends don't exist in wars!" thundered one general on a Saturday to a gathering of journalists he left nonplussed. The climate of militarization and police vigilance imposed on the whole country has triggered an outbreak of police violence on the streets and of neighbors spying on neighbors, encouraged by a government that likes to describe itself as "progressive." Informing on others is firmly on the agenda. Of course, there are also very many examples of solidarity, empathy, and kindness among neighbors, but this kind of informing activity, typical of totalitarian societies, is worrying and affords little hope in terms of the future that awaits us.

There is no shortage of examples. Like the individual who denounced a mother who had gone to the supermarket to buy candles for the birthday cake she'd baked for her daughter: birthday candles are not "essential items." Or the shocking concert of threats and insults which a group of neighbors struck up from their balconies aimed at a man who'd simply sat on a bench by himself (whom someone filmed and put on social media). Or the insults directed at some health workers or supermarket staff when they go into the street in order to go to work because the neighbor shouting at them from their window doesn't realize they are essential workers. . . . The fact that some citizens are acting like a frenzied mob and spend their time spying on how often, how long, and why their neighbor goes into the street—and triumphantly call on the police to intervene—is extremely worrying and should put us on our guard. Even more so when this behavior is being encouraged and applauded by those whose responsibility it is to exercise power.

These days, when there is much talk of issuing "immunity certificates" and various initiatives are being discussed to control the movements and interactions of the population through cell phone apps, the debate over security—health safety, in this case—and freedom is back on the table. This debate, which arose in 2001 as a consequence of the attacks on New York's twin towers, assumes special importance in countries with a tendency to crave authoritarian solutions in times of crisis. In terms of controlling the pandemic, there is no doubt that such measures can be efficient, as shown by the example of China and Korea, but the issues posed in relation to ethical outcomes and the impact they may have on Western democracies should compel us to engage in a broader dialogue in which not only politicians and scientists should have the right to participate. The perspectives of scientists are indispensable, but we must also listen to philosophers, anthropologists, intellectuals, artists, and creators. . . . And beyond the strictly health-centric debate, we should be asking ourselves what kind of society we wish to live in.

*

The most optimistic are confident that, sooner or later, science will defeat the coronavirus through the longed-for vaccine and that, once the unprecedented economic crisis we must now confront is over, our lives will return to more or less what they once were. We will travel and attend mass events again, and the recent months of lockdown will become a collective memory to share with our descendants. Conversely, the most pessimistic are anticipating a future of totalitarian, technologically advanced societies, like the ones that appear in *Black Mirror*, a series that updates the scary dystopias imagined by twentieth-century writers like George Orwell, Ray Bradbury, Anthony Burgess, or Aldous Huxley. Globalization and the randomness introduced into the way we live and relate to others are both sources of wonder and fear, and today more than ever, futuristic dystopian fictions act as a kind of warning to those who travel the Web.

The modern dystopian novel, inaugurated by Yevgueny Zamyatin with *We* (1924), invites us to reflect on apparently utopian, authoritarian societies where the basic needs of individuals are satisfied and everything is perfectly regulated and controlled by the state. Societies with a high level of conformity, where violence and machismo have apparently been eradicated alongside hunger and incurable diseases, where collective well-being is prioritized over individual happiness. Societies that are theoretically perfect, though inhabited by uncritical, apathetic, unhappy individuals, societies where betrayal rules, and which have no impulses, divergent opinions, democracy, or history (in the Fukuyama sense), or that spirit of rebellion and creativity which characterizes us as human beings. Namely, a *brave new world* where no one would like to live.

Imagining worlds and posing dilemmas is what we writers have done since the ancient times of the rhapsodes. Contrary to what was believed by Plato, who proposed banning of poets from his ideal republic, accusing them of being "lie-makers," we fablers are indispensable, not only because we provide *entertainment*—without which it would have been hard for us to endure these tedious days of lockdown!—but because fiction, whatever the format it adopts, helps us to reflect on our longings and limitations, and to think of ourselves as society and as individuals. Even fictions as absurd as those involving vampires, werewolves, extraterrestrials in the form of giant insects, and the living dead, so popular over recent years, pose interesting situations and moral dilemmas. They are the contemporary versions of Hydra and Medusa, the Minotaur, the dragon, ogre, or Siren. Of the monsters, at the end of the day, who threaten *civilization*, and who are none other than ourselves.

Nietzsche imagined, in ancient Greece, a perpetual tension between Apollo and Dionysius, between the world of the civilized and the world of the wild. Plowed (that is, orderly) fields and the city with their constituted systems of government and justice stood against the dangers in forests inhabited by drunken gods with unruly temperaments like Dionysius or Pan. In the twentieth century, the Apollonian dystopias of the writers I previously mentioned find their counterpoint in the Dionysian dystopia recreated in *Mad Max*, where the concept of civilization disappears and chaos overcomes order in a world ruled by base passions and instincts; that is, by violence and not by an ideal of justice. However, in the society imagined by Nietzsche, Dionysian madness and Apollonian rationality complement each other. Apollo and Dionysius cannot exist without each other, and their "coupling" finally gives birth to Attic tragedy (F. Nietzsche, *The Birth of Tragedy*, 1872) that, not at all coincidentally, reaches its climax in fifth-century BC Athens, parallel with the introduction of democracy as a political system replacing the old aristocratic tyrannies.

None of us would want to live in the London of *A Brave New World* or the arid, dusty landscapes of *Mad Max*. Between totalitarian dictatorship and the brutal anarchy of extreme individualism we encounter the space for performances of Attic tragedy that are our imperfect Western democracies. History has taught us that in times of fear and crisis, authoritarian solutions find supporters, and, in the globalized world where we live, which possesses the necessary technology to keep a constant eye on us—and, consequently, to limit our freedom—it is vital to tackle the question of which values we want to invoke in order to build the future we will bequeath to our descendants. At the present time, none of us can say what the world will be like after this pandemic and, yet again, we confront the uncertainty of the unknown. Around the corner is that other big threat hanging over us, climate change, a threat that will inevitably force us to live our lives differently, one already stirring the consciences of young people, many of who have voluntarily begun to introduce important changes into their lives in order to save the planet, such as not eating meat or traveling by airplane (matters, that, in my case, as a relentless carnivore and traveler, remain pending).

Now, as I jot down these reflections, I don't know when I will be able to visit my family and friends, or whether in fact, or to what extent, my life will change after the pandemic. Meanwhile, tied to a ship's mast, I will continue to invent stories, pursuing, in Kafka's words, the "expedition in search of truth" that is literature. A "truth," as Catalan poet Salvador Espriu writes, that is a mirror shattered into a thousand pieces, of which each and every one of us possesses a fragment.

OXFORD, ENGLAND
MAY 1, 2020

The Intrusion

NAIVO

Translated from the French by Allison M. Charette

Naivo (Antananarivo, Madagascar, 1960), is a journalist, novelist, and scholar from Madagascar. His historical novel Beyond the Rice Fields *(2017), about the devastating effects that colonialism wrought upon the country in the early nineteenth century, is the first novel from Madagascar ever to be translated into English. Naivo is also the author of the collection of stories* Madagascar entre poivre et vanilla: Petits portraits à plume débridée *(2016). He lives in Ottawa, Canada.*

Coughing fit
In an empty street,
It marks a memory
Of a different time,
Tense and inventive and scrawled.
I called, but knew it not,
This blood of mine leaking out.
The nights of toil and vigil
With syrupy
Lullabies,
Which my coughing and
Raspy throat
Pester to no end,
To no connection.
For all that we have,
The wall is there, almost wondering, waiting for
This forgotten life soon
Lost,
These life-saving fears
This multitude with keen ears
Crushed in the long silence, long.
Silence.
Lights. Sirens.
Shadows frightened by
The spiral of leaves,
Stilled.

OTTAWA
MAY 2020

Augury

FREDERIKA RANDALL

Frederika Randall (New Castle, Pennsylvania, 1948–2020) was a writer, reporter, and translator. Among her numerous translations are Ippolito Nievo's Confessions of an Italian *(2015); Giacomo Sartori's* I Am God *(2019), and his forthcoming* Bug *(2021), both published by Restless Books; and two novels by Guido Morselli,* The Communist *(2017) and* Dissipatio H. G. *(2020). Randall received grants from the National Endowment for the Arts and PEN/ Heim Translation Fund and was awarded the 2011 Cundill History Prize, with Sergio Luzzatto, for the English translation of* Padre Pio: Miracles and Politics in a Secular Age. *She died in Rome in May 2020.*

EVERY MORNING at about 6 a.m. a chalky white dove lands on my bedroom windowsill and begins cooing very loudly. Beady eyes peer in the open window. Does he/she think I don't notice that a largish bird is contemplating broaching my domestic space—and boasting about it? The cooing is certainly more welcome than the assorted dog music that is our usual fare: hordes of unseen neighborhood canines, each alone with his or her own human family, that periodically excite each other to paroxysms of nervous barking. But mostly—ever since Italy was laid low by the COVID-19 virus and a countrywide lockdown was ordered on March 9, we've been hearing from the birds.

Gulls with something of a bad attitude, wheeling above, shrieking out their raucous claims to the upper air; crows and their melancholy cawing, masters of the middle air and colonizers of the tall cypress across the street, where a pair of them make their nest every year; squadrons of feral rose-ringed green parakeets, escaped from cages, that bomb in nearer the ground and settle on a bush or a tree, yapping excitedly among themselves.

We hear the birds because the streets are free of automobiles, the sky brighter and cleaner and quieter without a steady stream of airplanes landing at Fiumicino. We hear thrushes and finches and a blackbird, singing his heart out right now, it's a long story, every line of his song is a different chapter from the one before. An Odyssey of a tale. And what has possessed the white dove to want to share his or her joy—or whatever it is—with us? Virgil, my Italian husband, spotted a white bird yesterday on top of the air-conditioning unit on the balcony off our living room. The dove couple have made their nest there; maybe that's why they're in good spirits. I suspect the one who comes to the windowsill is the male because his call is so loud. Apparently they share the brooding of the eggs, so perhaps he stops there when he's off duty.

I admit, I have a bad conscience about the air conditioner, one of those human gadgets made for our comfort that pump carbon into the atmosphere. But with climate change, in the nearly thirty years since we moved from Milan to Rome, summers have become much more stifling than they once were.

*

It seems we've been fortunate here in Rome; infection rates and deaths have been very contained compared to Milan and other hard-hit Lombard cities like Bergamo and Brescia. We Romans put our good fortune down to the fact that that we're not workaholics like the northerners, traveling all over creation hawking our products, visiting our factories, putting in ten- and twelve-hour days and keeping up a healthy social-cum-business life with lunch in one city and the evening *aperitivo* in another. There are plenty of businesses here in Rome too, but the dominant ethos is that of the civil servant: nine to five, dinner at home, sometimes lunch. This is not the productive heart of the country but its administrative backside, so to speak. But will our lethargic streak keep us out of trouble as Italy cautiously reopens?

I wonder if the birds know something? A month has now gone by since we listened, charmed, to the dove's morning call; he or she has left us although I can still hear that loud cooing, somewhere in the distance. The nest is empty too, the fledglings have flown. But the times are out of joint: doves don't normally sit on windowsills and eye human living quarters with proprietary intent. They're sizing up our spaces, maybe planning on invading us as we have them. COVID-19, it's said, is the result of humans invading nature: shrinking wild habitats and a huge trade in illegal wildlife have allowed the virus to jump species. "This is not nature's revenge, we did it to ourselves," said the biologist Thomas Lovejoy, who pioneered the concept of biodiversity, and who advises us to show more respect for nature.

A tall order for sapiens. We humans are fatally anthropocentric when thinking our important human thoughts: about the economy, about politics, even about worthy matters such as injustice and inequality. When push comes to shove, our loyalty to our own species always trumps concern for the others. Even the best among us believe we must first resolve our species problems—humans cheating and exploiting other humans—and then, when all is well, address the coral, the whales, the insects, the bees, the rhinos, the trees, the birds and all. I'm not sure there's time.

Trouble is, we don't know much about other species. We don't know their languages. We don't understand them and we can't talk to them. A translator myself, I don't think it's impossible we might learn. Jane Goodall lived with our fellow primates, chimpanzees, for thirty years in the wild. The cohabitation revealed many chimpanzee characteristics that our species didn't know about. Individual humans who've lived with several different species of birds have also learned how to interpret some of their avian sounds and gestures.

African gray parrots are popular pets, there's a vast illegal trade that has decimated their numbers. Grays have an unusual ability to mimic human language and can learn up to 250 words and use them appropriately. Humans profit from the species' intense sociability and capacity to communicate with flock mates about location, predators, food sources and safety. Two grays recorded in the wild in Zaire could reproduce over two hundred different sounds, including nine imitations of other wild bird songs and one of a bat. When using human language to communicate with humans, grays choose their words carefully, using expressions that are socially appropriate as well as lexically correct. In captivity they need a lot of stimulation and attention and suffer if neglected. Although our experience with African grays demonstrates no human ability to make ourselves understood in another species' language, it does show that creatures can communicate across species lines.

In *H Is for Hawk* Helen Macdonald tells of the tempestuous time after her father's sudden death when she acquired a goshawk, a difficult bird of prey, and set about training it. The bird's nervous temperament in some ways mirrors her own, and they arrive at a kind of understanding. The language she has to master is not one of sound, but of motion. J. A. Baker too, in his astonishing description of another raptor in *The Peregrine*, is alive to how a falcon moves, as it hovers, falls like a deadweight, stoops (swoops) down from far above the gulls' stratum to snap the neck of its prey, perhaps a pigeon or the unfortunate doves of peace the Pope released in St Peter's Square one Easter.

If these high-flying birds had been flying over lockdown Rome, the streets empty of humans and of the perennial convoys of cars, what would they think had happened? There's a video made of central Rome in March—the Colosseum, the Capitoline, the Forum—dazzlingly empty and beautiful, eerie, postapocalyptic. It reminds me of the highbrow sci-fi novel *Dissipatio H.G.* by the Italian writer Guido Morselli I recently translated. Morselli believed Western thought was intellectually decadent, that European philosophy had become arrogantly and misguidedly anthropocentric. In his novel, people suddenly vanish and the birds celebrate the disappearance of the human race.

I've always thought the beautiful murmurations of starlings you see in the skies of Rome were celebrations, too. Celebrations of their numbers, their life force, their indifference to us. When you've walked the streets of the city where those avian swarms have come to roost in the trees, the air smelling powerfully of ammonia and the pavement slick with guano, you can't pretend these others come merely to amuse and entertain us.

The Romans of antiquity thought birds bore messages for humans. From the city's earliest days, they never made a decision without consulting the auspices. It's a very old custom; it may have been practiced by the Latins and the Etruscans who lived near these hills before Romulus and Remus. The Romans codified the auspices, considered expressions of Jupiter's will. No magistrate could be appointed, or campaign undertaken, without a positive *auspicium*.

The augurs, officials who interpreted patterns of thunder and lightning, avian cries and maneuvers in the sky and other signs, kept records of their interpretations, like legal precedents, to guide decisions. They watched two types of birds: Oscines, which were studied for how they sang, and Alites, observed for how they flew. Oscines included owls, ravens, crows, and hens; alites eagles, vultures, and ospreys. The cries and the movements of these birds were meticulously classified according to time of year and other circumstances.

I think I can interpret what the springtime "Caw, caw" of the hooded crows nesting in the cypress across the street means, as I watch them furl their wings and settle down to part the tree's deep branches. They're warning us and other dangerous and predatory species to stay away from their tree, from which their fledglings still have to fly. But I truthfully haven't a clue about the loud cooing of those doves who built their nest on top of my air conditioner and sat on my windowsill. Was that contentment? A love song? Triumph? A diversion, to draw attention away from a nest that was too exposed? A lament? A reminder we're not alone on this earth, that birds need shelter too?

Not long ago I saw a video with clips of wildlife and other animals around the world invading human spaces, presumably because all the humans were shut up indoors. There were herds of elephants marching down an urban street in Thailand, prides of lions sunning on the tarmac, huge pink clouds of flamingoes whirling over suburban Mumbai, a rhino pursuing a man in a village of lowland Nepal. The quality of the video was poor, and when a Korean translator acquaintance replied to my retweet: "I didn't know there were rhinos in Nepal" I thought: "How gullible I am." But then I consulted Wikipedia and found there are some six hundred greater one-horned rhinos in Nepal. It turned out the Korean translator wasn't doubting the claim, he was merely surprised.

My son the ecological-change biologist likes to take me to task for promoting false claims about natural phenomena. I'm no expert but I don't like to spread fake news. Were those clips of elephants and lions and flamingoes really proof that animals are reclaiming our space while we're on lockdown? I don't know, they could have been filmed at any time. Still, I think it's a good thing that some humans, however anecdotally, however virtually, even if just on social media, are thinking beyond our sapiens-centric world, imagining one more multispecied. For as worrying as we find this virus, it and we are only two species of the millions in our biosphere. We need to spend some time worrying about the others.

ROME
MAY 9, 2020

Our Old Normal

KHALID ALBAIH

Romanian-born and Qatari-raised, Sudanese artist and political cartoonist Khalid Albaih (Bucharest, Romania, 1980) is based in Copenhagen, Denmark, where he is the International Cities of Refuge Network (ICORN) PEN Artist-in-Residence. His cartoons have appeared in the New York Times, *the* Atlantic, NPR, *and the* BBC. *His commentary is published in the* Guardian, CNN, *and* Al Jazeera.

I WAS IN the last months of my guest artist residency in the city of Copenhagen when the COVID-19 pandemic broke out. I was supposed to leave for Sudan in February but travel abroad was suspended by the Danish government.

So I have had to stay a little longer in Denmark, which has given me the chance to observe firsthand how the "first world" is coping with a pandemic.

Just like everyone else around me, I have been quite anxious and worried about what is happening. But I have also been quite amused by the countless articles from American and European experts explaining how the various restrictions on public life which governments have imposed will become the "new normal" across the world.

I am sorry to break it to you, but your "new normal" has been the "old normal" for billions of Brown and Black people around the world. For many of us, restrictions, repression, and deprivation have been a constant feature of our whole lives.

Cannot travel wherever you want anymore? Well, the majority of us were never able to travel anywhere we wanted either—many simply because they cannot afford to do so, and the few who can—because of travel restrictions. That is right—declared and undeclared travel bans are nothing new to us.

To be able to get through those restrictions, we would have to fill out piles of papers asking us about all kinds of things—from the number of household dependents, to recent travel to "hot zones," contact with "suspicious people," and all the way to past participation in "terrorist activities." Not to mention that we would have to prove ourselves "disease-free" with all various certificates, such as the yellow fever card, the absence of which would land us in quarantine at the airport.

Throughout the visa application process, we would be kept at a (social) distance. We would submit our papers online, pay fees at a separate cashier at the bank, and wait outside the embassy in the scorching heat because we might be a danger to embassy staff.

And of course, once we got the visa, it would be no guarantee we would be allowed in. At arrival, we might very well be escorted to a small room to join other Black and Brown people for further questioning. And if they did not like us, they might make us leave. Cutting short your stay abroad in order to board a plane home happened to many people in this pandemic. It has happened for a long time to many Brown and Black people, too. You call it "evacuation"; we have had to call it "deportation."

Some Brown and Black people have tried to make it to their desired destinations by boat, and in many cases they have not been allowed to dock. In a very similar way, many cruise ships full of Westerners have not been not allowed to dock anywhere because of COVID-19 fears. Under the present circumstances, they, too, were "undesirables." Oh, the irony.

There is of course much anxiety in the West about children missing out on education because of closed schools and universities. Well, many Brown and Black kids cannot go to school even if there is one open near them, or they have to drop out before graduating because of poverty. And where I am from, universities have been shut down every time the governing regime has decided some suspicious political activity is happening on campuses.

There has been much noise about service industry businesses closing down, too. All of a sudden, Westerners have been forced to live without restaurants, hair salons, spas, gyms, cinemas, etc.—indeed a hard life, one that many Brown and Black people know all too well because it has been their normal forever.

Another thing I have found quite entertaining is the proliferation of speculations about a changing world order and China coming to dominate the West. We too know this fear. Foreign domination has been all too real for us, whether it has been by China, the United States, the United Kingdom, France, or any other colonial or neocolonial power.

Indeed, it is quite demoralizing and disempowering to know that your people do not have their own fate in their hands and that it is someone else sitting in a faraway capital taking decisions that will determine—most often devastate—your life.

Now many are also worried about growing surveillance, police repression, state of emergencies, and "increased powers" of governments as a result of the pandemic. Well, many Brown and Black people are intimately acquainted with mass surveillance and unlimited power, having lived under dictatorships for extensive periods of time. Many have spent their whole lives under a state of emergency.

Indeed, it seems the pandemic will give many in the "first world" a taste of dictatorship and perhaps mobilize them to resist. I can already see individuals, groups, and organizations uniting to support each other in hope of a better future, singing together, praying together, remembering the names of the martyrs who risked their lives to warn us, only to succumb to the deadly enemy.

There is a feeling of uncertainty about the future, which is not only scaring people but also making them hopeful, inviting them to imagine the world differently, to rethink political systems, the economy, to exchange ideas with others, to debate on social media and read countless analyses of what could and should happen.

I have seen all this before, and so have many other Brown and Black people who have witnessed and been part of resistance movements in their countries. This was my reality throughout last year as the Sudanese Revolution was raging on. It was also the case almost ten years ago during the Arab Spring.

And today I have the same fear I had last year, and almost a decade ago—that once the dust settles—inshAllah soon—things may not change at all, that we may go back to the "old normal."

While for us Brown and Black people it has been clear that we do not want to go back, I fear that many Westerners, while indulging in daydreaming about a different world today, will rush to go back to "business as usual" once the restrictions are lifted. They will forget all those discussions and realizations that their "old normal," while comfortable for the privileged, was ultimately unsustainable.

I do hope that the Western world and the rest of us will treat this experience as a wake-up call and keep our promises for change. We should remember that we are all in this together. The global political and economic system needs to change; we need to start investing in social justice, equality, and solidarity.

This should be the "new normal" we seek to establish.

COPENHAGEN
APRIL 2020

A Certain Slant of Light

HAMID ISMAILOV

Translated from the Uzbek by Shelley Fairweather-Vega

Hamid Ismailov (Tokmak, Kyrgyzstan, 1954) was born into a deeply religious Uzbek family of mullahs and khojas, many of whom lost their lives during the Stalin-era persecution. He was the BBC World Service's first Writer in Residence. He is the author of many novels including The Underground *(2015) and* The Railway *(2015), both published by Restless Books. Critics have compared his books to the best of Russian classics, Sufi parables, and works of Western postmodernism. His works are still banned in Uzbekistan.*

ZOMIN HAD A DREAM. In the dream he seemed to be riding a bicycle. The road was dark but flashed with light. As he rode a stern shade of a woman dressed in black was following him, and when she was even with his bicycle she gave Zomin a shove, and he toppled over on the side of the road, and suddenly he seemed to realize this woman was Death. With that dreadful thought, covered in a black sweat, Zomin woke up. . . .

Now the lightening sky began to edge out the darkness, and other than the rustling of rain, there was silence all around. Zomin listened. From far away, the sound of a train started up. It came closer, knocking and clanking as it passed. It moved away. Upstairs, his wife was making noise with something. That woke up the cat, who went to nudge at the door to the living room. When it didn't open the cat went back to its basket. Zomin turned onto his right side and all of it—like rainwater on a greased windowpane—washed out of his memory, and he went back to sleep. This time it was a heavy, dark, dreamless sleep.

When he awoke, time had somehow flown. True, today was Sunday, he thought to himself, he didn't have to hurry to work. His wife must be busy with the housework, so luckily she hadn't woken him. Zomin opened the door of his downstairs bedroom and focused on the sound of voices in the house. Those voices seemed to be of people weeping upstairs. And there were so many shoes piled outside the door. Probably his wife's friends had gathered to complain about their husbands, Zomin thought to himself, and he used the downstairs bathroom to wash up. Not bothering to say hello to the women, he stepped out of the house.

Though the weather was in a terrible mood, the night's rain had cleared, and the grass and leaves were damp and gave off a sad aroma. Zomin exercised a little, stretched, relaxed. Then his eye fell on their cat sitting hidden under the juniper in the yard. "Mosh!" he called to it. Ordinarily the cat ran to him when he called and rubbed against his legs, but this time it didn't move. Zomin called it again. The cat didn't budge, didn't even flick an ear. "What is she, deaf?" Zomin wondered

114

with a scowl, and he tore a couple of yellowing leaves off a plant, cupped them in his hands, and then left the inner courtyard and walked away from the house. As he walked past, it wasn't sobbing he heard now, but something like people reciting their prayers. "Sure, now even they have turned religious all of a sudden!" he thought, and threw those yellowing leaves into the trash can. Instead of going back inside, he figured he'd let the women have their own conversation, and until they dispersed he might as well take a walk, so Zomin set out for the park across the street.

It was late Sunday afternoon. Everyone was busy with their own thing. Some were out walking their dogs, some their children. Thank God that this time, unusually, neither the dogs nor the children paid any attention to Zomin: the dogs didn't bark at him, the toddlers didn't get scared of his beard and run away screaming. And the sun came out for a moment. Zomin sat quietly for a long while on that bench, facing the sun.

He remembered how he used to bring his son and daughter to this park. Now they were both grown up, one was married, the other off in a university in another city. Zomin and his wife were all alone in their house. This life was one of displacement. He'd like to hear from the children, but they were far away; he'd like to give them a call, but it turned out that he had left his telephone at home, and even if he'd had it now, neither of them ever answered when it rang. . . .

Zomin walked around the park one more time, and when dusk was just starting to fall he returned home. Perhaps the women had already left. Downstairs he stopped to listen. Just as before there was a commotion upstairs. He shut himself in his room, thinking he'd read a book, but even though he could feel his eyes running over the page, no matter what letter or line he stumbled across it seemed empty or false.

When the dusk grew dark and was slinking into evening, they left. They were still weeping and sobbing a little outside the door. Zomin listened to their voices from his room, and in between he thought he could make out the voices of his son and daughter too. "Are they here?" he wondered, surprised. If he were to walk out now, his wife would surely rain down anger on him: "We had guests all afternoon! Where did you disappear to?" she would say. Fine, let the guests leave first.

When the house went quiet, Zomin carefully walked up the stairs into the living room. Yes, his son and daughter truly were there. They were in the middle of discussing something with their mother. Zomin was about to say hello to them, but for some contradictory reason, thinking "Does the bull hang its head before the calf?" he simply stood there, mouth shut, waiting for them to greet him. If only one of them would turn his way! Nothing happened. Their conversation went on. At that, Zomin lost his temper. The words burst inside him. "You're both so big now that at your age you can't spare your father a glance, much less say hello? To hell with both of you!" And he turned around and went back downstairs to his own room. The cat was usually yowling underfoot when Zomin walked down the stairs, but this time, as if it were conspiring with the others, not even its tail moved when Zomin's foot jostled it.

Locked up in his room, Zomin lay down. For a long time, he was much too angry to sleep; yet with the rain rustling again, his eyes began to close and he fell into a pitch black slumber.

Early the next morning he washed up downstairs, and rather than going up to the kitchen or waking his wife and children, Zomin left for work. In his anger he said hello to nobody at the office. He didn't so much as join them for a smoke break. He spent all day at his computer and his paperwork, never lifting his head. He didn't go out for lunch, either. When he thought about it, he realized he hadn't eaten anything all day, but he didn't feel hungry at all. Even during days of plenty, Zomin was not in the habit of gluttony; how could he have the slightest appetite now, when his family was rejecting him?

He had finished work and stepped outside when suddenly he recalled that, there at the office, he had seen a flash of someone he hadn't seen in a very long time. Could he really have seen the shade of his old English friend Graves? No, wait, wait, people said he had died ages ago! Could it possibly have been him? Or had he just run across someone who looked like Graves? If it was Graves, wouldn't he have given Zomin a look, or embraced him? So it must have been someone else.

For some reason, he did not feel like going home. Everything he did he had done for his family, and look at the ingratitude they had displayed yesterday! When he had come into the room and stood there, they hadn't said a word in greeting, or even turned their heads! Again Zomin grew angry. Was he supposed to go now and make them do their duty?! To hell with that! These grievous thoughts in his head, he walked into a movie theater. "Up till now I've never lived for myself, and this is my revenge," he thought, and he bought tickets not just for one film, but for two in a row. True, he retained no memory of the movies he had seen, they might have been about some kind of ghosts on the rampage, and Zomin sat there, buried in his own thoughts, as the two films played.

When they ended, it was the middle of the night. Zomin cut through the city, which was still bustling and mostly drunken, and walked home. The lights were out, so they must have gone to bed. Zomin carefully went into his downstairs bedroom. The door to the room was open and the light was on. He saw his wife had changed all the sheets and bedding, and the cat was there, curled up in a ball, snoring. Zomin washed up hastily, got undressed, and went to move the cat off the quilt. But then, lamenting to himself that naturally the cat of an inconsiderate family could never be considerate, he pulled the covers back without jostling the cat and carefully got in bed. The cat did not move a muscle. That night too, Zomin dreamed nothing.

In the morning, Zomin awoke to rude voices upstairs. Those voices would usually have woken the cat, sending it clawing at the living room door to get out, but now the cat was still lying there the same way it had been last night. Maybe this creature, who before had always jumped off the bed with a thump as soon as Zomin got up, had become infected with its masters' indifference and couldn't be bothered to move! Zomin walked into the bathroom, relieved himself, washed his face and hands, and glanced in the mirror—it was fogged, but he didn't care to wipe it clean. He walked out into the hall, and listened to the voices upstairs.

"Should I go and sort everything out?! I'll show you indifference! I'll show you disrespect!" he thought to himself, but as he stood there, he heard his son going into the kitchen. "So because my father is dead, I'm supposed to quit school?!" he said, clearly upset. Zomin stood where he was, struck dumb. What was he saying, that ungrateful child?!

Then his daughter came out too, and spoke to her younger brother. "We're not saying you have to drop out. All we're saying is you should just be with Mom during the mourning period!" What were they babbling on about? Furious, Zomin marched upstairs and burst into the kitchen. His daughter was embracing her younger brother, and tears were flowing from her eyes. "Here I am!" Zomin declared, awkwardly. But neither one of them turned in his direction. Just then his wife came into the kitchen too, and she also did not even glance in his direction, though she did go to the children and hug them both. Together, they cried. Zomin's mouth hung open. "Have they gone mad?!" he thought, and he left the kitchen and went into the living room.

Immediately, he saw it: his own photograph, framed, a black ribbon draped across it, on the table. All this nonsense made Zomin want to wake up from this nightmare. He tried hard, he put all his strength into it, he shuddered and shook, just to be able to physically heave this dream away! But if this was reality, then he understood nothing. Here he was, still, standing in his own house.

Zomin had been in states like this once or twice when he was younger. One winter afternoon, waiting alone for a bus going to the edge of his city, he had suddenly felt as if another Zomin, inside of him, had grown uncomfortable and stepped outside; he looked at the young man huddled in the cold, and finding nothing else to do outside himself, he slipped back inside that little body and short jacket. "I'm going out of my mind!" he had thought then, but the bus had pulled up, and his thoughts had been distracted and returned again to ordinary everyday life.

But this was more serious. It had already lasted for two days, not just a moment. Should he try beating down that madness with the ordinary fuss of everyday life, like he had before? Zomin went downstairs without saying a word to them. He picked up a pile of papers and decided to go to work. As soon as he left the house, every tiny little thing started grabbing his attention. The Indian neighbor who ordinarily nodded his head when he saw Zomin was busy plowing his garden and planting seedlings, showing him his back. He used to put extra zeal into cultivating the beds in front, near the door, just to keep track of the people coming and going, but now this master gardener acted as if he had no business with Zomin. "Fuck you!" thought Zomin, and out of revenge he didn't say hello as he walked by, either.

The bus also felt more crowded than usual. Though some seats were empty, the aisle was packed with people. At this hour old people seemed to be waiting everywhere, they were lined up near the door, but the ticket seller didn't give them a glance, moving on to investigate the tickets of the people in the seats. There among them . . . was that tall Qismet, the Turkish barber from the neighborhood? How many years had it been since he'd gone missing? Was he back now? Now the ticket seller came to stand right next to Zomin, but without looking at the ticket Zomin hurried to pull out of his breast pocket, he pushed on toward the driver. "What's troubling them?" Zomin wondered.

He decided he would definitely try to find Graves at work. As he walked around looking for him, he kept running into former coworkers. Zomin thought some of them had died and some had moved to the old folks' home, but here they all were at the office. In one nondescript place, he finally caught sight of Graves. Two young men were having some vulgar conversation in front of him, laughing, as if Graves weren't even there and they could say whatever words came into their mouths. How could Zomin walk up to Graves and share his doubts and suspicions with him among the nonsense these lads were up to? What if he waited till they stopped bleating and snorting like young goats? But the jawing that was turning Zomin's stomach seemed to be getting on Graves' nerves too; he knit his brows, threw both men angry looks, and hurriedly walked away.

Should Zomin run after him? Well, there was no serious reason to trouble him; maybe he could discuss it with those irksome young men instead. He hadn't spoken to a living soul in two whole days. You know, that's really hard on a person. "Enough!" thought Zomin, and he walked up to the two young men who couldn't restrain their shameful thoughts and words. "My friend couldn't stand what you were saying," he shouted, leaping at them. "Now stop it!" But as if mocking him, the young men went on telling even more awful jokes, making a din like frogs in springtime. He would have said something else, but he could see they weren't taking him into account in the slightest. "Even your own family isn't paying you any attention, and how would these people know who you are?" Zomin asked himself, and his suspicions grew even deeper than before.

He walked up to one of the "former" employees, who was sitting there buried in his work, and said hello. The old man did not answer. He might have been hard of hearing, so he found a different, younger ex-coworker. This one, if you believed the stories, had drowned at sea the year before last. First Zomin was going to offer him some bottled water, then he remembered that story and thought it might be better to invite the man out for a smoke, and he said to him, "Why don't we step outside and dirty the air?" But the drowned man did not answer. His eyes were stabbing so hard into the screen he might have been drowning in the computer. Suddenly, Zomin felt something dawn on him. He glanced at the curtained window behind the drowned man. The sky had cleared, the sun was coming out, and dropping the pile of papers in his hand right there, he hurried to leave the building.

Breathless and bewildered, as if reaching out for a great discovery, he stepped outside. The sunlight hit his face. His eyes were dazzled by the light. Eagerly, he turned around. Zomin had no shadow.

PRAGUE
LATE MARCH, 2020

Genesis, COVID.19

ANDRÉS NEUMAN

Translated from the Spanish by Ilan Stavans

Andrés Neuman (Buenos Aires, Argentina, 1977) is a poet, translator, columnist, and blogger. The son of Argentinian émigré musicians, he went into exile with his family to Granada, Spain. He is the author of novels, short stories, poems, aphorisms, and the travel book How to Travel Without Seeing, *published by Restless Books in 2016. His many accolades include being selected as one of* Granta's Best of Young Spanish-Language Novelists *and named to the Bogotá39 list, the Alfaguara Prize and Spain's National Critics Prize for* Traveler of the Century *(2012), and the Community of Literary Magazines and Presses Firecracker Award for* The Things We Don't Do *(2015). His most recent title translated into English is* Fracture.

And the Pope said amen in the empty square
and no one answered from the clouds
and no one answered from the mirror
because all voices were beneath the ground
sweetly cradled to cease existence.

And the Stock Exchange swelled its lung
and counted the oxygen in coins
and rerouted its wind toward some islands
sewn to the sea with sutured wounds
only for lizards and exceptions.

And all countries became one
but specially themselves
since many needed to choose
between virus and bread and a few saved
a piece of future in the freezer.

And supermarkets were crowded
with animals in search of animals
with families in white that grazed
in a field of alcohol paper and plastic
and gloves keying the fear code.

And each hospital became tempest
and roofs rained and doors flew
and the thread of life became clear-cut
and truth came and went in hallways
without being asked any questions.

And grandparents could see
with skin like fishing nets
and hands stained with memory
and eyes blinded by lucidity
their rights turn into numbers.

And technology was flesh
in those who already had it and ghost
in those with only body
and we sang rhyming songs
promising never to forget.

And very soon our voices went quiet
in the usual places in multiple corners
with a fly's buzz in that devil's limbo
which is the border between song and silence
between mourning and amnesia.

GRANADA, SPAIN
MARCH 27, 2020

@Coronarratives

NADIA CHRISTIDI

Nadia Christidi (Damascus, Syria, 1984) is a Syrian, Palestinian, and Greek researcher, writer, and artist who studies how cities that face increasing water supply challenges due to the effects of climate change—Los Angeles, Dubai, and Cape Town—are imagining, planning, and preparing for the future of water. Her artwork has been exhibited at Beirut Art Center, SALT Galata (Istanbul), and SALT Ulus (Ankara), and her writing has been published by ArteEast and ArtAsiaPacific. Christidi divides her time between Cambridge, MA and Beirut, Lebanon.

THE FOLLOWING PHOTO ESSAY presents a selection of contributions to @Coronarratives, an Instagram project I started in March 2020. The project grew out of a desire to build a much-needed community at a time of isolation; to get glimpses into what experiences of the pandemic and lockdown were like around the world; and to develop a firsthand archive of a historical moment. Contributors took over the account for a day and assumed an ethnographic lens onto COVID-19 in the cities where they are based. Here, selections from six contributions present insights into the lived experience of the social, political, economic, and infrastructural facets of the pandemic in various locales in Asia, the Middle East, and North America.

Anthropologist Elena Sobrino's contribution sheds light on how the pandemic has exacerbated the already difficult task of sourcing and distributing water in Flint, Michigan, where residents have been struggling with water toxicity issues for over five years now. Sobrino documents the compounded vulnerability of marginalized communities like Flint under the current pandemic and the creative solutions they have been developing to meet their needs. Artist Ala Younis's photographs poetically explore the distinctive sounds of the strict lockdown in Amman, Jordan—from the 6 p.m. siren marking the beginning of the nighttime curfew to silent skies empty of planes to the sounds of vehicles granted exceptional permission to move at night. Younis effectively captures the sonic through the visual, conveying the suffocating stillness of the lockdown and the fear and paranoia accompanying the state of emergency. Media scholar Eylül İşcen probes the politics of image production and circulation within debates on class inequalities and the pandemic in Istanbul, Turkey. İşcen does this by putting into conversation well-circulated images like a map illustrating divisions in "who stayed at home" in Istanbul, which has been mobilized in classist arguments and critiques alike, and a sign by the Construction Workers' Union dissenting to pressures to keep construction work going, putting workers' lives at risk.

Artist-courier Elaine W. Ho's "coronarrative as a chain letter" departs from @Coronarratives' chain letter-like structure for recruiting contributors to muse on the early days of chain letters and their resurgence today; the potential for building solidarities on the Web, and internet overload; and how to mobilize anew in a time of immobilization in the wake of the recent Hong Kong protests. Anthropologist Timothy Loh presents the reformulation of public space and publics in Singapore from newly instated safe distancing measures and social distancing ambassadors to a questioning of who gets included and excluded in increasingly common slogans like #SGUnited and "Singapore First." Software engineer Tim Nosov and designer and illustrator Tanya Nosova's contribution focuses on mobility and its containment through policing, surveillance, and technology in Moscow, Russia. Nosov and Nosova showcase present mobility realities alongside speculative future visions by Moscow-based §Knife Studio, asking what our speculations might tell of our current dreams and fears.

BEIRUT, LEBANON
JUNE 1, 2020

Coronarratives
Flint, Michigan

...

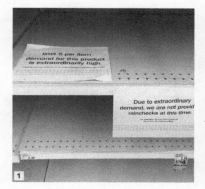

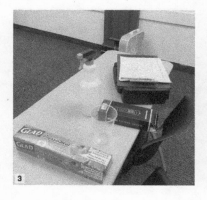

Getting clean water is hard in Flint, and now it's even harder. Organizations that distribute bottled water are running into shortages and rationing.

1. is a picture from Meijer, the local grocery chain, this week. As I checked out I overheard a worker gently tell a man buying water, "Sorry, you can only buy two gallons at a time." The pandemic has also made it even harder to coordinate the labor of distributing water. Volunteers and residents involved in water pick-ups have to somehow maintain social distancing. And like many essential workers right now, volunteers at these water distributions don't have personal protective equipment. Because Flint has been dealing with water toxicity for almost five years now, there have been creative ideas in place to get water moving through the city to people who need it. I'll share here just one example that I've used myself. 2. shows the Water Box, a portable filtration system that dispenses drinkable water. 3. shows some of the sanitation and testing equipment—the water that flows through box is tested every week, and the results are posted online publicly. 4. shows the five-gallon plastic jug I use to collect the water from the Box, sitting on my kitchen counter this morning. It's incredibly heavy when full, but at the moment it's actually almost empty. *By Elena Sobrino @eucat on March 28, 2020.*

Coronarratives
Amman, Jordan

•••

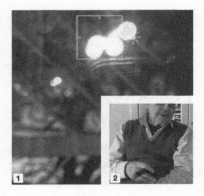

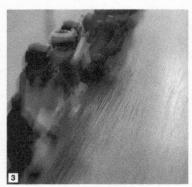

1. Sirens everyday at 6pm 2. Awaiting the 8pm daily update from minister of health 3. Queues 4. Bread bus 5. Silent skies 6. Night sounds of people with permits #ammancoronasounds #amman #covid19 #curfew *By Ala Younis @alayounis on April 10, 2020.*

Coronarratives
Istanbul, Turkey

•••

Kadikoy, Atasehir, Camlica, Fatih, Atakoy, Bakirkoy, Florya, Etiler and Sisli **THANK YOU**.
Esenyurt, Bagcilar, Sancaktepe, Sultanbeyli, Pendik, Beykoz **YOU CAN DO BETTER**.

In Turkey, citizens are asked to "declare their own state of emergency" and stay home (except some restrictions imposed on the oldest and youngest). Despite multiple calls from Istanbul mayor Imamoglu (affiliated with the opposition party), there is no announcement of a strict lockdown in Istanbul while 2 million people still go out every day. Erdogan follows the motto "production must continue" and puts the state's own responsibility on the shoulders of citizens. 3. The government asks for aid while spending their budget (our taxes) on the wars we oppose or going ahead with the controversial urban projects. Even though it is voluntary based, the aid campaign could easily become a means to pressure or blacklist citizens. Despite the outbreak, the government did not slow down their oppressive

Biz Bize Yeteriz Turkiyem Milli Dayanisma Kampanyasi'na "KORONA" yazip bu mesaja cevap vererek veya "8119"a kisa mesaj atarak, 10 TL katki saglayabilirsiniz. B002

and polarizing agenda. **1.** Who could afford staying home? **3.** Who are "we" in the national aid campaign slogan that Erdogan launched? **2.** Workers are forced to work at unsafe workspaces (if they are not already unemployed or not laid off yet). The state is still attacking Kurdish municipalities and holding political prisoners locked (some at higher risk) by excluding them from the new bill aimed at releasing inmates. Taking doctors into custody for speaking up about the current insufficiencies at hospitals. And refugees, who have become a political game rather than lives to be protected. The list goes on...
1. Image courtesy of Veloxity. **2.** Image courtesy of İnşaat-İş Sendikası / Twitter. *By Eylül Işcen @ eyuliscen on April 4, 2020.*

Coronarratives
Hong Kong (1/2)

• • •

On Government Service text and photographs:

香港政府公函 ON GOVERNMENT SERVICE

Planning Department

We began this narrative as a chain letter. From the simultaneously sharp, spicy and caring Ala Younis in Amman to me in Hong Kong, we make an attempt, amidst pandemic, for staggered solidarities. Our host called it 'internet memory lane', but these days I am so overwhelmed by WWW, I wish more of it could disappear and be forgotten.

Our data traces, and plastic wrap, will survive us all.

Coronarrative as chain letter. *By #何穎雅 #ElaineWHo @light.logistics on April 17, 2020.*

The chain letter was perhaps something like an intentionally spread virus of the early days of e-mail, maybe fun the first time you tried it except that they became annoying after a time and I, probably like most of you, decided to stop spreading it. And they faded out after awhile, but this recent resurgence in a time of pandemic makes perfect sense somehow, like sentimentality + misplaced longings for connection + boredom, all in one.

(insight/poem/quote/t don't know them). It s Don't agonise over it

Talked a lot with @vervaz the last months about what possibilities transnational solidarity can bring.

(This is what's left of our movement)

Coronarratives
Hong Kong (2/2)

...

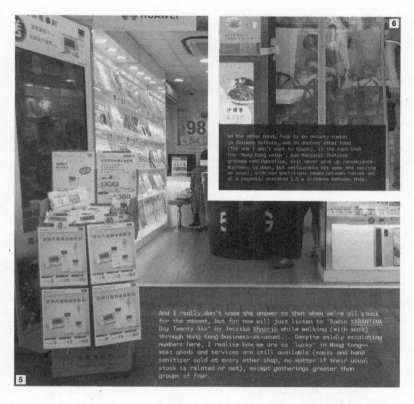

On the other hand, four is an unlucky number in Chinese culture. And on another other hand (the one I don't want to touch), is the fact that the 'Hong Kong value', our Margaret Thatcher groomed neoliberalism, will never give up convenience. Business is down, but restaurants are open and serving as usual, with new partitions added between tables set at a recently instated 1.5 m distance between them.

And I really don't know the answer to that when we're all stuck for the moment, but for now will just listen to "Radio KARANTINA Day Twenty Six" by Jessika Khazrik while walking (with mask) through Hong Kong business-as-usual... Despite mildly escalating numbers here, I realise how we are so 'lucky' in Hong Kong— most goods and services are still available (masks and hand sanitiser sold at every other shop, no matter if their usual stock is related or not), except gatherings greater than groups of four.

I am an artist-courier by trade. So person-to-person networks, movement, and maybe the metaphor of chain letters, are something important to me. But like every-one else these days, all of that is on hold, so with apologetic burden to the postal services of the world, I have made a few exceptions to our usual form of LIGHT LOGISTICS and visited the post office a few times recently. Exceptions in solidarity with stay-at-home-reading.

Transiently, I received two e-mail chain letters in the time since this quarantinism began. We are all walking down internet memory lane, alone and longing.) One of the letters was called 'Words for Women', and the other 'Recipes for Quarantine'. I haven't forwarded either yet, but for now this coronarrative chain snakes from Hong Kong to Yogyakarta, to Rohan of @indoscenepart1, for your thoughtfulness, boredom and beautiful, shy solidarity.

In solidarity,

何雨遠 ❦

Coronarratives
Singapore

···

1 2 3

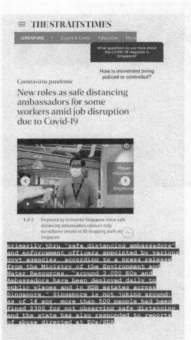

≡ **THE STRAITS TIMES**

SINGAPORE > Courts & Crime Education Mor

What question do you have about the COVID-19 response in Singapore?

How is movement being policed or controlled?

Coronavirus pandemic

New roles as safe distancing ambassadors for some workers amid job disruption due to Covid-19

1 of 2   Employed by Enterprise Singapore, these safe distancing ambassadors conduct daily surveillance checks at 92 shopping malls ac Singapore

4

Here in Singapore, as with everywhere else, #COVID19 has left an indelible mark on society. In a story that replicates itself in a multitude of places, it is the most vulnerable who bear the brunt of emergency—refugees in one place, the disabled in another, and migrant workers in ours. And, of course, often more than one group must be counted among the most vulnerable. Under conditions of structural inequality, the fault lines that run through our social fabric are brought into sharp relief, forcing the more privileged among us to confront the unjust situations we had previously ignored—and our own complicity in them. Even the rallying cry of #sgunited—for a united response to the pandemic—can carry multiple, contradictory valences, both/either a universalist call for brotherhood and/or a nativist insistence on "Singapore First!", reminiscent of a particular presidential campaign. What we can expect in life-after-pandemic depends on the extent to which we are willing to shift both mindsets as well as material resources in order to (re)create a different future. *By Timothy Loh @timloh on April 30, 2020.*

Coronarratives
Moscow, Russia

...

Everyone is Moscow is ordered to stay home. You're only allowed to walk to the nearest grocery store or pharmacy.

Any other trip you're required to register with the government by providing your passport information, information about where you live, where you're going, the route you're taking and why you're going there.

Police and video surveillance are deployed to harass people and hand out fines.

I needed to go to the bank today. I's unclear whether you need to get a permission to do so but I decided not to apply.

Wise decision not to notify the government of my trip?

YES	NO
67%	33%

1

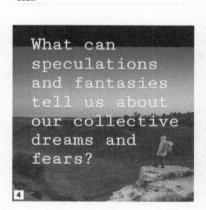

What do you want to know about Moscow on quarantine?

Did the military have to intervene

2

What do you want to know about Moscow on quarantine?

How is the government using tech to control movement?

3

4. Image source unknown. 5. Image courtesy of @studioknife. *By Timofey Nosov @getamongst and Tatiana Nosova @tatnostatnos on April 20, 2020.*

What can speculations and fantasies tell us about our collective dreams and fears?

4

By @studioknife

5

Plague Days

LYNNE TILLMAN

Lynne Tillman (Woodmere, New York, 1947) is the author of many works of fiction and nonfiction including The Velvet Years: Warhol's Factory 1965–1967 *(1995), with photographs by Stephen Shore,* No Lease on Life *(1998), a finalist for the National Book Critics Circle Award in Fiction, and* American Genius, A Comedy *(2019), and* What Would Lynne Tillman Do? *(2014), a finalist for the National Book Critics Circle Award in Criticism. The recipient of a Guggenheim Foundation Fellowship and a Creative Capital / Andy Warhol Arts Writer Fellowship, Tillman is Professor/Writer-in-Residence in the Department of English at the University of Albany. She lives in Manhattan with bass player David Hofstra.*

I AM MYSELF, because I do the same things every day. I do them now, make the bed, a pot of tea. There are things I don't do, never do, things other people do, cook fish, for example. I don't need to know why I don't do them, but often I do know, and this is what makes me.

In a room, I think about what I will do, myself, about others. I remember others, memory includes others, friends lovers sisters father mother ex-friends. Figures in mind, like Kafka, who abjures himself, and the dead, they live with me now.

In a room, I am reading, glancing out of the window, or I am looking at what I am writing. Then I stop. Discouraged, distracted, I am exhausted, lie down, sit up, touch my toes, swing my arms, make a phone call, ignore a call, hear a voice, see a message, answer it, don't, there is plenty of time, too much time. Only time.

In a room, I am restive, restless, and bore myself.

I look at my books, shelves overwhelmed, actually I watch them, I am their guardian. I read this, that, Natalia Ginzburg, Lyndall Gordon on Charlotte Bronte and Virginia Woolf, a book on spies. Books live for me to read, books are alive when they are read, but mostly I fail them, and they rebuke me.

I look for distractions. I look at my cat, my cat is not worried, and I am I.

*

Now, as I did yesterday, and the day before, I shower, dress in my over-sized jeans, a loose cotton shirt, then give myself a task, to go outside, and walk. Fresh air is good. I find out the temperature. I will go to the post office.

I pull on a pair of white, sticky, latex gloves. I carry a bag with a small spray bottle of fluid to vanquish invisible bacteria, because the virus awaits. I walk down three flights of stairs, not holding the handrail, though I fear, and have always feared, tripping and falling down a flight of stairs, breaking my neck. I know I will die this way, if the virus doesn't kill me. Still, I don't hold the handrail.

I reach the street, I walk, watch everyone, create the mandated social distance, and weave a path on the sidewalk. I will keep six feet away, I try to, some people don't, many, children don't. I reach the near-empty post office, and wish I had packages to mail, there are no long lines, when there are always long lines, but I don't have a package, just a letter I slip into a slot in a wall, disappointingly.

I walk to the door, push the door open with my shoulder, it's heavy, when a woman suddenly is close beside me and breathes on me. I walk away fast, then look back at her. Who is she to endanger me?

She is very old, wearing a misshapen black cloth coat.

Everyone is an enemy in a virtual war.

I look back at the very old woman. She has stopped walking, bent over, maybe catching her breath, and watching me. She is wondering why I am fleeing her. I think, You are not keeping enough distance between us. Do you want to make me sick. Will I make you sick. Are you sick. Now I feel sick, but I am not sick.

I walk home, wary, avoiding humanity, and reach the front door of my building, wipe the doorknob, and wonder if I should post a message to the other tenants, let us know if you are sick. If you are sick, stay away.

Upstairs, I brush off the soles of my shoes on a rug, unlock the door, carefully take off the gloves, and wonder if they should be washed, can be washed, can be reused, and if I can waste a pair of gloves, or how many will I need. I wash my hands, happy birthday happy birthday, lather up, consoled by the hot water, wonder if there will continue to be running water, wash my hands, happy birthday happy birthday, singing too fast I think, and wonder who will be saved.

NEW YORK
MARCH 16, 2020

The Song of
the Stormy Petrel:
A Cautionary Tale

MAXIM OSIPOV

Translated from the Russian by Boris Dralyuk

Maxim Osipov (Moscow, Russia, 1963), who received his medical training at the Russian National Research Medical University, lives in the town of Tarusa, where he established a charitable foundation to ensure the local hospital's survival and to improve its standard of care. His debut collection in English, Rock, Paper, Scissors: and Other Stories, *translated by Boris Dralyuk, Alex Fleming, and Anne Marie Jackson, appeared in April 2019 from NYRB Classics.*

THERE ONCE WAS A MAN who lived in terrible fear of the novel coronavirus. Actually, when he first learned of the virus back in January or February, he wasn't so terribly afraid (he'd read on Facebook that it was no worse than the flu), but his fear grew steadily in March and, by April, had reached terrible proportions. The man wasn't old and didn't suffer from lung disease, diabetes, or, knock on wood, cancer. He wasn't worried about himself, but only about his eighty-year-old mother. When the holidays came, he moved in with her so as to isolate jointly and keep a close watch on her health, measure her temperature and blood pressure, make sure she had plenty of food and medicine.

The man wasn't a smoker, drank in moderation, adhered to a strict diet, took walks with a pair of ski poles, and even had a little nest egg—that is, he had prepared for disaster. To tell the truth, his concern for his mother's well-being was accompanied by a growing sense of curiosity: the price of crude oil was plummeting, the ruble collapsing, and the economy going to hell in a handbasket—soon to be followed, surely, by the political system itself. Consequently, along with a sense of dread (again, his mother), he also felt, for the first time in many years, restrained optimism. After all, what did people expect? In order for things to improve down the road, they first had to get worse, much worse. But Mother—just imagine what she was going through: old age, diabetes, vascular problems, blood pressure affected by the weather. Still, she got along without caregivers. Good for her.

And so, back in March, the man began telling anyone who would listen that he was worried about his mother. What else would he be worried about? No sense in thinking of the children (they weren't vulnerable), his wife was eleven years younger than him, and, needless to say, he wasn't concerned about himself. Do the math: what were the chances of him croaking? One percent, maybe one point five. A real man doesn't lose his head over trifles. *If I die in a combat zone, box me up and ship me home.* . . . Oh, speaking of, he'd prefer to be cremated—everyone clear on that? People had always told him he had a pleasant voice, and now he was growing convinced of it. He kept singing and singing—vigorous, patriotic songs. He'd have loved to sing democratic ones, but there just weren't any. A nervous reaction? Maybe. . . . But it was his mother he was worried about, not himself.

One fine April morning, his mother made him his favorite break-fast—pancakes smeared with strawberry jam, just how he liked them. He bent over his plate and inhaled deeply through his nose: no smell. He took a bite: no taste. The horror, the horror. . . . His throat closed up and he gasped for breath. What he wanted to say, in his deep, resonant voice, was: "It seems I've caught it." But what came out, in a falsetto, was: "Mom, the thermometer."

The rest was a blur. Since he couldn't choke down the pill for his fever, his mother had to crush it up. Good lord, so bitter! And then someone showed up in a spacesuit, drew his blood, and declared: "Positive." But by that time he was getting better. And so he was entered in the statistical record as "Recovered." His case was over.

Now he spent most of his time sitting in the kitchen, eating pancakes with strawberry jam or smoking cigars (yes, he did smoke, but only occa-sionally), and browsing Facebook. From time to time he himself composed witty comments. "Poor little thing," he wrote on the wall of one socialite who'd complained of shortages, "looks like there isn't enough coconut water for everybody."

"It's really fun to watch. I'm telling you, they're kaput," he told his mother, who had zero interest in politics. "Completely washed up! Oh yes, my dears, now you'll have to get your hands off Venezuela, off of everything, and come begging to Camdessus. We'll see how powerful you are when the president of North Macedonia starts talking down to you." He wiped his mouth with a napkin: that's right—the bitterer the pill, the better you'll feel. *Let the tempest come strike harder!* That's the stuff! *Lock your doors, shut 'em tight, they'll be looting through the night!* (He was fairly well-read.)

But what about Mother? Come to think of it, she was already eighty, and had survived far worse. True, some of the older people did die from this thing, but most recovered. Best to keep a cool head. Nothing to fear.

One morning, when he was still barely awake, he pulled up Facebook and learned that a well-known evildoing politico—who always voted for all the bad policies and against all the good ones—had fallen ill and been placed in an artificial coma. Well, served him right. Still in bed, the man wrote: "A dog's death for a dog." Then he had second thoughts and deleted the comment. But it also occurred to him that the critical cases, like this politico's, were widely reported, yet few people spoke out about the relatively mild ones. Yes, he should share his own story with the frightened citizenry, tell them that he too had been afraid of the coronavirus before catching it and recovering without a hitch. In the end, it was no worse—in fact, it was better—than the flu.

At that point another person read the man's story, lifted his fingers from the keyboard, and kept touching his nose, mouth, and eyes. A few days later this second person developed a high fever and had trouble breathing. Then he stopped breathing altogether. He wasn't entered into the statistical record, since he died before the specialists could get to him. And you, dear reader, will also die if you don't send this story to ten or twelve others.

TARUSA, RUSSIA
APRIL 11, 2020

Today, When I Could Do Nothing

JANE HIRSHFIELD

Jane Hirshfield (New York, New York, 1953) is the author of nine much-honored books of poetry, most recently Ledger *(2020). She has also written two now-classic books of essays,* Nine Gates: Entering the Mind of Poetry *(1997) and* Ten Windows: How Great Poems Transform the World *(2015), and edited and co-translated four books collecting world poets of the past. Her poems regularly appear in the* New Yorker, *the* New York Review of Books, *and other publications. A former chancellor of the Academy of American Poets, Hirshfield was inducted into the American Academy of Arts and Sciences in 2019.*

Today, when I could do nothing,
I saved an ant.

It must have come in with the morning paper,
still being delivered
to those who shelter in place.

A morning paper is still an essential service.

I am not an essential service.

I have coffee and books,
time,
a garden,
silence enough to fill cisterns.

It must have first walked
the morning paper, as if loosened ink
taking the shape of an ant.

Then across the laptop computer—warm—
then onto the back of a cushion.

Small black ant, alone,
crossing a navy cushion,
moving steadily because that is what it could do.

Set outside in the sun,
it could not have found again its nest.
What then did I save?

It did not look as if it was frightened,
even while walking my hand,
which moved it through swiftness and air.

Ant, alone, without companions,
whose ant-heart I could not fathom—
how is your life, I wanted to ask.

I lifted it, took it outside.

This first day when I could do nothing,
contribute nothing

beyond staying distant from my own kind,
I did this.

MILL VALLEY, CALIFORNIA
MARCH 17, 2020

The Virus of Hasty Cover-Up

GYÖRGY SPIRÓ

Translated from the Hungarian by Bernard Adams

György Spiró (Budapest, Hungary, 1946) is the author of Captivity, *published by Restless Books in 2015. He is an award-winning dramatist, novelist, and translator and has earned a reputation as one of postwar Hungary's most prominent and prolific literary figures. He teaches at ELTE University of Budapest, where he specializes in Slavic literature.*

IN OCTOBER 1973, when the oil crisis broke out, the socialist Hungarian press trumpeted that the ripple effect of the price explosion was not going to reach us. My father, an engineer and economist, who died a month later, said: "In every crisis it's the middling economies that are ruined. The developed ones fend it off; the undeveloped don't even notice it. We shall be ruined."

The 1956 revolution had been a profound political experience for Kádár, and so to raise the standard of living he begged money from both the Soviets and the West, creating serious debt. At the same time, he tied Hungarian energy provision to the Soviet (Russian) oil, gas, and nuclear industries for a good hundred years beyond the change of regime and the collapse of the USSR.

In 1990 the second (socialist) world lost its ring-fenced international market and, despite its scientific and technical efforts and achievements, became part of the third world and in a form of state capitalism or state feudalism nicknamed "parliamentary democracy" was integrated into the globalized world market.

In the twentieth century most of the countries of the third world— Greece, Turkey, and states in South America, the Middle East, Africa, and Asia—alternated between phony democracy and overt military dictatorship. Apart from the paid work typical of modern colonies, the copying of scientific and technical innovations originating in more developed countries, and a number of professions requiring little material outlay, a hopeless second-class status awaited the former socialist countries. The three decades of peace that began in 1990 have set off a slow spiritual decline and fading of hope. The marketable workforce, together with the elite of the intelligentsia, has partly emigrated to the West, a third of society has slipped into dire poverty, social mobility has ceased, and public health and education have been cut back. The top tenth of society has done well, two or three percent have been enriched, and thus the condition of the interwar years, generally typical of the third world, has returned.

The socialist utopia had advantages over Nazism and fascism: it set out humane goals in which it was, for a time, possible to believe, and over which the regime could be called to account, sometimes with success. In 1990 this way of thinking became obsolete. In Eastern Europe, when parliamentary democracy began, the right of the individual to housing and employment was withdrawn and, in its stead, chauvinism was strengthened; this brought Europe to ruin twice in the twentieth century. That a number of countries joined the European Union did not alter this.

During the fifty years since the oil crisis the world that was divisible into developed, undeveloped, and middling has changed: globalization has swallowed up everybody. Apart from the Atlantic world almost all states are reckoned as middling, very poor or less so, and for that reason a world crisis threatens the foundations of their existence.

Unemployment, famine, impoverishment, political blackmail by epidemic, and a workforce that will become cheaper than ever awaits the countries that are for the most part forced into monocultural production, whether Bangladesh or Russia.

The great powers have transferred military tensions to Middle Eastern theaters (the latest is Syria), where weapon systems more advanced than ever could be tried out. The great and middling powers, in possession of all the advanced technology, have built up arsenals of inconceivable destructive power at incredible expense. Crises have broken out again and again, various terrorist organizations have been generously financed and spectacularly fought against; sensational atrocities have concealed the fact that millions have fled their homes to escape famine and war. It has seemed that by present means dreaded atomic war can be avoided. There has been much talk of climatic disaster, which has expanded the famine zones, but nothing has been done to stop it.

The extreme instability of the whole world order has been revealed by the coronavirus epidemic. Inhabitants of almost all the Earth have been put under house arrest (as of April 23, 2020, 2.7 billion people), and political leaders—having taken no precautions against the epidemic despite the warnings of experts—have sought refuge headlong in fake activity and shut down the entire world economy. They shrug off responsibility onto the victims through a hasty cover-up, and their ambition is tyranny.

The apocalypse only renders visible what already exists. The evidence of history shows that there is no immediate consequence when secrets are brought into the daylight. Forty years on, even the Second World War has been forgotten, and nowadays there is not a single leader in the world with any conception of what a serious crisis entails or how to handle it. For thousands of years writers of history have endeavored to cover up when incompetent leaders have talked rubbish. Today it is broadcast live to thousands of millions that a president recommends injecting disinfectants to treat a viral infection.

The developed countries will struggle through the world economic crisis at the cost of huge sacrifices, but those of middling development—the rest of the world—will slide steeply into bottomless darkness. In countries where the virus and the crisis are handled intelligently, loss may be minimized. Such countries are very few. The previously wide split between the developed and what may tactfully be called the developing countries will grow exponentially. Unemployment in the third world will be enormous, exacerbated by a further move toward automation. The whole political and economic system of the world will have failed. Something usually turns up, sometimes a wildly irrational faith will help as did Christianity two thousand years ago. Mankind, religious beast that he is, usually deals with objectively insoluble problems by means of a radically new blind faith, but on this occasion no such religion is in sight.

Throughout the European Union, great economic potential is matched by indecisiveness; the stronger European states react to stimuli redolent of the First World War and retreat into national statehood, and there is no sign of their being able to break this habit. If the USA succeeds in surviving the recession that threatens it with civil war, it will join China in carving up the world. Core-Europe and Russia will belong to the upper band of the endangered zone of middling development. To the detriment of the other small states and to the grief of the Poles, the alliance of Germans and Russians that has been forged again and again over the centuries will be able to regain strength and an attempt may be made to build a second world on the ruins of the EU.

The countries that are closer to feudalism may lapse into a state of medieval anarchy. Warlords (mafia chiefs) will oppose central authority with their private armies. Gangs will murder the civilian population and reduce the majority to serfdom or servitude. We know the recipe from the histories of the South American and African countries which are today's theaters of war, but Italy, to name but one, is on the same road. Civil and religious life may also once more become entangled where they became separate after the French Revolution, and in other parts—in the countries ruled by organized crime and theocratic governments—will bring about famine and progressive state bankruptcy.

Where those in power themselves have wound down the most important functions of the capitalist nation-state—public health, public education, state bureaucracy—or where it was never really built up, the very existence of the state may be jeopardized. The sort of agreement may arise between the forces struggling for power that brought about the dissolution of Yugoslavia or the collapse of the Soviet Union. Similar tensions may arise with the dying out of the epidemic in Spain and Great Britain—oppositions of North and South, Spanish and Catalan, English–Irish–Scottish. All this is bound to happen if the European Union is incapable of putting its basic principles into practice.

The World Food Programme report of April 2020 puts the anticipated number of starving people in the countries of low national income at 265 million. Before coronavirus, fifty-five countries—in particular Nigeria, South Sudan, Syria, and Yemen—were suffering from famine due to war, drought (resulting from climate change), and economic crisis. Especially grave situations are foreseen as a result of the virus in Zimbabwe, Yemen, Iran, Iraq, Lebanon, and Syria. China, where the ending of famine was regarded with justifiable pride as the greatest achievement of the past thirty years, has also come to a halt but is not within the purview of the

WFP; nor does the report mention Bangladesh, India, or Pakistan, nor the Romany populations of Eastern Europe.

The crisis has revealed that in the globalized world societies that are differently structured in principle function in similar ways. The ability to surveil the individual and to make them subservient to the central will can be perfectly attained by technical means. Ideologies based on the blessings of the right of individual freedom have departed a long way from the practice. Where respect for the individual has never existed, modern technology may be introduced against anyone without a qualm.

In the very beginning, when its outbreak was being kept secret, the pandemic became a worldwide epidemic of lies. Since then, with the exception of the honest elites of one or two more fortunate countries, lying has become the global norm. As the result of a range of substitutes for action—which appeared expedient at the time—whether deliberately or not, hundreds of millions may easily be wiped out. Even in the twentieth century that which our ancestors had painstakingly built up since the Declaration of the Rights of Man was constantly being undermined, and now may be finally destroyed. The survivors will find out what it means to inhabit the technically advanced Middle Ages.

BUDAPEST, HUNGARY
APRIL 26, 2020

PART III

I'm Not Alone in Misery

The Longest Shift: A New Doctor Faces the Coronavirus in Queens

RIVKA GALCHEN

Rivka Galchen (Toronto, Canada, 1976) is a New Yorker *contributor and the author of* Atmospheric Disturbances *(2008),* American Innovations *(2014),* Little Labors *(2016), and* Rat Rule 79, *published by Restless Books in 2019, her first book for young readers.*

She has received numerous prizes and fellowships, including a Guggenheim Fellowship, a Rona Jaffe Fellowship, the Berlin Prize and the William Saroyan International Prize in Fiction. Galchen also holds an MD from Mount Sinai School of Medicine.

EARLY IN THE CORONAVIRUS CRISIS, before New York shut down and the schools closed, when people still shared opinions about Marie Kondo and the timing of the Iowa caucuses, Elmhurst Hospital, in Queens, began rearranging its emergency room. The section for less acutely ill patients became a screening room for patients with symptoms of COVID-19. Within days, a new wall had been built. The critical-care area was doubled, then tripled. A triage tent soon went up outside. And the family room—where doctors and families can have difficult conversations in relative privacy—was turned into a place for the distribution of personal protective equipment, a transition from a "cold zone" to a "hot zone." "You walk into your shift and are handed a bag with your PPE for the day, like it's your lunch box when you show up to school," Hashem Zikry, an ER doctor, told me, adding, "It's a little bit surreal. We all have perspective for a moment on how truly insane what's going on is. That our life is picking up this PPE and changing into it, and that everyone out there is so sick."

At the beginning of a recent shift at Elmhurst, Zikry took over the care of a forty-five-year-old man who had a wife and four children. Although the man was on high levels of oxygen, he was short of breath. He had written out several paragraphs in Spanish specifying that he did not want to be intubated or resuscitated. "Normally, I don't push back on that too much, because I think people don't understand the futility of those efforts in most cases," Zikry said. "I pushed back on him, though. Because he was only forty-five." The man reiterated his wishes. "When he came in, he was well enough to speak in full sentences," Zikry said. "Two hours later, when he was at the point where we would have intubated him, I asked him again." Too breathless to speak, the patient shook his head; he was resolute. Zikry called the man's wife, who said that she trusted her husband to decide. "It was a horrendous shift," Zikry said. "So many people were dying." The man was visibly in agony, as is every patient struggling for air. Zikry and other doctors tried to help him find positions that might let more air into his lungs. The man rolled and bucked; eventually, he was still. By the end of the shift, he was dead. Zikry called the wife again. She didn't shout; she thanked him and the other doctors and nurses. "It was very hard to hear someone thank you for standing there and watching her husband die," Zikry said. "I felt very helpless."

Zikry has been working as a doctor for nine months. He is twenty-nine years old, an intern in the emergency-medicine residency program at Mount Sinai Hospital. As part of his training, he rotates through different hospitals and specialties. In late February, he began a six-week rotation in the ER at Elmhurst Hospital, a place he loves and describes as the soul of medicine. The neighborhood around the hospital is one of the most diverse on the planet. Nearby blocks are crowded with Thai noodle shops, Colombian bakeries, and groceries that sell lotus and taro root. The neighborhood, which has a large working-class immigrant population, was hit earlier and harder by the pandemic than most of the rest of the city. "It's become very clear to me what a socioeconomic disease this is," Zikry told me. "People hear that term 'essential workers.' Short-order cooks, doormen, cleaners, deli workers—that is the patient population here. Other people were at home, but my patients were still working. A few weeks ago, when they were told to socially isolate, they still had to go back to an apartment with ten other people. Now they are in our cardiac room dying." Zikry, whom I have spoken to regularly in the past month, has extraordinary resilience and good humor; on this day, he sounded despondent. "After my shift, I went for a run in Central Park, and I see these two women out in, like, full hazmat suits, basically, and gloves, screaming at people to keep six feet away while they're power walking. And I'm thinking, You know what, you're not the ones who are at risk."

Before Zikry went to medical school, he had been in an ER only once. When he was thirteen, he shut his front door on his left middle finger. There was so much blood that his mother almost fainted, and Zikry remembers going to the ER with his younger brother. An orthopedic surgeon said that there was nothing to be done—he would lose the finger. By then,

155

his mom had arrived, "like a mother on a mission," and she said, "My son is a pianist, don't tell me there's nothing to be done!" A plastic surgeon was brought in—Jess Ting, who had studied music at Juilliard. Zikry had never played piano in his life. He told Ting that his parents were the worst people in the world, and liars. ("I was very . . . hormonal.") Zikry recalled, "Then Ting said to me—and he became my mentor, he's the one who kept encouraging me to go to medical school over the years—'Well, I'm here now, let's see if I can help.'"

Zikry went to Hamilton College, where he studied English and ran cross-country, before going to Mount Sinai's Icahn Medical School. He loves Jane Austen. He still reads before bed, and trains for and runs marathons—his favorite is Grandma's Marathon, in Minnesota. Through the majority of the pandemic, Zikry worked an average of six days a week at Elmhurst. His shifts often lasted thirteen hours, an exhausting schedule that is typical for a first-year physician.

Even after New York's schools were closed, on March 16, many hospitals in the city were at the eerie stage of preparing and waiting for a surge in COVID-19 patients. "I would say our ER looks, well, more orderly than usual," Jolion McGreevy, who directs Mount Sinai Hospital's ER, told me, on March 18. Elaine Rabin, the head of the hospital's emergency-medicine residency program, recalled being an intern during 9/11, and said, "This is different from that. It very much feels like a tsunami is about to hit us." But, for the time being, the patient volume at Sinai was down. The non-corona cases—the broken bones, the belly pains, even the chest pains—were not turning up in their usual numbers. (Telemedicine had off-loaded some of those patients, but people were also afraid of the hospital, as evidenced later in the dramatic increase of deaths at home.) Elmhurst Hospital, however, was already four people deep into its sick-call list for staffing. It had many COVID-19 patients, but they were accompanied by the usual load of "normal" cases. "The drunk falls, the chest pains—those numbers have been inelastic here," Zikry told me, in late March.

The PPE bags that Elmhurst doctors received at the start of their shifts contained a papery yellow gown, blue gloves, a face shield, and an N95 mask. The mask had to suffice for a whole day, although as recently as February the CDC recommended putting on a new one for each patient. An N95 mask fits the face more tightly than a regular surgical mask, and has a metal strip on top to hold it in place. "The bridge of my nose is bleeding from wearing it all day," Zikry told me. "I tried to MacGyver it with a Band-Aid, but it's not working." The PPE that ER doctors in New York have been wearing more closely resembles a poor man's welding gear than the astronaut-like outfits seen in photos of medical workers in South Korea.

When Zikry came on shift on the evening of March 21, one of the COVID-19 patients signed out to his team seemed not as sick as some of the others he'd seen. "He walked by the desk during sign-out," Zikry told me. "He walked by again fifteen minutes later. Asked us where the bathroom was. He was walking—that's a great sign. Talking—that's a great sign. These are very reassuring things to a physician. I wrote down, 'Ambulatory, Conversant.'" A short time later, a hospital police officer approached Zikry to say that a man had collapsed in the bathroom. When Zikry reached him, the man had no pulse. He began chest compressions. "Nothing like this had ever happened to me," Zikry said. "I had seen him walking minutes before." The man was taken on a stretcher to the critical-care area, where resuscitation equipment was on hand. Despite the efforts of Zikry and others, the patient died about fifteen minutes later. Zikry recalled turning back toward the rest of the ER He said, "We look back on this sea of, like, three hundred people that expected us to treat them immediately, to figure out what was wrong with them." This was around 3:15 a.m.

Zikry had been in the middle of a presentation—describing to a team of providers how a different patient was doing, so that they could make a plan for care. "I had to pick up in the middle of that conversation as if it had been about a basketball game the night before," he said.

That day, a headline in the *Washington Post* read "In hard-hit areas, testing restricted to health care workers, hospital patients." Anthony Fauci, the director of the National Institute of Allergy and Infectious Diseases, said, "When you go in and get tested, you are consuming personal protective equipment, masks and gowns—those are high priority for the health care workers."

But Zikry's patients—and patients across the country—wanted to be tested. "I got yelled at a lot," Zikry said. "I understand the anger." The PPE makes communication more difficult—all that a patient sees is eyes behind a plastic shield. "It's that much more distance between patient and provider." At Elmhurst, which offers translation in dozens of languages, conversations often occur through an interpreter. "The most difficult thing has been describing to patients what is going on," Zikry said. "We ourselves are so confused and scared, and every day when we come on shift it seems like there's a different protocol"—the guidance comes from the state Department of Health—"for who are we testing, who are we admitting."

Repeatedly, Zikry had to explain to patients that they probably did have the coronavirus, but that there wasn't much the hospital could do for them—they needed to go home and take Tylenol, and come back if they were in respiratory distress. "These patients are well informed," he said. "They say we're not testing enough and that's why it's spreading so much, and there I am trying to explain, maybe with a video interpreter in Mandarin, the intricacies of why we are past the point of testing, that we don't have those resources."

Some patients, frustrated and frightened, told Zikry that this would never happen in another country, and that he didn't care about them. "That is so hard," he said. "I often think about what mistakes I may have made, what I could do better. But the one mistake I know I never make is the mistake of not caring." These encounters can exacerbate a sense of loneliness, one that paradoxically persists alongside a heightened camaraderie among ER doctors—all in it together, day after day. "Even co-residents—people with the exact same lived experience—we don't get to talk to each other much," Zikry said. "We're working so hard. And we're also on quarantine." The residents used to meet up at a bar or a coffee shop. "That has completely dissipated. And it feels strange. Because they are the only people who know what my days are like."

After his shifts, Zikry took off his PPE, showered at the hospital, then changed his clothes completely before turning off his phone and running some six miles to the Upper East Side, where he shares an apartment with his younger brother, Bassel. Bassel has kept their refrigerator stocked. That week, Zikry's bedtime reading was *Duel in the Sun*, an account of the 1982 Boston Marathon, in which Alberto Salazar and Dick Beardsley had one last great race, before problems—illness, addiction—pulled them down. Zikry says that his runs home help him reach a reconciliation with the day, "which is not a peace, it's different from peace." Reading helps his mind change tracks. "I'm a big dreamer," Zikry said. "And I love sleep." Most nights, he gets a break from the hospital in his dreams.

Every day in an ER is potentially traumatic. Dan Egan, an ER physician at New York-Presbyterian/Columbia Hospital, has been a doctor for more than fifteen years. "We work with disasters, we see horrible things all the time," he told me. "We see unexpected deaths as part of our regular job." Still, he said, colleagues were now calling him crying in fear—something that had never happened before. "I think it's that it's unknown. I remember the time of Ebola. Of course we were scared—and that was a more deadly disease—but it didn't feel like it does now."

Egan and I went to medical school together. I was there for the classic wrong reason: to fulfill parental expectations. (I had not even been able to handle the fertilized-egg dissection, back in fifth grade.) Egan was the magnificent opposite. "Honestly, I loved all of medical school," he said lightly, as if it were a goofy attribute. He has a beautiful voice and sings in choirs, but he has a disarming way of speaking like a teenager when it suits the situation. If our medical school class had had a homecoming king, it would have been him. He was kind to everyone, and he never complained—a popular medical student pastime. He has loved the ER since he was a kid, when his mother was an ER nurse. When we were in school together, I thought—and still think—that if I were sick and scared I would want Dan to be my doctor. I told him that. He laughed. "I don't want this to sound strange, but one of the things I treasure is being able

159

to communicate bad news to patients in a compassionate and human way," he said. Sometimes a patient comes in with a headache, which turns out to be something awful. Patients come in with a rash, and leave with the news that they have cancer. "My father died of metastatic esophageal cancer, and I still remember that conversation with the oncologist," Egan said. "It was so not compassionate. So not humanistic. I couldn't believe it was happening in that way. I know my patients will remember these conversations, and it's important to me that the human piece be there."

Egan was exposed to COVID-19 on March 12, and went into quarantine. He did telemedicine while out, but, he said, he felt "almost guilty that I couldn't be there to step up." When the quarantine protocol for health-care providers with mild symptoms was reduced, from fourteen days to seven, he returned early. He felt well, and wanted to work. I heard again and again that, despite doctors' stress and fear, they were glad to have something to offer. When I asked Zikry why he chose to specialize in emergency medicine, he replied, "For times like this." Yvette Calderon, an ER doctor at Mount Sinai, who grew up in the Chelsea projects, a few miles south of the hospital, said, "This is the door to the hospital. The ER is what faces the community. I grew up seeing that there was a need, and I wanted to be in the part of the hospital that serves literally everyone."

On March 24, New York had been shut down for four days. Governor Andrew Cuomo said, "We haven't flattened the curve, and the curve is actually increasing." Cuomo cited estimates that New York State might need as many as a hundred and forty thousand hospital beds. The city had some twenty-three thousand beds in use, and hospitals were converting surgical and pediatric units into space for COVID-19 patients. Work was beginning on a four-thousand-bed facility at the Jacob K. Javits Convention Center to decant non-COVID-19 patients from hospitals—but even at Elmhurst there were now very few of these.

"I'm truly exhausted," Zikry told me that day, at the end of another overnight shift. "I'm starting to see patients I've already seen, now in worse condition. A patient who four days ago had an oxygen saturation of a hundred per cent and an OK chest X-ray, then two days later their saturation is low nineties and it's not a great chest X-ray—well, they come in now with a saturation in the high eighties and with horrendous chest X-rays, and we need to admit them to the hospital." Zikry knows that medical language can obscure as well as explain: "The term used for what you see on the X-rays is 'ground-glass opacities.' I have no idea what actual ground glass looks like. I can tell you that on the X-ray it looks like a snowed-out background, or like when I go out in the rain—I wear glasses—and I can't really see, because of the water on my glasses. There are these patchy opacities. That's what the chest X-rays look like."

Each ER has a board that notes who has been seen and who remains to be seen, and clearing the board constitutes part of ER doctors' collective sense of well-being. "We never caught up on the board," Zikry told me, after a shift. "All of us were working so hard, but we were about forty people behind all night." As the crisis progressed, it was taking longer and longer for patients to be admitted to a ward in the hospital—and more critically ill patients were remaining in the ER to receive care. There were stretchers in hallways and the common spaces, wherever space could be found.

"I miss the sunsets."

"What strikes me is the deterioration of what is normal," Zikry said. Walking by some stretchers, he noticed two patients who were not in visible distress but who had oxygen saturations in the seventies. They needed to go into the critical-care area immediately. Soon after, "I hear this guy calling me by name, he's smiling and waving," Zikry said. "And it's this man—I've seen him three times this week. I have friends who would be so jealous of how much more time I have spent hanging out with this guy than with them. So I was feeling amused and also maybe dismissive—that I have already counseled this guy so many times to go home and watch his symptoms."

The man, to the eye, seemed unchanged. "I go ahead and order his chest X-ray again, not expecting to see a change—and it was atrocious." The man was on the verge of crashing—of not being able to breathe properly without medical assistance. "It was so scary. And he had looked so well."

Many doctors had described to me the grave contrast, in many COVID-19 cases, between a patient who can sit comfortably in a chair and a chest X-ray that shows pneumonia in both lungs. Soon, those patients can abruptly crash. "You see the patient using the full energy of the body to breathe," Zikry said. "Neck muscles are distending. You see the muscles around the ribs."

At around 3:45 a.m., Zikry received a text from his mother: "I'm in tears thinking of you." She was worried that he wouldn't take care of himself. She said that he was the most important. The text made him laugh a little. Zikry is not much of a crier. He recalled crying only once in the past ten years, while studying for the Step One exam, a comprehensive all-day test at the end of the second year of medical school. "I just hated it so much, I wanted to quit medical school. I had composed the email," Zikry said. "I called my mom and was saying I wanted to quit, and she was in a car with my brother, and I think he had been yelling at her, too." His mother dropped the phone accidentally. He called back, telling her that she didn't care about him, and that he was going to quit then and there. "She said—and I give her so much credit—she said, 'Look, OK, if you want to quit, you can quit tomorrow morning.'" He didn't quit. His third year of training changed his perspective: he kept meeting physicians about whom he thought, That's the kind of adult I'd like to be.

Zikry took an Uber home from his shift that day, instead of running. That was unusual for him, but he was unusually tired. His residency program was paying for rides for residents, as a gesture of support. It was around 7:45 a.m., the beginning of a kind of day off. Interns call this a doma—day off, my ass. He would get home around eight-thirty, have breakfast with his brother, try to rest, and then be back at work by 7 a.m. the next day.

Throughout the crisis, doctors have made clear their dismay at the lack of proper supplies—both for their own protection and for the health of their patients. "The systemic frustrations are the most exhausting," Zikry told me. "Today, we ran out of oxygen masks for the patients to use. So much work goes into trying to locate and obtain more. We had a shortage of oxygen tanks, so we connected more than one patient to larger tanks—stuff we normally wouldn't do. Will we run out of masks entirely? People can give you answers, but they are not witnessing what is happening in front of you. People can tell you it will be O.K, and it is solvable, but this has never happened before."

Physicians in other cities watched New York for a sense of what was headed their way. David DiBardino, a pulmonologist at the University of Pennsylvania Medical Center, described how the process of entering his hospital had changed for employees. "We're funneled through an entrance that hasn't been open for years," he said. "It has this black metal gate that looks so gothic. It's like a near-future dystopian scene, like something you would watch on Netflix. Some people are trying to distance in line, but also it's a line, you can't be that far away—so distance, but not wanting to get cut." On March 26, the third day of the new entrance policy, the line was three blocks long. "Three city blocks of people in scrubs panicking. This anesthesiologist who is older saw the line and started screaming—he was anxious about how close people were standing in the line."

As at Elmhurst, doctors receive only one set of PPE for the day. "The PPE has actually been put under lock and key," DiBardino said, and laughed. "I have to deal with these things with humor, because it's all so weird and scary." In subsequent days, the line to enter the hospital grew short, then long again; instructions for hand hygiene, temperature taking, and mask distribution kept shifting. "What has really been startling is this gap between the protocols—between how we used to throw the mask away after every procedure and the really difficult practical challenge of, how do you avoid contaminating yourself with the new conservation protocol," he said. "It's hilarious how tedious it is. You touch the back of your neck, and then you're, like, Is the back of my neck contaminated now?"

DiBardino, who with his wife has three children—fifteen-month-old twins and a three-year-old—does not typically work in the ICU. "As interventional pulmonologists, we are board certified in critical-care medicine, but it's not something we do on a daily basis." On April 6, that changed.

"It's really, personally, scary," he said. "There's a really good chance that I will contract COVID-19—and I think, you know, you and I should be fine if we catch it, but whether to bring that home to my family? Should I just stay at work and not come home?"

DiBardino was asked to lead a team at a neurology ward that was transformed into an ICU for COVID-19 care—a seven-day tour of duty. An anesthesiologist was assigned to head one half of the ward, and DiBardino the other. "The rooms have this pretty loud hum to them," he said, because negative pressure is used to keep the covid air from escaping. The doors to the patients' rooms are kept shut, and typically only one medical worker goes in at a time, while the rest watch through the glass. "It's like a fishbowl," DiBardino said. He described his first day of training there: "So the nurse goes into the room with a whiteboard. She'll write, 'BP is super low. Max norepi?' Or she'll write, 'I need a new IV bag,' and so someone runs to get it." Coming in and out of the room is slowed by the donning and doffing of gloves, a gown, the N95 mask, and a face shield.

Emergencies occur all the time in an ICU. "An alarm seems to go off every five minutes, but then only one person goes into the room for the response—it's so weird," DiBardino said. "It's almost like we're running as fast as we can, but with one foot nailed to the ground." Since the doors of the rooms are glass, doctors standing outside sometimes direct the provider inside by writing backward on the glass doors, so that the person inside can read it. "I know this is stupid," DiBardino said, "but one of the first thoughts I had was: I can't write backward!"

By early April, funeral homes in New York were overwhelmed, and the city had deployed forty-five mobile morgues. The Javits Center switched from serving only non-COVID-19 patients to serving exclusively COVID-19 patients. More than six million Americans filed for unemployment in one week. A midlife-crisis film called *Phoenix, Oregon* topped the box office, making $2,903 from showings on twenty-seven screens. Half the planet was under lockdown orders. People mixed quarantinis, didn't quite educate their children. Guidance on masks was still changing. My mom wrote to my brother and me about ordering tonic water, because she had read that it had quinine, which was getting talked about as a remedy.

At Elmhurst, as at many publicly funded hospitals in poor communities throughout the country, the situation was deteriorating. In the best of times, these hospitals are underfunded and overwhelmed. Yaagnik Kosuri, a general-surgery intern at Mount Sinai Hospital, who has been working at Elmhurst during the pandemic, described much of his work as a "hundred-per-cent Sisyphean task. That is the situation at baseline. It just wasn't set up for success in the setting of something so catastrophic."

So many patients were in the ER that a resident was assigned to walk around checking their oxygen levels, to make sure that they weren't crashing. This job had never existed before. "I thought the volume could not be worse," Zikry said. "I thought we had reached an asymptote. We have superseded that. The other day, we had thirty-one intubated patients in our ER, which is twenty-eight to thirty-one more than normal." Now when he left the hospital each day a dozen reporters were there to ask questions, as if the doctors were some dark version of Broadway actors exiting the stage door. "I just show up to work," Zikry said. "I am very scared to do it. I am scared something is going to happen. On my way over, I say to myself, I'm going to show up. If I just keep showing up, something good will come of it compounded over time."

It had been Bassel's birthday, so Zikry decided to try to cook spicy fish tacos, one of his brother's favorite meals. At Citarella, Zikry had walked past the mustard he wanted, then taken a few steps backward to get it, and in the process bumped into someone, who started shouting at him: How could he be walking backward at a time like this? "I had to let that one go," Zikry said.

In the ER, the work had become "sadly algorithmic." Typically, the glory of working in an ER is that you never know who will come in the door, what kinds of problems they will have. "We now presume they all have COVID," Zikry said. "You don't have to be Dr. House to figure it out." He said that he tries to tell a patient early in the conversation, "'I think you have coronavirus and you need to be admitted to the hospital.' I think it's a shocking conversation for them. Especially if they've been waiting for eight hours and I've been seeing them for thirty seconds."

In normal times, a nurse or a technician draws blood for lab tests, a task that doctors tend to be not that good at, but now, because of staff shortages, it's part of the job. Zikry described drawing labs from a patient, then taking the patient to get a chest X-ray. Hospital stretchers drive worse than grocery carts. "I hit his bed against a corner," Zikry said. "And this guy, who hadn't spoken any English up to that point, turned and said, 'Is this your first fucking day?'" Zikry has a youthful face. "I have the same questions he does. I don't know how I ended up in this situation."

To contain the spread of the virus, family members are not allowed in the ER or on ICU floors. People are in distress alone. ERs, which are often in basements, sometimes don't have good cell phone reception, and worried families have no choice but to call doctors. When I spoke with Dan Egan at the end of March, he was coming off two consecutive night shifts. Over the weeks, more staff arrived—Egan worked with a pediatrician and with an orthopedic physician assistant—but the work remained overwhelming. Egan said, "I have never put more patients on a ventilator in one shift in my life, and of course I was thinking, If this is how it is now, and with what the models are predicting for a week or two from now—it makes me really scared."

He described the barring of visitors as a secondary trauma. "Families are calling me all night for updates," he said. As an ER doctor in New York, he's accustomed to being yelled at. The current situation is not like that: "Instead, they are like, Doctor, I know how busy you are, I just want an update on how he's doing." One young patient struck him as the sickest person he had seen that night. "And I'm trying to relay that over the phone to the family, who thinks he's at the hospital with, like, 'a little coronavirus.'" The patient was on a ventilator. "I wanted to be honest about how sick he was, but I didn't want to take away hope. They're asking me, 'Will I be able to talk to him tomorrow?' And, because they're not here, it's so much more difficult to explain what it means to be on a ventilator—that a machine is breathing for him." Egan wants to be empathetic, but he's taking care of many patients at once. "Multiple times last night, I had to say, 'I am so sorry, but I have to get off the phone, because someone really sick is coming in right now.'"

The medicine is the medicine, Egan explained. Everyone is on oxygen, and everyone is there for the same thing. "But people are dying, and the family is not there." That night, he had an older patient who was critically ill, on a ventilator. He was not expected to live much longer. Egan had had multiple phone conversations with the man's daughter about how sick he was, and what the family's goals of care were—they wanted him to be free of pain. The daughter got off the phone to contact her siblings. "Then she called me back and asked me if I could do her a favor. I say, 'Yes, of course.' She says to me, 'Would you go in and put the phone to his ear so we can all say goodbye?'"

He put on his gown and gloves and full PPE, and went into the patient's room. "I had the phone on speaker, because I couldn't really hold it to his ear with all of the equipment. I felt like I was intruding, but that's what it was." The words were mostly Spanish. Six or seven family members, all telling the man how much they loved him. "I thought, My God, this is real. This is what everyone is doing now."

NEW YORK
APRIL 20, 2020

Not Without

FORREST GANDER

*Forrest Gander (Barstow, California, 1956), a writer and translator with degrees
in geology and literature, taught for many years at Brown University. His recent
books include* The Trace *(2014), a border novel, and* Be With *(2018), winner
of the Pulitzer Prize in poetry. Gander has translated books by poets from Spain,
Latin America, and Japan. He lives in California.*

Not grasping your hand * on pause

Not coming closer * taking a detour

Not to dock no dock * more than arm's length

Neither seen with nor transparent * locked in lockdown

No double shadow * fingertips stopped short of gratitude

Not two redwoods * emerging from fog

Nor tracing surfaces lightly * as headlights stroke the garage door

Neither lapsing, nor * like a tide gone out

Not the way color, say the neighbor's tree * of persimmons speaks

Not without portent * from a distance

Not as the wind plunges itself * into its own pocket

Not the cloud * but where the cloud was

Not yet the end * of "we"

PETALUMA, CALIFORNIA
APRIL 2020

Toiling Under the Canopy of Empire

LILYA KALAUS

Translated from the Russian by Shelley Fairweather-Vega

Lilya Kalaus (Almaty, Kazakhstan, 1969) is a philologist, author, literary editor, script writer, radio presenter, and artist. Her writing has been published in print and online journals in Kazakhstan, Russia, Uzbekistan, Germany, Ukraine and the USA. The author of seven books for adults and children, Kalaus is a member of Kazakhstani Union of Writers, the Kazakhstani PEN club, and the director of her own publishing company.

THEY TAUGHT US LATIN our first year in the philology program. I loved it; I always studied, practically the whole class copied my homework. "So what good did Latin ever do you?" you're asking (meanly). You're asking. I know you. And here's my answer: it has done me plenty of good. It gave me my daily bread for five years after I finished university. The new age dawned, and in the 1990s they started opening new colleges with new programs of study, and the new deans took pleasure in resurrecting half-forgotten subjects. Latin for lawyers, for example. I fed Latin to future prosecutors, attorneys, judges, and notaries at a brand-new legal college. I fed myself, too, thanks to what my own instructors had taught me so well. So there's that. As a student I also translated, more or less, some long dull text from Latin about a farmworker, about an ordinary day in his life. He got up at four in the morning, fed the pigs, ground a handful of grain, sifted the flour, milked the cow, kneaded the dough, cooked some bread and ate it. Then he went out to the fields. Breakfast à la antiquity. I'd kill myself, I thought as I slogged through that translation. I'd rather die of hunger and all that was rubbish.

Life, as the great poet once said, turned out to be long. The now former students of that college have made themselves into real people and retooled themselves from jurists into famous bloggers, and the college doesn't exist anymore, and Latin has been tossed aside and forgotten, though it still sends me a quick note now and then.

Let me paint you a bucolic picture of today's morning in quarantine. I got up at four because my furry-tailed livestock were demanding cat food. I fed them and went out to the fields. I wasn't even half sleepy anyway. I harnessed up good spelling and punctuation and sowed a huge plot of somebody else's text with seeds of wisdom in the form of editorial correc-tions. Then the next batch of mouths to feed stirred in their warm nests. They'd be up soon, demanding breakfast. The latest nuisance is that we have no bread. There's no going to the store because I'm in a high-risk group, and my family would have my head if I usurped power like that.

And so I baked some bread using kefir. Hail! or whatever you should say there. The denizens of my apartment all rose to the aroma and warmth of baking bread, still sleepy, not talking, like zombies. They started digging into the hot kefir bread and ate so much the sun is already setting on the second loaf. And meanwhile I'm back in the fields, again sowing what is good, wise, and eternal. Remotely, as usual.

And, as usual, from time to time I use WhatsApp to talk to my husband and children, who are in the same apartment. Under our own canopy of empire, so to speak.

Working from home is my modus vivendi. For all time.

ALMATY, KAZAKHSTAN
APRIL 12, 2020

Chronicle from the Vortex of a Global Tragedy

GABRIELA WIENER

Translated from the Spanish by Jessica Powell

Gabriela Wiener (Lima, Peru, 1975) is the author of books of poetry and prose including the crónicas collection Sexographies *(2018) and the memoir* Nine Moons *(2020), both published by Restless Books. A columnist for* El País *(Spain) and* La República *(Peru) and a contributor to several American and European publications such as* Etiqueta Negra *(Peru),* Anfibia *(Argentina),* Corriere della Sera *(Italy),* XXI *(France), and* Virginia Quarterly Review *(United States), she was editor of the Spanish edition of* Marie Claire *until 2014.*

EVER SINCE THIS ALL BEGAN, I suspect we've have all had some dystopian, apocalyptic fiction in our heads that we keep coming back to, something that allows us to draw absurd parallels, to laugh to ourselves or disconnect from what we are experiencing in real life. The one that sticks with me is *Ben-Hur*. So many times I've wanted to ignore the possibility of contagion and enter those pestilent caves, lift my husband and *hije* in my arms, and take them out of there, like Judah does with his mother and sister, restoring their humanity, driving away marginalization and stigma. But I don't do it. The "impure ones." That's what we call Jaime and Coco as a little joke. Half of our house is the Valley of the Lepers. The other half is still the "country of the well," as Christopher Hitchens called that place from which he departed, plunging definitively into the "land of malady."

We're hot-blooded, boisterous people, kissy, tickly people who like to roll our tangled, massed bodies all over the place. And now we communicate with one another through a barred window. Three times a day, we healthy ones leave trays of food on the floor for the COVIDs. How did this become our lives? The pandemic curve evolves in different ways behind our doors. The logarithmic scale does not measure small, daily tragedies. Luckily, we have the perfect house for the coronavirus. This is one of the hundreds of new thoughts I now have per day, thoughts that, for the past two weeks, have reshaped what we understood the world to be: a house with two very distinct atmospheres, separated by a small patio, the borderland.

The day the lockdown began and the kids stopped going to school, filling the house with noise, Jaime got sick. We didn't even have time to get our hopes up for a family Sunday that would stretch out indefinitely. He had the already dreaded fever that hovers around 101.3. The scratchy throat. The muscle aches. On the third day, Coco (age thirteen) developed a fever and cough. By that point, we'd already assumed that our theater production about polyamory, *What Madness to Fall in Love with You*, had been canceled, that we'd have to refund the money for at least four sold-out shows and reimagine the next few months in a very different way. A friend proposed renaming the play *What Madness to Be Infected by You*.

Life in the apartheid of your own family begins with resistance. Roci and I took it for granted that we'd been infected and that the symptoms would soon appear; when that didn't happen, we started to think we were asymptomatic. One day, we decided we were healthy and that we, along with Amaru (age four), the three unvanquished ones, should entrench ourselves at a distance, just in case. We called and called the community health services until finally a facility answered and marked our door with the blood of the lamb. They counted us, we were a statistic, but they warned us that we would have to suffer through it at home, without tests, medical care, or a hospital. That's why we waited, maybe for too long.

Jaime had had the same fever, the same pain for a full week when it occurred to me that not only had he been lying in bed that whole time, but that he had been sleeping too many hours during the day and that, when he was awake, he couldn't stop coughing. I think that's what triggered me, that he seemed unrecognizable, reminding me of my father sleeping all day in the weeks before his death, the projection of an absence in his presence. My husband couldn't finish a sentence without starting to cough. When you know they are caused by the virus, the violent breaths of the people you love most in your life rattle inside your own chest.

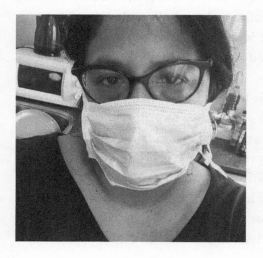

I stopped sleeping. The news about entire families admitted to the hospital or children ending up with social services because their parents had been hospitalized gnawed away at us. The stories of people who couldn't be with their seriously ill loved ones, the stories about people enduring their illnesses all alone, deaths without goodbyes, the closing of the overrun Madrid Municipal Funeral Service, terrified and fortified us.

Roci and I became revolutionaries fighting on the liberation front against COVID, with masks instead of balaclavas and blazing eyes. We used all the tools of our militant feminism to organize our resistance. Every day, we talked to an anti-racism comrade's parents—his father, a virologist and his mother, a nurse—to Roci's extremely gifted aunt, a cardiologist, also a victim of coronavirus; we listened to our pediatrician sister-in-law Gloria's recommendations about Coco; we cried with Lola, an aunt who's a nurse in the Canary Islands. We got ahold of a pulse oximeter through our network of dyke friends. We learned to measure oxygen saturation. We learned that ninety-five and above is good and below ninety is bad, and that at sixty, you die. And one morning, the pulse oximeter said eighty-seven and we called an ambulance.

I had never been so close to the vortex of a personal tragedy, not to mention a national tragedy, much less a global one. Madrid had become Spain's Valley of the Lepers. A morgue for five hundred people per day. Health workers were receiving applause every night, but we were also beginning to learn about what they were not receiving, about what they lacked, their exposure, their frustration. The same day that Jaime started having trouble breathing due to the infection, we read that every hospital in the city was on the verge of collapse. It took the ambulance five hours to arrive. But still we couldn't imagine all that lay ahead of us. Men dressed as astronauts who looked like they'd come to pick up ET took my husband away.

They took him to the nearest hospital, the Hospital Universitario 12 de Octubre. They wouldn't let Roci in. They took him to the emergency room, where they are isolating coronavirus patients. I know that hospital well. It's where I had gone every other day for my shoulder rehab. It's an enormous hospital, almost unfathomably so. The newspapers said it was one of the few hospitals that still had beds available, but they informed us that he'd have to wait twenty-four hours to get one. And that day of hours became an eternity with the arrival of dozens of infected people, some of

them elderly and asphyxiating, falling out of their chairs; people crying with uncertainty and helplessness.

Jaime sent us this message from the 12 de Octubre: "A doctor just broke down sobbing and told everyone in the waiting room that it's excruciating for them to leave us out here like this, that it's horrible for them too, and then she couldn't go on talking. And the waiting room applauded her for like five minutes." I posted it on Twitter. At home, we searched desperately for friends of friends of friends of friends of doctors who worked at the 12 de Octubre. But no one could do anything. They took X-rays and he sent us the message we'd so feared: "don't be scared, I have pneumonia in both lungs." Jaime, forty-five years old, healthy, with no underlying medical conditions. Hundreds of coronavirus patients die every day from pneumonia, many of them young people, though older people make up the larger percentage and their deaths are more publicized.

I cried in the shower, in the kitchen, on Twitter, while I splashed bleach around and wiped everything down and took the garbage out; I told Coco that Daddy was going to be okay without really knowing if it was true; I hugged Roci, we caressed one another with our gloves on and she told me that she'd take care of everything, that I should go to bed. I would go lie down and write to Jaime to ask him about his saturation levels—he wasn't going to die, he couldn't die—and to the religious wing of my family's WhatsApp groups, asking them to pray, and to the doctors I knew, begging for information and miracles. I didn't want to talk to my mom yet because, in that moment, I couldn't allow myself to revert to being ten years old, and I couldn't press myself against her breasts because she lives thousands of miles away and she's also in quarantine. Amaru stared at me and I gave him cookies. I sobbed silently, murmuring the same thing over and over: "my poor sweet love, my poor sweet love, my poor sweet love." And more than anything, I was scared to death.

Jaime sat in a chair for thirty-two hours waiting to be seen. Not even on a stretcher, after a full week of fever, his body wracked with pain. And finally, at one thirty in the morning, they called us from the hospital, or maybe it was God, to tell us that they'd admitted him, and Roci and I clung to one another through our insomnia, and to our remnants of hope. At least he wasn't in the ICU, at least he was breathing on his own, at least his saturation levels were good, at least his fever wasn't too high, at least they're finally treating him. At least Coco's better, two days without symptoms and now playing the flute as if there were no tomorrow, having learned dozens of new songs while in seclusion, hammering our brains with them as evidence of intact lungs. Feeling better, trying to break the rules of social distancing: "Mama, Mama, it's been forever since I hugged anyone, please, please." And face to face, standing three feet apart, we embraced one another's ghosts.

They tested Jaime again and this time there it was, *la corona-virus*, as Amaru calls it, the unmistakable pointed crown. And so we began to hear about hydroxychloroquine, the malaria drug that helps but doesn't cure, about "false negatives" like Jaime, whose tests come back negative despite the presence of all the symptoms. About his hospital roommate, another false negative who was coughing his lungs out, who was much worse off than Jaime, and whom Jaime was caring for the best he could in his own fragile state. And also, as the days passed, we started hearing his voice, sounding more and more clear, more like Jaime, more animated, more determined to get out of there. At home, we'd run out of games to make up to play with Amaru, who was now wearing a cape around the clock and answering to the name Bat Boy of the Coronavirus. At his tender age, he already knows perfectly well which areas of the house he's allowed and not allowed to fly through in order to stay safe.

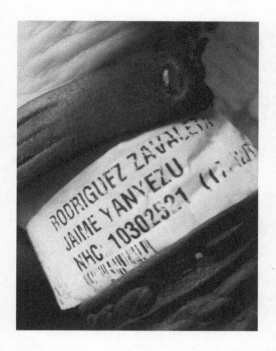

One of the most terrible things about a contagious illness is the impotence of the caretaker: we learn to offer comfort without touching, without talking up close, almost just through our gazes, with subtle, invisible gestures that at first might seem cold and rejecting, but which are exactly the opposite.

Yesterday, the doctors at the 12 de Octubre discharged him, five days after that first hellish night. The same astronauts who came to take him away in an ambulance now brought him back, but this time, arriving home, ET had gotten his color back. He's here with us, with his children, but he still has two more weeks of medicines and quarantine, confinement within confinement. How do you greet someone you love so much and whom you feared you might lose without taking him in your arms, without melting into him, without talking for hours together in bed? I don't know. I don't know how we did it. These are things that only happen in the land of malady, the new rules of the game that you grudgingly learn to play.

Before he arrived, we'd already divided the house in two, organized systematically, with turns and strict rules for the few common areas. As if welcoming him with flowers and balloons, we gave him instead plastic bags, soap, and disinfectant. We do not take off our balaclavas. We've learned to be cold in order to triumph. I sent him a message: "For these two weeks I'm going to love you like this, I want you to feel this part of my love, we're going to take care of each other ferociously."

Now love is disinfection. Love is that plate that you don't hand to him. Love extends in strange ways across the border between the healthy and the sick. Last night Amaru cried before bed without really knowing why. He said to me: "You know what's wrong, Gabi? I just remembered Christmas Eve." It's what we're waiting for, that blessed night when we'll again break down the walls that separate us.

MADRID
MARCH 2020

The Age of Calamity

JON LEE ANDERSON AND ILAN STAVANS IN DIALOGUE

Jon Lee Anderson (Long Beach, California, 1957) has been a staff writer for the New Yorker *since 1998. He has covered numerous conflicts in the Middle East and Africa, reported frequently from Latin America and the Caribbean, and written profiles of Augusto Pinochet, Fidel Castro, Hugo Chávez, and Gabriel García Márquez. He is the author of several books, including* Guerrillas: Journeys in the Insurgent World *(1992),* Che Guevara: A Revolutionary Life *(1997),* The Lion's Grave: Dispatches from Afghanistan *(2002), and* The Fall of Baghdad *(2004). He lives in West Dorset, England.*

Ilan Stavans (Mexico City, Mexico, 1961) is the publisher of Restless Books, the Lewis-Sebring Professor of Humanities and Latin American and Latino Culture at Amherst College, and the host of the NPR podcast In Contrast.

ILAN STAVANS: It has started now. Nothing will look the same. Will we remember who we were after it ends?

As I write this, in mid-March, much of Europe, Asia, the United States, Africa, and Latin America is in a stage of epidemic containment. The coronavirus, also known as COVID-19, is spreading at fast speed. The world as we know it, it is fair to say, will not be the same afterward. I am bunkered down in Amherst with my wife Alison and second son Isaiah and his girlfriend Amara. Life has come to a standstill: students and workers have been sent home; streets are empty; bars and restaurants are closed. There are confirmed cases in the hospital a dozen miles from here. Tents are being built next to those facilities to expand the number of beds. Let me first ask, where are you? And more importantly, *how* are you? Describe for me what you see from your end.

—March 11, 2020

JON LEE ANDERSON: I'm in Dorset, England, or more aptly, west Dorset, which is the more rural corner of this county in Southwest England. Dorset is next door to the better-known county of Devon, on the way down the boot of England, heading westward to Cornwall. There is no motorway (highway) into this area, just a winding two-lane road and its pretty, hilly countryside and wild coast with pebble beaches, cold water, and limestone cliffs. I live in a small market town called Bridport that has its own little harbor, West Bay, about a twenty-minute walk away. I'm here with my wife, Erica, who is Cornish, and our son Máximo, who flew in from California a few days ago to be here with us. Our daughter Rosie lives in Oakland, which is where Máximo had been, visiting, and Bella, our eldest child, is in Siberia, in Russia.

I am at my desk and am looking out at a cold but glisteningly sunny day, thankfully, because that's not always the case here. Since yesterday, the sun has been fully out, though, and with it, life changes for the better.

I went for a two-hour hike with my friend Nic earlier this morning. We go every day during the week. He lives a couple of streets away, just up the hill, and usually waits for me outside my house, on the high street, and we head off in one of three or four different directions. Some days we head to the sea, down through the streets of the town onto the paths that follow the river that flows through water meadows to West Bay. Sometimes we come back along the old railway tracks, or over the hills through some fields.

Today we did a more ambitious walk, to the neighboring hamlet of Walditch, and then up an old holloway—an overgrown, almost Arcadian pathway that probably once was a road for horse-drawn carts—up to the top of the hill there and across its spine above the village of Bothenhampton, with the sea in the near distance and all the town below us, and then we dropped down through the edges of the town and back home again.

We met a number of other people out walking, some with their dogs, and both noticed that everyone was keeping well away from one another. When we met people on the narrower brushy trails, either we found a perch to stand aside, and waited for them to come past, or they politely did that for us.

Everyone still says hello, I noticed, but there is a new wariness, as if even speaking or prolonged eye contact somehow carries danger. Everyone is now more on edge, even here, proverbially "far from the madding crowd" (it was precisely this area that Thomas Hardy was writing about in his novels, by the way) because Boris Johnson's ministers were all over BBC Radio this morning issuing admonitions. It seems a good many Brits spent the nice weekend weather outside in the parks and on beaches, but in a number of places did so very much cheek to jowl, not observing the coronavirus guidelines of keeping a six-foot distance from one another. If people don't behave, they said, a stricter regime will be enforced, as it has been in Italy, preventing people from going outside much at all. I'm frankly most concerned about that possibility, because although I live in a big house with a fairly decent sized walled garden, I crave the daily outings with Nic, and also my separate walks with my two rambunctious dogs, Stig and Tug, both for exercise but also because the walking helps lift my mood, especially when the weather is bad, as it so often is here.

—*March 18, 2020*

IS: I envy those walks, although we live in a forest. But the general mood in the United States is one of hysteria. Workers have been laid off and unemployment has skyrocketed. Whole industries are paralyzed. Even ordering takeout at restaurants is being dissuaded, since the virus apparently travels on plastic, metal, and other hard surfaces. The situation in Italy, France, and Spain is desperate, and the same goes for Iran. Natural calamities, including pandemics, are a fixture of humankind, and literature figures out how to become a record of it. The Bible is full of scenes of despair. So is Boccaccio's *Decameron*. I had read, not long ago, Daniel Defoe's *Journal of the Plague Year*, about London in 1665. Also serendipitously, a month ago I watched the film *The Andromeda Strain*, based on a thriller by Michael Crichton. And two of my favorite books, *One Hundred Years of Solitude* and *Blindness*, are directly about epidemics, in both cases quite mysterious: in the former, an outbreak of insomnia blankets Macondo; and in the latter, people suddenly and without reason lose their sense of sight. We take for granted what we have; and we have almost nothing except ourselves.

All this, in other words, was expected. Each culture responds to fear in different ways. I'm not only talking about spontaneous reactions. People grieve in context: some laugh, others cry. Social distancing is making it impossible for people to grieve together. In Spain, an enormous number of dead are piling up in morgues, next to churches and conference centers. There is no time to bury them. Nor is there any way to do so, since funerals are forbidden. In Jewish culture, people gather for seven days in the *shiva* to accompany the relatives of the departed; but *shivas*, like all other religious rituals, are forbidden. The daughter of a friend of mine committed suicide last week. Only the parents and brothers were allowed to attend the burial.

Still, for now I feel safe in Massachusetts, even though the state has been quite affected, with the number of COVID-19 cases increasing exponentially every day. We aren't quite in the extreme emergency that New York, California, and Washington find themselves in, but we are getting close. Yet in Mexico and Brazil, where presidents Andrés Manuel López Obrador and Jair Bolsonaro for weeks and more mocked the severity of the epidemic, I suspect the impact will be unique. In Mexico City, people are finally in self-quarantine. Poverty is widespread. I hear of *atracos*, armed robberies of Costco, Walmart, and other stores. *Invasiones domésticas*, house invasions, are increasing.

—*March 21, 2020*

JLA: Ilan, what you say about how different societies react to fear is very true. This reminds me that you and I both live in countries other than the ones we were born in, which offers us an additional, although not necessarily easier, perspective on the world around us. We also live in an era when technology has allowed us to be aware, almost in real-time, of what is happening in the farthest reaches of the world. We're cognizant of how others are faring across the planet. Everyone's lives are on hold, at different stages of limbo, and if we share a human condition right now, all of us, it is one of dread. We live with it and adapt to it in different ways, but it is there all the time, an existential dread that is ineradicable, as in the historic literary plague chronicles you cite, because none of us know what the future will bring.

This may be a bit of a tangent, but just very briefly, circling back to that national duality we share, and the topic of fear: I'd say that a certain type of Brit has a national myth, and a corresponding self-faith, that they are not fearful people, and they look over their shoulder to Churchill's "we shall fight in the streets" clarion call and the way they stoically withstood the Blitz as evidence of that spirit. No national myths are quite entirely real, of course, and nor do they last forever; Brexit, more than anything else, shows a collective fear response to being overwhelmed by the Other. In the modern British context, this was triggered by the specter of being subsumed by a European Super Nation ruled by others, roiling with an unchecked tidal wave of immigrants. And when the Brexit referendum was held, four years ago, there was also a fear of the Islamist terrorism that had erupted and was associated with those immigrants.

In the end, this is an island nation, which, allegorically speaking, must be perceived as a fortress or castle, surrounded by a great moat. When the Great Beyond gets too close, the drawbridges come up, the boats are sunk, and the gates are closed. Psychologically, then, with Brexit, many Brits were already in the process of quarantining themselves, so to speak, well before the coronavirus came along.

Most Americans also believe they are not fearful people, and they point to their wars, their possession of weapons, and their willingness to use them as evidence of that. If the United States has a national myth it is that it is a victorious nation, a winner in everything—Number One in the world. Trump's presidency, however, is all about fear—fear of the other, fear of no longer being "great," and so forth. Despite its constant wars abroad, America's inclination toward isolationism has never gone away, and paradoxically, since the US is practically a continent in scale, Americans have also created an island fortress for themselves, as well as a bunker mentality, and feel themselves to be surrounded and besieged by dangerous Outsiders. Trump's presidency is at once America's Brexit and also proof that fear, not bravery, is what rules the day.

There are places in the world where the coronavirus has opened up a Pandora's box of unknown contents, in which anything might happen. Brazil immediately comes to mind in this context. I have Brazilian friends who are self-isolating despite their absurd, irresponsible president Bolsonaro, who is actively encouraging them to do the opposite, for his own inexplicable reasons, and against the advice of his own health minister. Brazilians, then, must contend with a double measure of foreboding—not only of the pandemic itself, which is still just beginning to spread in that country, but for the day of reckoning they must face with the imbecile they chose to lead them. Clearly, they must get rid of him, sooner rather than later—one way or another. It's a very analogous predicament to that faced by Americans with Trump, who happens to be Bolsonaro's role model.

Just in the last few days, in Mexico, fortunately, President Andrés Manuel López Obrador, who as you say had also taken a laissez-faire attitude to the pandemic threat—suggesting that Mexicans were blessed with a unique culture that would somehow protect them from it—has done a 180-degree turn and is now on board with the kinds of protective measures we are seeing in most other countries. This is a huge relief, and one only hopes it has not come too late. You mention Mexico's poverty, and it's a good point. In Mexico and beyond, what is going to happen when the virus spreads through the crowded slums, favelas, and refugee camps where so many millions of people now live, and where there are few doctors, much less hospital beds or the vaunted ventilators we are hearing so much about? What happens in Haiti, Venezuela, the Philippines, and the Congo? It seems likely that in such places the virus will wreak havoc. In places where people cannot simply stop working, where they have no food stores, and live hand to mouth, how can they survive under quarantine? There will be no government subsidy check coming in the mail for them. It seems inevitable that there will be upsurges in crime, and potentially significant social and political upheaval as well.

—*March 23, 2020*

IS: I heard this morning that Boris Johnson, Britain's prime minister, has contracted the virus and is now leading the country in isolation. He too dismissed news of the pandemic for much longer than other cautious politicians. The obfuscation is frightening. Such hubris! Of course England, which literally just left the European Union after a protracted period known as Brexit, likes to do things its own way. Weeks later, the nation is paralyzed. Infections are rapidly spreading. It is not only Johnson who has tested positive; other cabinet members and MPs have also done so. Prince Charles too is infected.

—*March 27, 2020*

JLA: That's right. Not only Johnson; the British health minister has also contracted the virus. That's a lot of symbolism for a government that, as you say, was taking a far more casual approach than most of its European neighbors right up until a fortnight ago. When we look back to early March—as the virus began to make its way into Europe and across the world from China, we can see that Johnson and his Tory coterie were affecting nonchalance, still patting themselves on the back after securing Brexit and fortifying themselves in the recent election in which they achieved a historic victory over Labour. Then suddenly, everything changed, as it seemed to dawn on them what was really occurring. Hard to believe, but it was just last Monday, March 23—a week ago—that Johnson announced the national quarantine.

I've been interested to see how my British friends have reacted to the changed circumstances, and, for the most part, they have done so well. It's in their social DNA to do so, really, again, derived in part from that national mythos of the Brits being brave and stoic, to Keep Calm and Carry On, to have stiff upper lips, and not to whinge, as they say—not to complain, and to "soldier on," come what may. Their ability to get on with things and be self-sufficient, and to understate, rather than to exaggerate, *is* admirable. But obviously such posturing has its limits and it can be a double-edged sword. In the weeks prior to the quarantine, Johnson had affected an air of bravado, trying to reassure his countrymen that everything would be all right, even boasting about how he had shaken the hands of patients ill with coronavirus in a hospital ward. Now, of course, and probably as a direct result of that, he has contracted the virus too, and presents a less-than-convincing model of national leadership—just as the virus begins to spike in Great Britain.

Johnson bears a huge degree of responsibility for the unprepared-ness of the United Kingdom in dealing with the coronavirus, but the political punishment for this negligence has been held in abeyance for now. Many Brits who are very critical of their government's deficien-cies and also what they see as their society's failings, have moved into a different mindset ever since the quarantine was announced. There is a sense that "we are all in this together." Many remain critical of their government, yes, but have directed their criticism toward practical matters, not politics. Why don't the NHS doctors and nurses have the personal protective equipment they need? How can they be obtained? What about more ventilators and ICU beds? Now that there is a national course of action—now that a decision has been made, they have gotten into a kind of national lockstep, which seems to gratify them by offering them a sense of shared national purpose. In this context, the national mythology has produced some markedly positive results: The government asked for 250,000 volunteers to help the NHS, and in a week, 750,000 have come forward.

One day last week, at 8 p.m., everyone came to their front doors and clapped, applauded, cheered, and banged pots in praise of the NHS doc-tors and nurses, the frontline soldiers in Britain's battlefield of the new world war.

—*March 28, 2020*

IS: Almost daily, I have been keeping a journal. I started it the day Alison and I were no longer allowed to leave the house. To me, it felt like the Holocaust. A large number of my ancestors perished in concentration camps. I used to think—and express those thoughts openly—that compared to previous generations in my family, I had been lucky to be an actor in a relatively calm period in history. Yet things began to feel far less stable a few years ago, in 2016, when Donald Trump was elected president. One of the side effects of ideological polarization in the United States was the increase of anti-Hispanic and anti-Semitic feelings. I wrote about them frequently in the *New York Times* and elsewhere.

When I was young, I used to look with awe at Hannah Arendt, Gershom Scholem, Walter Benjamin, Theodor Adorno, and other public intellectuals in Europe whose plight was defined by the rise of Nazism. As a generation, they had been tested in fundamental ways. Some had chosen exile right away, while others bunkered down and only later sought ways to escape. Now it is us who are tested. The future will remember how we reacted in our volatile age.

—March 29, 2020

JLA: Our societies have become more fragile, Ilan, it is true. The old hatreds and bigotry, most of which we thought—or perhaps merely hoped—were long-buried, turn out to have remained alive—and have been reignited. That is what we have learned in the Trump era, and it is both alarming and infuriating to behold. The idea that democracy itself, not to mention its civilities and its protections, is somehow available to be questioned and even ransacked by a new generation of hateful Know-Nothings is extremely difficult to stomach. Perhaps this crisis will be an opportunity to reset the necessary balance of things; I sincerely hope so.

—March 30, 2020

IS: The morning after COVID-19 will feel like V-day. Even though pandemics are a fixture of the planet, this one more than any other in recent memory—maybe since the Spanish Flu of 1918—will reconfigure our Weltanschauung. Europe and the United States have aging societies. It is being said that 2020 will be the first year in which there is a negative population growth: old people are dying in hordes; immigration has decreased in dramatic ways; and the young, for an assortment of reasons, are postponing having babies. Not having a vigorous old generation will deprive society of the wisdom that comes from the elders. While impalpable to many, this, in my view, will create a sense of uncertainty.

—April 1, 2020

JLA: "Days after" are always precious and very fleeting opportunities for profound transformation. With the end of World War Two came a necessary purging at Nuremberg, and also the groundwork for a new world order that was to be fairer and which, through shared institutions, would ward off the threat of nationalist totalitarianisms and devastating wars: In a few short years, the Marshall Plan, the United Nations, NATO, and the foundation stones of the European Union were all created. These became the bulwarks of Western civilization for the next three generations, withstanding and surviving even the pressures of the Cold War. We now stand on a threshold, one in which those collective institutions that remain are seriously weakened, their very survival open to question, often from within. When this new global crisis is over, there must come a reassertion of democracy and a strengthening of its essential instruments of civic freedom and rule of law—or there will be a consolidation of power by the new authoritarians, who are on the rise everywhere.

—April 2, 2020

IS: This morning, the tally for the virus was over one million people, with around 60,000 deaths worldwide. In the U.S., the Center for Disease Control and Prevention has predicted twice that amount, maybe more. The numbers are staggering, Jon Lee. More than ever, the early decades of the twentieth century look now like the Gilded Age: excessive, irresponsible. The general feeling was that humans were invincible. Money was easily made. I think of the so-called FIRE entrepreneurs, who retired at twenty-eight or thirty, secure that with their million or two in stocks they could live four or five decades in relatively inexpensive places like Bali. Life is upside down: empty-pocketed, they are trapped in remote locations, unable to return home.

Especially worrisome is the ideological divide we all are part of. People of divergent political views already existed in cocoons, intransigent, belligerent, fed with self-serving news, suspicious of the other side. How to react to COVID-19 depends on which TV channel to tune into. Scientists, who now more than ever hold the key to our existence, are being ridiculed. And religion is being reembraced wholeheartedly. I heard that a London synagogue that in normal times has trouble congregating a *minyan* of ten people for early morning prayer had two thousand a Saturday or two ago. This last topic interests me dearly. You and I have seen the degree to which this age of calamity has been portrayed, on the global scale, as an apocalypse of biblical proportions. This, it is being repeated, is the end of times. We all have sinned and are paying for our deviated—i.e., immoral—behavior. In other words, the Almighty is punishing us. One hears this scandalizing tone among evangelicals in the U.S., *Haredi* in Israel, fundamentalist Christians in Chile and Argentina, among proselytizing groups in Africa, and so on. The phenomenon could be laughed at, yet it is unquestionable that in periods such as these, faith plays an enlarged role. I myself am a skeptical rationalist. I find the talk of religious salvation obnoxious. But I also understand it, and, in moments of despair, even sympathize with it a bit.

I am exposed to a lot of this apocalyptic chatter in my native Mexico, where I keep strong ties. I regularly receive messages about *Armagedón*: with López Obrador as erratic as he is, I read emails about the upper class, *la aristocracia mexicana*, always traveling the world like busy bees, bringing the devil into poor neighborhoods in Ciudad de México. Sometimes the target is more concrete: Mexican Jews. And, as is the case in other parts of the globe, I read about magical cures concocted by *curanderas* and other indigenous figures.

—April 3, 2020

JLA: As we look on in horror at the soaring U.S. mortality rates, especially those in New York—not to mention the political chaos caused by Trump and the lack of a true national health system—here in Britain there is a sense that things are approaching a critical stage. The news, on Sunday afternoon, that Boris Johnson was taken to a London hospital from Downing Street triggered a greater sense of national emergency. Government officials were characteristically discreet, saying only that Johnson had been taken to hospital for "routine tests" due to "persistent symptoms of coronavirus," ten days after contracting COVID-19 and going into self-isolation. Throughout the day, minions spoke to the BBC to declare that Johnson "continued to run the government" from his hospital bed. But such reassurances were obviously intended to soothe the fears of a worried population, and fooled no one. If Johnson had to be hospitalized, as everyone knew, his condition was serious.

Also on Sunday night, Queen Elizabeth, who is now ninety-three, addressed the nation in a televised broadcast. It was an unusual thing for her to do. She always records an annual Christmas message but otherwise does not often make such addresses. Her message was aimed at instilling a sense of calm national purpose: "Together we are tackling this disease, and I want to reassure you that if we remain united and resolute, then we will overcome it," she said. (For me, as an American, the contrast between such a dignified public statement to the latest outrage from Donald Trump was, as ever, jarring and mortifying. The latest, from him, was that he wouldn't be wearing a mask during the pandemic despite the decision by U.S. government health experts that all Americans should do so for the duration of the pandemic. So much for leadership.)

Yesterday, Monday, April 6, went by in a strained limbo. Brits got on with their lives, such as they live them now, in constrained circumstances but with an ear cocked to the news. In the evening, the breaking news came that Boris Johnson had been moved to intensive care. He remains there today, with more attempts at reassuring news being doled out that he "remains conscious" and that "although he had required oxygen, he is not on a ventilator." His foreign minister Dominic Raab, had been "deputized" to carry out the PM's functions "should that be required."

Messages of sympathy and support from everyone who's anyone across Britain's political spectrum have poured in, including from new Labour leader, Keir Starmer, who replaced the outgoing Jeremy Corbyn after a leadership vote just yesterday. Starmer, a doughty centrist, has reassured Labourites who had long felt dismayed and alienated by Corbyn's hard left ideology and whiff of anti-Semitism that had swirled around him.

In such ways, almost serendipitously, there is a sense of the British finally pulling together again, much as Johnson had willed them to before over Brexit, but unconvincingly and unsuccessfully. If he dies this week—a possibility—there will be widespread public shock and many expressions of regret for a life—and an ambitious political career cut short—but there will also be many Britons who will note that it was Johnson's hubris that brought about his demise. It was less than three weeks ago, at the outside of this pandemic crisis, that he appeared at one of his first ever coronavirus daily briefings to relay in enthused tones how he had been to a hospital with coronavirus patients and had shaken their hands, and how he would continue to do so. The air of irresponsibility that has always clung to Johnson, endearing him to many for his good humor and air of irrepressible adolescence, therefore, will also inevitably color his epitaph. But if he survives and returns in good health to lead the country from 10 Downing Street, he may well pull off the Churchillian moment he has sought but failed to achieve because of his character failings. If he can acknowledge the recklessness and arrogance that were his main identifiable traits before his near-death experience, he might finally command wide respect. Right now, his future, and the sense of well-being of the United Kingdom, rests on the outcome of his ability to keep his lungs going.

—April 7, 2020

IS: Boris Johnson is back at home. He bounced back from the abyss and has been in the public eye, thanking the nurses who cared for him in the ICU. Meanwhile, in the United States Trump's endless sequence of blunders continues. Just last week he was in a back-and-forth with various state governors—a group on the West Coast that includes California, Oregon, and Washington, and another in the Northeast from New York, Connecticut, New Jersey, and others—arguing that it is up to him, a supreme leader like North Korea's Kim Jong-un, to decide when Americans are allowed to leave isolation. The tension goes back to the Republic's federalist foundation. How should the balance of power between the federal and state governments be understood? Except that with Trump, an erratic, mercurial tyrant, this isn't a dialogue but a series of deafening soliloquies. In the middle of it all are the American people, themselves a boisterous bunch pulling in every possible direction. Libertarians are standing up to mayors and other politicians, portraying the lockdown as a curtailing of individual liberty. Forget about the well-being of the country as a whole, which is what scientists have been pushing since this nightmarish standstill began: if all of us stay home, the death toll will be much smaller. But these American ruffians in Idaho and elsewhere believe it's all a strategy by the government to limit their freedom. And Trump is encouraging them. Last night, after finally accepting that governors have the last word in these matters and not the president of the United States, he sent a bunch of incendiary tweets encouraging discontent in Michigan and other states. "Liberate yourselves!" was his message. "Bring down the democratic governors!" My God, at a time when we need unity and forbearance, he opens the doors to anarchy and rebellions.

The largest number of victims is in prisons, old people's homes, and other similar environments. News of dozens of corpses found in these facilities show up every time one reads the paper or turns on the TV. Just before the lockdown, I was teaching Shakespeare at a local prison. But six weeks ago or so I was forbidden to enter the facility out of fear of contagion. A few days ago, I read in the local newspaper that a few cases had appeared at the Hampshire County Jail. This morning the number was twelve. My heart aches. I think of my "inside" students all the time.

Our connection was interrupted just as we were reading *Hamlet* together. We were going to stage the play. They were already beginning to memorize their respective parts. The connection between theater and reality is eerie. In my mind, it feels as if we are part of a larger-than-life play, just as Shakespeare inserts in Hamlet a play within a play.

You won't believe what I've been doing to anesthetize myself, Jon Lee. I've been watching telenovelas from Latin America. They are, as you know, the lowest of artistic forms, that is, if one even begins to see them through the prism of art. I've always been fascinated with the emphasis they place on overwrought emotions. I've spent long hours watching *Sin senos sí hay paraíso*, *Frontera verde*, and *Rosario Tijeras* from Colombia, *Club de Cuervos*, *La Casa de las flores*, *Luis Miguel: La serie*, *El clon*, *La Reina del Sur* and *The Day I Met El Chapo* from Mexico, and *Cuatro estaciones en La Habana* from Cuba. Each of these miniseries (such are recent developments that it is almost impossible to distinguish between a standard telenovela in what is called "open TV," meaning evening prime time from Monday to Friday, and a Netflix-style narrative) has between thirteen and sixty-three episodes of roughly thirty minutes to almost two hours. This means that cumulatively I have been in front of the damn screen for more than two complete weeks without intermission. Crazy! Yet it has been enormously rewarding. I'm doing the exercise with fifteen students. The exploration has enabled us all to appreciate what makes these countries tick. In one word, *amarillismo*, what Germans call *Schadenfreude*: finding delight in the pain of others. Do you know how many scenes I have seen in these artifacts in which a daughter is abused by her father, a maid finds herself pregnant by her boss, someone tries to kill a rival, and so on?

I say all this because, bizarrely, I wonder if our own global calamity isn't somehow *telenovelesca*? As the public waited for news about Boris Johnson's health, it wasn't difficult to detect, in a portion of the public, a desire for his death. Likewise, I have heard countless complaints that COVID-19 isn't finding the "right" victims. Why, if Trump, Vice President Mike Pence, and Senate Majority Leader Mitch McConnell refuse to wear masks, haven't they been infected? Is the virus a tool of the Republican Party? Of course, one hears the exact same complaint from the other side: Bill Gates' foundation started it all; the whole epidemic is a ploy orchestrated by Nancy Pelosi. Extreme politics in the United States is a deafening cacophony politicizing every significant and innocuous move.

Talking about telenovelas, I was told yesterday that certain Latin American nations have ordered that on even-numbered days, men are allowed outside from their homes, whereas women go out on odd-numbered days. Other than cutting the population on the street in half, I've tried to understand the logic but it evades me. Honestly, it doesn't surprise me that such absurd rules come from Latin America. What is the point of going out if the world is reduced in such a monochromatic way?

Tomorrow is five weeks since Alison and I have been indoors with Isaiah. The passing of time is weird. Were it not for Jewish rituals, a Friday night would feel anodyne. Indeed, the passage of time feels heavier, less a cycle than an impossibility. I have been having lucid dreams in which I see people from my childhood I have not thought about for decades. I wonder if in the months of the plague dreams have an altogether different grammar. Do they speak to us differently? Are they deeper? Do we unconsciously acknowledge that our dreams are the only way we can actually travel now, other than while watching a Netflix program?

—*April 18, 2020*

JLA: In the days since you wrote me, Ilan, the Trump-instigated protests against the lockdown in various American states have picked up steam and acquired gruesomely cartoonish proportions, with groups of armed men and women, garbed in paramilitary gear and in some cases wearing masks, swaggering around in public. In one unforgettable image that went viral yesterday I saw an armed group occupying the steps of the State Capitol building in Philadelphia, led by a man armed with an AR-15, his face concealed behind a mask of George Washington. In another, a busload of armed louts poured into the State Capitol in Kentucky, observed by uniformed police in a scene that made a mockery of the very idea of law enforcement, not to mention the rights of freedom of assembly and of speech.

As seen from Europe, such spectacles are frighteningly loaded with bellicose symbolism, and obviously a perversion of the constitutional rights Americans profess to hold so dear. The sight of protesters armed with guns taking over public spaces in defiance of those who think differently is extremely alarming. This kind of thing has been happening in the United States for a while, of course, but the fact that these shows of armed force are taking place now—in protest over coronavirus quarantines that are intended to save lives—makes them especially grotesque.

I am always shocked and humiliated, as an American, to see such acts of stupidity, and feel anger at my—at our—inability to alter the status quo that allows such things to occur. Quite beyond the obviousness of the increasingly urgent need to extricate Trump from the White House, and, ideally, into a jail somewhere, I despair when I ponder the damage he has done to the social fabric of the United States. Even if Trump loses and Joe Biden becomes president in the next elections, what happens with the ginned-up oafs like the armed man in the George Washington mask? Will they continue to be egged on by the likes of Hannity and Huckabee and Laura Ingraham and Franklin Graham and the other rabble-rousers of this American era? And what about Trump himself? Will he retire to his gilded Jacuzzi in Trump Tower or will he continue to barnstorm the country, hurling accusations and spreading conspiracy theories about the Deep State and the Fake Press and Rapist Mexicans? One suspects it will be the latter, unless he becomes so embroiled in legal problems that he has to spend all his time going to court. But even then, of course, he'll be mouthing off to a waiting press scrum that will be as eager as it ever was to provide him with a microphone to do so. Think Roger Stone.

In less than a generation, the Us and Them line in the sand that was initially drawn globally by George W. Bush with his post-9/11 "you're either with us or against us" speech has been brought home. It has divided the

United States in a way I haven't seen since I was a boy, when the country was riven and bloodied by Vietnam and the battles over civil rights.

I know this sounds alarmist—so be it. But I am certain that if Trump wins another term in office and has four more years to undermine democracy and spread his bile among Americans, there will be a significant deterioration of American civic life, and the groundwork laid for potentially violent polarization on a scale we have not seen since the Civil War. If Trump has made anything more possible, it is the possibility of armed conflict between Americans who regard one another as enemies. If Biden wins, he will have a huge task to repair America's damaged institutions, and to recreate the idea of a binding national ethos that unites all its citizens. If he cannot achieve that, I fear for the future of the United States.

That some human beings are expendable is part and parcel of the "end the lockdown, everyone has to die sometime" argument now being propagated by Trump and his cohorts—and it is being actively echoed by Trump's Brazilian Mini-Me, Bolsonaro, by the way, with huge mounting costs to human life. Two of the most vulnerable groups you mentioned— the elderly who live in old people's homes and the inmates of prisons—are clearly the expendables of the new era. (May I call it the Deplorable Era, to paraphrase Hilary Clinton?) The obviousness of this reality raises the question, in turn, as to how much of a priority they will be in the post-pandemic period, especially during the coming economic recession.

I commend you for your telenovela solution to the challenge of teaching your students in this plague-time; what a wonderful idea! I confess to having felt no compulsion these past few weeks to watch much of anything, though I have tried. Having heard about the American frenzy over *Tiger King*, I did watch a couple of episodes, but then stopped, feeling depressed at what felt like a voyeur's prowl through a trailer park. At the encouragement of my son, I recently began watching *The Last Kingdom*, a Netflix series about Saxons and Vikings, and I must say, the scenes of slashing and hanging and rough sex in the forest have been a useful, if temporary, antidote to the rage I feel about Trump's America. The depiction

199

of politics in ancient Britain as a ceaseless and entirely virtueless battle for power and survival, also feels very *now*, somehow, as well.

On this note, since you mentioned Boris Johnson and his health, which were the main topic of my preoccupations when I last wrote, it's true that he is now out of the ICU, no longer in mortal danger, and has been said to be recovering at Chequers, the prime ministerial mansion in the country-side outside London. He has been little heard of since then, with a young minister deputized to speak for him and handle things in his absence. There is a sense that things are being dealt with more seriously and with more gravitas in Johnson's absence; nonetheless, there was a great flurry at the news that Johnson had attended a virtual cabinet meeting lasting two hours and had expressed caution on the issue of ending the British lockdown. Perhaps his near-death experience has chastened Johnson. It seems essential that it does.

Even so, there are worrying signs that the "old Boris" has not entirely gone away. Yesterday morning in Whitehall, signs appeared saying "Boris is Awesome," having apparently been put up by something calling itself the "Boris Is Awesome Committee." Speculation has been rife on Twitter that the "Committee" is none other than Johnson's chief of staff, Dominic Cummings, an antisocial, Rasputinesque figure—in American terms, the equivalent of Steve Bannon—an unelected advisor who operates behind the scenes but exercises huge influence over Boris Johnson. It remains a matter of conjecture whether, as the media is now suggesting, he is the brains behind the Boris is Awesome campaign. Public or commercial campaigns that champion Britishness, whether it's the quality of the beef or carrot juice—have become ubiquitous in the Brexit era, but the idea that someone—anyone—in the British government would think it OK to go around cheerleading Boris as an "awesome guy," which is an Americanism anyway, is almost beyond belief.

It is also patently clear to anyone with the faculties of memory and reason that Boris Johnson may be many things—he may be smart, entertaining, and even likeable, as his fans would have us believe, but he has not been an "awesome" prime minister, and when it comes to the COVID-19 pandemic, he has been an utter failure, to the point of endangering his own life out of a negligent approach to the threat. This has played out in a steady stream of revelations about the government's lack of preparedness, the under-equipped medical staff at hospitals, the absence of tests and testing, the high mortality rate, and the deaths of NHS doctors and nurses who have been infected by the patients they are treating because of inadequate protective gear. This is not awesome, but awful, and that is really the only adjective to attach to Johnson's government thus far.

In any case, we live in a time in which disbelief has been suspended, and the antics of politicians that once would have seen their careers ended no longer has consequences. In the West, now, in addition to Trump, we have Bolsonaro, and in little El Salvador, Nayib Bukele, a young man in Armani and a clipped beard whose Twitter handle, until recently, said he was "the coolest president," and who uses his Tweets to send orders to his military officers, and threatens anyone disobeying his quarantine orders with thirty days in jail. Where is this all going, Ilan? Is theatrical buffoonery always a feature of populism? Will the pandemic bring us more authoritarians, more people willing to believe in the snake oil that they sell, do you think? Latin America has entered a post-ideological era with the collapse of the Left, and now, also, of American leadership in the hemisphere in the sense of it being a model or beacon of any sort. If the United States is no longer the City on a Hill, what replaces it? Why are there not any new Latin leaders emerging to topple the big-mouthed buffoons? Or will they now emerge and make themselves known during this pandemic? What about all the social protests that rocked Latin America last year? The protestors are locked down, along with everyone else, because of the coronavirus. When this is over, will they renew their demands, or will they have new ones? What happens next?

—*April 21, 2020*

IS: I had a bizarre dream last night. Before going to bed, I occasionally read a couple of pages of the *Babylonian Talmud*. It's an exercise I picked up decades ago, as a student. The *Talmud* is a nonlinear narrative written between 500 BC and 200 CE, that is, over a long stretch of time. There is no single author; instead, a symphony—or maybe I should say a cacophony—of rabbinical voices digress on a variety of legalistic, religious, and political issues. The rabbis making the arguments, the Amoraim and the Tanaim, didn't know each other; still, in these pages, they talk to one another as if they were in the same room. There is little patience for building a character the way we are accustomed to in a novel. A certain rabbi, say Rabbi Eliezer, will show up making a big pronouncement, to which an assortment of sages will react. We don't know who Rabbi Eliezer is; nor do we know much about the other commentators.

These exercises allow my mind to rest. Last night, I was reading about a feud between two rabbis, one of whom courts the other's wife. The first one, the owner of a far more portentous mind, dies at one point; the other is still in love with his wife but doesn't want to interfere in her mourning rituals. But the wife for a variety of reasons can't bury her husband. I mean this literally. Her husband's corpse lies in his bedroom for more than a year in a process of slow decomposition. At one point, worms emerge from his ears.

I couldn't get this frightening image out of my mind. Somehow, it felt intricately linked to everything in the news now. Anyway, I finally relaxed and made my way to bed. But then I had this ominous dream. I will describe it succinctly. I was in an empty parking lot, as big as the eye could see. I was alone. In the dream I didn't know how I had gotten there. I felt desolate. Suddenly, I felt something tickling me on my left ear. I touched it and found a worm. I then saw my feet—I was barefoot—and could see them become roots. I have a beautiful katsura tree in my backyard. In the last few years, its roots have become quite visible. At this point some of them look just like branches whose ends are buried in the ground. My feet looked the same way.

I wanted to walk but couldn't. I also wanted to scream but my throat wouldn't emit any sound. I got upset. Or maybe I got angry. I no longer know the difference between these two emotions. And then, out of breath and in a sweat, I woke up.

It took me hours to go back to sleep.

Somehow, the last few questions in your latest comment made me think of the dream. I clearly felt close to death in it, like the rabbi in the *Tractate Bava Metzia*, Part III, that I have been submerging myself in. And I felt paralyzed, as if I had lost all my freedom. I have thought about all this a lot. Will we regain what we're losing now? The isolation has brought along a few benefits. I love spending more time at home with Alison and Isiah. I love cooking. I even love teaching remotely, although I never thought I would one day say it. But, like everyone else, I feel fractured, upended, rooted to the degree that the very roots appear to be killing me.

—*April 29, 2020*

JLA: You are lucky to remember your dreams, Ilan, or perhaps not, given the nature of your latest ones, which seem to have been nightmares brought on by existential anxiety. And fair enough; we all have a quota of anxiety we carry with us; now, no doubt, more than ever. If I do have dreams—and I suppose I must—I carry no memory of them in the morning, although I sometimes awaken with a sore shoulder and bicep, which my dentist tells me is from grinding my teeth at night. I am lucky, I guess, to suffer only abstract physical symptoms from my anxieties, if that is what they are, while no memories of them plague me.

Like you, I feel suspended, in limbo, and like you, a part of me enjoys this suspension, the slowing down of time and the opportunity to spend more time at home and with my loved ones. I am usually traveling around the world; last year I probably visited twenty-five or more countries, and flew over a hundred times. I both love that existence—exploring the world is my preferred natural state of being, and always thrills me—but I also know that it keeps me from living according to a more productive and healthier daily routine. Nowadays, I am doing just that, waking up early, writing for a bit, walking Stig and Tug (here in England we can have outings for exercise) and then settling into a full writing day, followed by another longer walk in the afternoon, and then dinner with Máximo and Erica. It is a good, almost luxurious rhythm of life, and perhaps because of its enjoyable novelty, I have not yet grown bored with it. Although I feel somewhat guilty saying so, a part of me would like the quarantine, if not the COVID-19, to go on for as long as possible.

—*April 30, 2020*

WEST DORSET, ENGLAND,
AND AMHERST, MASSACHUSETTS
MARCH 11–APRIL 30, 2020

Peregrination

LOUIS-PHILIPPE DALEMBERT

Translated from the French by Ghjulia Romiti

Louis-Philippe Dalembert (Port-au-Prince, Haiti, 1962) is among the most important Haitian writers of his generation. He is a poet, novelist, short story writer, and essayist. His books, praised by critics in France and abroad, have been translated into several languages and include L'île du bout des rêves *(2003),* Noires blessures *(2011),* Avant que les ombres s'effacent *(2017), and* Mur Méditerranée *(2019). His novel* Epi oun jou konsa tèt Pastè Bab pati *(2007) is written in Haitian Creole. The English translation of his novel* The Other Side of the Sea *was published in 2014. Dalembert lives in Paris and Port-au-Prince.*

I wander through paris, empty
of our laughter of our frenzy
absent from our absence
the spring sun
shines uselessly
stripped of our meanderings
of the lovers' kisses
and their knowing hands
along the canal saint-martin

I wander through paris
who no longer knows our names
silent from our laughter
and our pale anguish
the black and naked sun
has a faded smell of hunger
in the eyes of a child from my island
one-eyed and dirty
with silence
with lost arrogance and banter
like a harlot from another time
worn out with syphilis and artificial paradises
paris ultimate refuge
paris with the empty rhythm
of our planetary doubts
nothing is certain anymore
neither the devil nor the good lord
nothing except the delusion
of slow days
of silence
on the shrunken balcony of the building across the street

a little girl in the flush of life
invents her first steps
suspended in the air

all to her discovery
eyes riveted on tomorrow
that opens underneath her feet
she brandishes an indifferent smile
to the adequate applause
of the neighbors from the building next door
as the crows
with their insolent sneers
rip open-throated
through the city's crushing silence

the night just like the toddler's steps
hesitates in this beginning of the spring

I wander through my room
cloistered
in the void

PARIS
APRIL 3, 2020

Draupadi
on the Mountaintop

PRIYANKA CHAMPANERI

Priyanka Champaneri (Virginia, 1983) received her MFA in creative writing from George Mason University and has been a fellow at the Virginia Center for the Creative Arts numerous times. She received the 2018 Restless Books Prize for New Immigrant Writing for her debut novel, The City of Good Death, *to be released in 2021.*

AT THE HEIGHT of my anxiety, I drive to a historic district near me. I find a parking spot far too easily for a late Saturday morning, and I walk around. I stop at my local yarn shop, a brick flatiron painted sky blue, and I knock on the paned glass door and wave at the woman inside. I step back, six feet away until the woman opens the door and hands me my order, and then I step forward and take it and step back again quickly, like a particularly stodgy bird performing a courtship dance.

The woman is a staff member I've spoken to before; she wears glasses and sometimes has a scarf wrapped around her hair. When she sees me, she smiles and confirms my name and says *Thank you* and *Stay safe out there*, but nothing else, and I realize I am disappointed. I continue to walk, until my legs slow and I turn around, my motivation to wander now redirected into a desire to leave. There is no one around to catch my eye, no one walking by with a coffee, chatting into the ether through cordless earbuds, no one to confirm that I am not the last person alive on this planet.

If you'd asked me months ago to define my normal—before the pandemic, before any stay-at-home order—I would have described the following: Struggling to wake up on time. Sitting in traffic. Eight hours of emails and meetings and office small talk. Startling when the nearby daycare lets its charges loose on the wide expanse of grass right outside the window abutting my cube, looking up from whatever I am doing to watch the little bodies run. Listening to their shrieks and panic, their wild laughter. Then, more traffic on the drive home. Watching the hours dwindle between errands and dinner and washing up, and finally sitting down to write or read, sometimes to knit, never for long enough. Feeling as if my time is not my own. Wishing for more of it, for peace in the incessant buzz. Too much noise, too much vitriol, too much hate and fear and angst and anguish.

Strange, I think now on the drive home from the yarn shop. The existence we think we want—the quiet, the emptiness, the stillness. And finding the reality quite different.

I feel foolish, not to have anticipated it.

209

*

There is a story in *The Mahabharata* about the previous life of Draupadi, the single consort of all five Pandava brothers. In that life before, she'd prayed and fasted for years, directing her mental energies toward Shiva, until her austerities provoked Him to appear before her and grant her a boon. Imagine sitting on a peak of the Himalayas, foregoing food and drink and speech, wearing rags, enduring every physical discomfort as you focus on one wish, your thoughts blank except for the thing that compels you to live entirely inside your mind. And then the Destroyer of the Universe appears, the first being you've seen in years, and one capable of incinerating entire planets with a single blink of His third eye. Suddenly, you must will your tongue, long dormant in your mouth, to move and speak the words you've carefully held in your throat all this time.

"I want a husband," Draupadi said. "I want a husband. I want a husband. I want a husband. I want a husband."

She said it five times. She couldn't help herself. The wish burst out of her; she'd been repeating it in her mind, why wouldn't she say the words more than once, to ensure she made her desire clear?

But Shiva heard each repeated utterance, and He granted her wish exactly as He heard it. He granted her five husbands, one for each time she made her request, all hers in the next life, all at once.

That's one version. Another version, the one I prefer, has Draupadi perfectly in control, as only a woman steeped in years of the intense *tapasya* capable of calling down the Destroyer must be. And when He appears, she is ready. She says she wants a husband, and then she lists the qualities she wants the man to have. She rattles off all the characteristics of moral, physical, and intellectual perfection. And when Shiva says such a man does not exist, she insists, to the point of rebuke. The work of her meditation demands a reward. This is the reward she wants.

The outcome is the same. One man cannot be everything Draupadi desires. So she will instead have five, the five Pandavas, who between them possess all the qualities she demanded. Five brothers, destined to be hers when she is reborn.

There is a lot more to the story than I am telling here, suffering that Draupadi endured in that life before she was Draupadi, before the point when she gives herself up to prayer, but the part that I am concerned with is the moment Shiva appears. The difference between what Draupadi asked for, and what she received. How the thing you want may not really be the thing you want.

I pick up my knitting, hold one needle in each hand, points up, and wrap the yarn twice around my left index finger, all in preparation to knit one stitch, then another. After twenty years of knitting, muscle memory renders the task as complicated as lifting a fork to my mouth while I'm watching TV. I look at the loops already anchored on my needle. And then I release it all and put it back on my lap. I do nothing.

When I read, my eyes slide over the words. I cannot listen to podcasts, have no appetite for music, and when I try to pick out a movie I instead spend hours scrolling through every single offering, adding films to my favorites list and then removing them. The only writing I can manage is to transcribe the pages from notebooks I've filled longhand in the preceding, pandemic-free months.

Sometimes, when I am walking outside, mask on, swinging a wide detour along the paved path when I see someone coming my way, avoiding their eyes and holding my breath until we're clear of each other, I imagine breaking into a sprint in time to all the emotions jostling in my head. Shrieks and panic. Wild laughter.

Ask me now what I remember about a normal day months ago, before the pandemic, before the stay-at-home orders, and I will describe this: Overhearing someone in the office summarize *Love at First Sight*, her voice filling with outrage, bafflement, unmitigated glee. Catching my colleague stifle a snort and an eye roll during a meeting. Finding an empty bench to read on during my lunch break. Getting distracted by the sun piercing a daffodil's petals, green stem buffeted by the breeze. Waiting at a stoplight on the way home, looking upward, and spotting a single red-brown hawk, talons gripping a tree branch, eyes fierce.

I attend video calls with coworkers, with friends, with my writing group, my knitting group. I watch authors do virtual events. I text everyone I know, and then I text them again. Each day, I peruse several different newspapers online. I read about reopening in April. Then, June. Autumn will be dangerous. The finish line stretches forward, hops further into the future. And still, my thoughts sidle toward a fantasy of normal, like an insect compelled to veer toward what it thinks is the sun.

I think about time a lot, when it seems we have so much of it to ourselves and the hours pass slowly and the days melt into one another. *All of that time*, I'd thought when this virus first began floating across oceans, coming our way. I didn't think of lives or money or jobs lost. Economies tanking, people pulled back into poverty and homelessness, death experienced in near isolation, last rites viewed on a screen.

I thought only of myself. I thought of time to think and to be. It's a supreme luxury to feel that way, a position of privilege that feels like guilt in my mouth, a taste I cannot wash away. And here it is, all that time, the price paid out by others and continuing to be paid, the sand slipping down the hourglass at exactly the same rate that it always did, each grain the same quality it was before, but there is a difference, and that difference is in me and the world and everyone I know.

Draupadi on the mountain, wishing for a thing so fervently that she neglected to confirm whether it fit within her own reality.

Other writers must also do this, see their thoughts pivot to creating conflict where there is none, out of a perversion to see what happens next. I think all storytelling is only that—creating a problem where there was none before, and seeing the problem through, all the cascading dominoes and how they tumble, the direction they fall.

Consider this moment from last summer: I was waiting in my car at a four-way stop sign in the middle of a busy town district, the kind with a movie theater, restaurants, two different cupcake shops. The stream of people walking in front of me was never-ending, and while my car idled, my mind did as well. The night was ripe with Virginia heat, days so hot you could roll your windows down at 10 p.m. and still feel the moist air bathe your face in sweaty dew. Everyone was happy, children on scooters, lovers with ice cream cones. I felt then that we were all lucky, in that place and time, and in the crystal calm of the moment I imagined a bomb, a meteor, an alien vessel—pick your disturbance of explosive proportions, but the end result was a collision of the unplanned into the calm of the complacent. And then I thought about what would happen after. Who ran? Who ended up curled in a ball in the middle of the intersection? Who continued to eat their ice cream, intent on finishing the last dregs even as life transformed into an entirely different thing?

I imagined this not because I wanted people to be hurt or killed, not because I wanted to mar their happiness, but because the calm triggered in me a need for catastrophe. I can't be the only one to think that way, to have the impulse to put a wrinkle into something smooth. To want something to happen. This is why people watch disaster movies, dystopian society movies, end-of-days movies, isn't it? I'm not drawn to seeing the triumph of the human spirit. I'm not looking at the woman offering her breast to nurse the dying man. My eyes linger instead on the charred city smoking just beyond.

If you know the story of what happens to Draupadi in the life after, when she is married to the Pandavas, you might think, as I do, that she was better off in the moment before she made her wish than she was thereafter. That her nature compelled her to ask for something to happen, to create conflict in the calm. As Draupadi, she received her husbands as promised, but she also suffered humiliation, degradation, a testing of womanhood that seems far beyond the testing she endured on that mountain and in the earlier years of that life before.

She didn't have to open her eyes to Shiva. She didn't have to ask for anything. In her state of extreme penance, she could have continued in prayer for years, picked her moment to release her soul from her body, and been done with all of it. Instead she asked for a change.

Subconsciously, perhaps I wanted something to happen, just for the sake of it, and now, it has. Consciously, I wanted quiet, and I have that as well. The things seem opposed, yet they coexist. *I want a husband: You shall have five husbands.*

The part of the story that I want to know, the part lost to us or more likely looked over, is how Draupadi felt *after* the Destroyer granted her boon and vanished. How did she pick herself up from realizing that the thing she'd focused on for so long was heading toward her, but in a mutation she never could have anticipated? How did she move forward with the rest of her years, right until the end, when she closed her eyes for the last time, knowing exactly what fate awaited her in the next life?

Once I realize that the despondency I feel is grief, that the little things I have lost in my day-to-day life are, indeed, losses, I am able to settle more fully into sadness. And after sadness fades—not entirely, not quite yet—I pick up my knitting needles. I knit an entire sweater, then another. I start inserting new writing into the notes I transcribe. I am able to read a page in a book, then another. All of this happens slowly, sporadically, and some days not at all. I move about with halting caution, as if brushing against something will shatter it and require me to adjust all over again. The difference I feel is still there, the presence of uncertainty is certain for a long while yet. It feels like waiting, and in the waiting I am compelled to occupy myself.

Sitting on my bed, paralyzed with what I should be doing, all the things I cannot do, I shut my eyes and I imagine all the noise in my head bursting forth into the quiet.

Maybe, after Shiva granted her wish in His way and vanished, Draupadi remained on the mountain a while longer. By that point, through the virtue of her prayer and the life she'd led before, she would have been half divine herself, imbued with her own power. Perhaps she descended the mountain, or else decided to return to her penance, living out the remaining time stretching before her.

When there is only one path before you, you can sit and think things over, but eventually you must get on with it.

I hope she allowed herself emotion: regret, grief at the loss of the life she envisioned, in its place a different reality, ready for her to live it. I imagine I can see her. Shivering, once again awake to the world, alone on the mountaintop. She might have rolled the divine words around in her head, wondering at herself, wondering at what she'd received. And her thoughts—after so long holding to one wish, what was the first feeling to rush into that newly vacated space in her mind?

Shrieks, perhaps. Panic. Wild, wild laughter.

VIRGINIA
MAY 1, 2020

Confronting the Pandemic in a Time of Revolt: Voices from Chile

ARIEL DORFMAN

Ariel Dorfman (Buenos Aires, Argentina, 1942) is a Chilean author whose books have been translated into more than fifty languages, and his plays, including Death and the Maiden, *which was made into a feature film (1991), have been produced in over one hundred countries. His writing frequently appears in the* New York Times, The Nation, *and many other papers internationally. His most recent books are* Cautivos *(2020), a novel about Cervantes, and* The Rabbits' Rebellion *(2020), a story for children and adults. He and his wife Angélica divide their time between their native Chile and Durham, North Carolina, where he is Distinguished Emeritus Professor at Duke University.*

IT IS ODDLY APPROPRIATE and perhaps ironic that Chile happens to be preparing to celebrate—in the midst of a pandemic that is drastically questioning all previous paradigms of behavior and human relationships—the centenary of the death of Alberto Blest Gana (1830–1920), the country's preeminent novelist of "manners" (*costumbres*) of the nineteenth century, who understood his moralizing work as part of a "high mission" that "brings civilization to the least educated classes of society," excoriates "vices," and teaches the public "healthy, wholesome lessons." It is even more paradoxical that exactly a hundred years after Blest Gana breathed his last, the founding myths of nationhood he helped to imagine and define have been shattered by a heroic social movement led by young people brought up on the works of this very author.

Like those youngsters in the streets, I first read Blest Gana's most famous and popular novel, *Martín Rivas*, in my Chilean high school, though that was back in the late 1950s. I confess that I immediately felt wary of the eponymous protagonist, who, coming from an impoverished provincial middle-class family, triumphs against all odds and manages to marry the haughty, albeit sparkling and sensitive, daughter of his aristocratic patron in Santiago. I found Martín too noble, too industrious and earnest, too tediously innocent, preferring his romantic friend, Rafael San Luis, rebellious and slightly satanic. I resented the fact that San Luis, because he breaks the rules of conformist existence and sexual monogamy, is condemned to die by the narrator (who at least bestowed upon him a gallant departure, combating a reactionary government), whereas the overly virtuous and mildly liberal Martín, after much intrigue and many misunderstandings, is rewarded with the girl and her family fortune.

Partly my disquiet came from the circumstance that I was reading Balzac and Stendhal at the time and thirsted for a Rastignac or a Julien Sorel to burst open the corset of social hierarchies. I also would have wanted the melodramatic and often prosaic Blest Gana to delve into some of the psychological complexity probed by the French and English novelists of

217

those years, the way, for instance, that Balzac himself and Dickens laid bare the corrosive influence of money on their characters.

But my distrust of the ascendancy of Martín ran deeper than a literary aversion. Already at the age of sixteen I was committed to critiquing the very society that Blest Gana's exemplary character personified. I saw the future of Chile (and humanity) not in the falsely meritocratic model presented by men like Martín, but forged by the struggle of millions of dispossessed people for a more just world, workers who, unsurprisingly, never make an appearance in the novel that celebrates the triumph of Martín and his incorporation into the dominant bourgeoisie of his era.

My dream for Chile would prevail during the three years (1970–73) of the presidency of Salvador Allende, a socialist whose peaceful revolution ended in a bloody coup by Gen. Augusto Pinochet. His dictatorship imposed the neoliberal model imported from the Chicago school of economics in thrall to Milton Friedman's ideas, a model of development and extreme privatization and exploitation that has ruled Chilean society (and much of the world) ever since, remaining prevalent even after democracy was restored to the country thirty years ago.

It is against that model that the Chilean people have rebelled since last October, demanding a new constitution and a system that works for the many and not for the privileged few at the top. (Chile is one of the most unequal nations in the world, with an appalling gap between the super-rich and the rest of the population.) And though the unexpected eruption of the COVID-19 pandemic has meant that the plebiscite that was supposed to lead to that new constitution (the first one to be forged by the people themselves, in the year when Chile celebrates the 210th anniversary of its independence) has been put on hold until late October, that same plague has confirmed to the people how the abysmal structural unfairness of the current social and economic system punishes the poor and helps the prosperous to thrive—a revelation about power that, one would hope, might also be central to the discussion regarding what the United States should learn from this crisis about its own national failings.

Though the considerate, upright, and austere nineteenth-century Martín Rivas, if he were to resurrect today, would probably deplore the greed and excesses of the cutthroat and all-too-real "Chicago boys" (among other things, Martín's progressive ideas and actions got him into trouble with the conservative authorities of his day, who are satirized in the novel), one can safely declare, nevertheless, that the current Chilean revolt is born out of a widespread rejection of the free-market, laissez-faire worldview that Blest Gana's hero represents. The youth of Chile had been promised that if they behaved like goody-goody Martín Rivas, benefits of all sorts would rain upon them. Instead, they live in a land where their education is discriminatory and underfunded; their families have dreadful health care; their parents are deeply in debt, earning Third World salaries to pay for goods with First World prices; and their grandparents have been immiserated by pension plans privatized by the dictatorship and devoted to taking advantage of pensioners rather than providing them with a comfortable old age. All the more reason to be enraged by the corruption and ostentatious luxury flaunted by the ruling elite.

As I recently returned to Blest Gana's novel during a prolonged visit to Chile, it did not seem far-fetched to interpret the uprising of Chile's youth—sustained by their elders in overwhelming numbers—as a rebellion against the paternalistic ideal of success through competition and individual accomplishment embodied by Martín Rivas that the activists read at school and that has been at the heart of how the ruling class wanted the people to dream of themselves during most of the republic's existence.

Of course, this view of Chilean identity—what my compatriots were supposed to collectively and personally aspire to—did not go uncontested in the country's society, nor in its literature. Besides the endless struggles for social justice by workers, miners, peasants, and intellectuals that would culminate in Allende's victory, the major novelists, poets, and playwrights in the hundred years since Blest Gana's death have channeled their creative energy into imagining an opposite, contrasting version of what Chile was and should be, vibrantly expressed in linguistic exploits that assail the prevailing certainties of sanctimonious and sanctioned history. The poetry of Neruda, both in his epic and surrealistic phases, and the mystical and covertly lesbian explorations of Gabriela Mistral, Chile's two Nobel Prize winners, are merely the most prominent of these endeavors. To these we can add an array of social-realist fiction devoted to the working class (Volodia Teitelboim, Francisco Coloane, Nicomedes Guzmán); the erotic narrative longings of María Luisa Bombal and Pía Barros; the acerbic verses of Nicanor Parra's "Anti-Poems" and José Donoso's phantasmagoric dissection of a decadent aristocracy; the freewheeling spirit expressed in the stories of Antonio Skármeta and Alejandro Zambra; the probing of marginal lives in novels by Manuel Rojas and Diamela Eltit; Raúl Zurita's hallucinatory love poems to a scarred and buried landscape of love and the glorious danger zones of the past conjured up by Tomás Harris in his *Cipango*; and the incisive plays of Jorge Díaz, Isidora Aguirre, and Egon Wolf. These and so many additional literary incursions (I think of Lihn and Lemebel, Isabel Allende and Marta Brunet) exposed a submerged country that did not believe that the road to liberation depended on imitating the conventional Martín Rivas archetype or the sort of unadventurous language in which his triumphant ascent and consolidation was transmitted.

But of all these authors, the one who best exemplifies a fierce and unbending rejection of Blest Gana's vision of what Chile should be is Carlos Droguett (1912–1996), who may not have been read by those who have flooded the streets for the past five months clamoring for justice, but who could be considered their secret godfather, a writer who predicted the rage of today's most militant protesters and their embrace of resistance, often violent, as a way of purging a corrupt and conformist social order.

Consistently and consciously outside the mainstream, the vitriolic and anti-establishment Droguett only received high-status recognition in 1970, exactly fifty years after Blest Gana's death and the year of Allende's victory, when he was awarded the National Prize for Literature. His most notorious novel continues to be *Eloy* (1960), a visceral, sympathetic, and tender stream-of-consciousness recreation of the last hours of a real-life bandit and murderer being hunted by the police, reflecting a fascination with the criminal and marginal sectors of society that Droguett never abandoned (he even has a novel in which Christ resurrects as a serial killer). More relevant, however, for fathoming today's revolt is another work, *Patas de Perro* (1965), which I consider his masterpiece (none of his work, alas, has been translated into English).

In that novel, the protagonist, Bobi, is born with the legs of a dog (that is, with *patas de perro*), and this radical symbolic and physical difference brings with it abuse, discrimination, persecution by every institution in the land (church, government, armed forces, politicians, entrepreneurs, educational system, the very ones being questioned by today's activists). Refusing to submit to society's way of dealing with him (he won't join a circus, will not put himself on display, will not market his divergence from the norm, will escape from an insane asylum where his murder is being planned), Bobi represents everything that official Chile has suppressed. His very existence epitomizes the spirit of defiance of those neglected by the powerful, ready to be martyred if need be. Droguett suggests that Bobi is alone now, but that a day will come when his example will be prophetic, when many others fight for the right to be different and rebellious.

As I reread *Patas de Perro* during my recent stay in Chile, I was acutely aware that not far from where I serenely sat with the novel, thousands of inadvertent emulators of Bobi were rising up and demanding recognition, that their countercultural voices be appreciated and their strangeness and desires be given legitimacy and respect. Like them, Droguett is furious and expresses that fury in a primeval, feverish flow of words and metaphors, eerily anticipating the wrath that has, as of late, been consuming a country whose elites have been blind for far too long to the needs and anguish of the greater part of the population.

With Droguett's ranting, lyrical, blood-filled indictment of Chilean society, we have traveled as far as it seems possible from the mundane, traditional realism of Blest Gana. Could this confrontation between these two acute opposites of Chile's halved identity bring to light anything about the crisis gripping this country at the end of the world, perhaps showing us ways in which a solution to its conflicts might be hammered out? Or am I engaging in an intellectually fanciful exercise by trying to examine present society's dilemmas through the prism of past literature, when so many other efforts and responsibilities await us? Indeed, do any of these fictional imaginings from decades ago speak to us, when the most immediate and harshly real tasks facing Chile—and humanity—are confronting the threats to our common survival in these times of pestilence?

I wager that there is something to be learned from the contrast between the extremes of Martín Rivas and Bobi, between Blest Gana's vision and Droguett's. For the immediate political trials facing Chile, it seems clear that without the explosive energy of the remote, unacknowledged disciples of the boy with the legs of a dog and his radical interrogation of established reality and societal norms, there is no likelihood of significant change. But that leaderless and anarchic insurrection against all forms of authority does not provide a blueprint for how, in concrete political terms, such real change might be implemented. For that to happen, Chile will need a meeting of sorts, a search for some kind of common ground. The followers of decent, honorable, hardworking, liberal Martín Rivas (and there are many of them, both in the middle class and among the disadvantaged, who continue to desperately crave, and believe in, upward social mobility) must be part of any long-lasting response to the challenges posed by the protests. The best among the elite that have ruled Chile are aware that the country cannot endure as a unified entity unless they reach some basic consensus with the multiple, passionate, contemporary avatars of Bobi and envision with them a strategy that maps out a future where the discordant parties disputing power can coexist, however uneasily, in the same land.

Until recently, I was uncertain if, given the chasm separating these contrary social actors and their antagonistic agendas, such an agreement could be worked out. The pandemic that now assails Chile, as it has the entire planet, has led me to believe that some sort of social pact, some semblance of an understanding, may not only be urgently necessary but practical and viable. A catastrophe of such epic dimensions will require both the dynamism and solidarity shown by the youth in the streets and the steadiness and efficiency of people in power who would probably define themselves as the distant descendants of Martín Rivas. If they do

indeed embody the worthiest principles and experience of that character—his constancy, his loyalty, his reliability—they can prove it by using
this moment of crisis as a way to learn about the enormous submerged
nation they have ignored. They can do what Martín never did: recognize
the permanent, defiant existence of that other Chile, the one Allende
once represented and gave a voice to, his vision of a society founded on
the principle that the needs of the many are more important than the
profits of the few.

For that to happen, enough Chileans of all classes would have to
realize that merely to survive the havoc of the virus will be meaningless
in the long term if the underlying causes of prevailing injustice and
inequality, revealed ever more starkly by the current calamities, are not
simultaneously addressed. The question then becomes whether Chile's
citizenry, as they pull together to defeat this plague, can also block the
authoritarian predisposition of those in charge to use the threat of this
dreadful disease as an excuse to put off much-needed reforms and endlessly defer the democratic and participatory discussion of a new constitution that would represent the great majority of the people. Will that
great majority, even in the throes of a pandemic, find ways of keeping
up the pressure for a better world while compromising enough, showing enough Rivas-like self-control, to ensure that Chile heals itself in
multiple ways and becomes a country where those who feel radically
alienated from the system are offered a place at the table, perhaps even
near the head of the table?

It would certainly be wondrous if the crisis, both political and medical,
ended up creating the conditions for a marriage between Martín Rivas,
with his moderate bourgeois dreams, and Bobi, with his implacable dog-
legs, an experiment worth looking forward to, a new form of dreaming
our identity, in both literature and reality—and not only in Chile, but
beyond its faraway frontiers.

CHILE
APRIL 6, 2020

The Parable of the Bread

JUAN VILLORO

Translated from the Spanish by Charlotte Coombe

Juan Villoro (Mexico City, Mexico 1956) has been recognized for his journalistic and literary work with such international prizes as the Premio Herralde de Novela, Premio Xavier Villaurrutia, Premio Rey de España, and the Prix Antonin Artaud. A columnist for the newspaper Reforma, *where the following essay first appeared, he is the author of* God Is Round *(2016) and* The Wild Book *(2017), both published by Restless Books.*

THE WORLD'S GOVERNMENTS are announcing funding cuts in the cultural sector, for the sake of the economy (the supreme being of contemporary theodicy). The irony is that people are surviving lockdown thanks to the arts. For centuries, the task of washing clothes has been made more bearable by singing.

Churchill claimed that Britain won the war because they decided not to close theaters. A people that puts on *Hamlet* during the bombardments is one that cannot be defeated. The prime minister's love of painting and literature was viewed by his colleagues as an extravagance akin to his consumption of cigars and whiskey, and it had certain unexpected repercussions (the name of the jazz-rock band Blood, Sweat & Tears was reportedly influenced by one of his more fiery speeches, and the Swedish Academy added the perfect touch to its laundry list of errors by awarding said speech the Nobel Prize in Literature). The contradictory and charismatic figure of the legendary English bulldog inspired endless films and TV series. Apart from his biography, one of his convictions is also worth retaining: that politics is meaningless without art. A few days ago, in a letter to Spain's Minister of Culture, the theater director Lluis Paqual recalled a quote often attributed to Churchill: "If we sacrifice the arts . . . then what are we fighting for?"

What is the point of emerging from lockdown into countries with no theaters, bookstores, or concert venues? Artists do not seem to be a priority in times of emergency. Support is taken away from them, overlooking the fact that people need aesthetic gratification. In times devoid of greatness, nobody is taking to the parliamentary rostrum with Churchill's spirit, or even his rhetoric.

And yet imagination is what is getting us through the crisis. To escape the mental imprisonment, some share memes, GIFs, or tweets, while others recite poems, dress up, sing, talk on the phone or Skype, dream, listen to the dreams of others. Thousands of artists have given away their plays, films, books, and concerts online. The species persists through forms of representation of reality (eliminated from public budgets as the most expendable part of reality).

In "The Grand Inquisitor," a chapter of *The Brothers Karamazov*, Dostoyevsky reflected on the eternal dilemma of human priorities. Ivan, the intellectual brother, recounts a parable to Alyosha, the religious brother. In sixteenth-century Seville, an old inquisitor sees Christ again, and imprisons him because his return calls into question the teachings of a Church that has veered away from his word. The old man points out the Messiah's worst mistakes. On hearing the voice of God in the desert, he could have asked for anything. The Eternal Father offered to give him bread for all humanity. Jesus could have fed humankind forever, controlled its economy, subjugated it. His reply was puzzling: "Man cannot live by bread alone." What did he mean? Jesus chose to promote freedom, even at the risk of it being used against him. On the cross, he could have resorted to a miracle, could have been escorted up to heaven by the angels. But he did not want to impose his faith using a gimmick. People should decide freely whether they believe in him or not. Miracles and distributing bread are coercive acts. Ivan frames the story as a failure for Christianity (a pointless sacrifice in the name of freedom); Alyosha understands it as a triumph for boundless faith. Imagining that wheat can be baked and sharing it are cultural acts. Putting a price on it is another matter. In 1929, Federico García Lorca wrote: "Man cannot live by bread alone. If I were hungry and helpless in the street, I would not ask for a loaf of bread; I would ask for half a loaf and a book. And here, I violently denounce those who talk only of economic needs without ever mentioning cultural needs, which is what people are crying out for at the tops of their voices." Half of our existence is imaginary: the taste of bread depends on freedom.

Civilization began around a fire. The world's governments should know that it served three essential purposes: warming hands, cooking, and telling stories.

MEXICO CITY
APRIL 24, 2020

Confinement

ANA SIMO

Ana Simo (Cuba, 1943) is the author of a dozen plays, a short feature film, and countless articles. Forced to leave the island during the political/homophobic witch hunts of the late 1960s, she first immigrated to France, where she studied with Roland Barthes and participated in early women's and gay/lesbian rights groups. In New York, she co-founded Medusa's Revenge theater, the direct-action group the Lesbian Avengers, the national cable program Dyke TV, and the groundbreaking online magazine The Gully. Heartland, her first novel, was published by Restless Books in 2018 It was a finalist for the Publishing Triangle's 2019 Edmund White Award for Debut Fiction.

"WHAT'S THAT?" Ludivina Cao asked the old man. He clutched the blackish purple thing against his heart and cleared his throat, trying to hide a malevolent sneer from her all-seeing eyes. A paroxysm of coughing threw him to the ground. Ludivina leaped over the crumbling gate and held his spastic head in between her knees, forcing his mouth open and depressing his tongue with the flat wooden stick that she always carried in her pocket. She had stolen it from the combat medic, the only other man in the camp, who had taught her how to spring like a Hyrcanian tiger. His name, which he despised, was Clyde, and he had lost his left eye in the battle of the Bosphorus.

"Are you pregnant? No? Then fuck off!" he had drooled when Ludivina, aged five, asked him to cure her bleeding, scraped knees. He was lying on his cot, a sliver of puke dangling perilously from the left corner of his mouth. Ludivina stared at it without blinking, counting the seconds before it would hit the ground. Overshadowed by the suspenseful puke, the combat medic's voice reverberated as if coming out of the bowels of a distant cave. He sang in a smoky countertenor voice:

> I'm a proud and bilious drunk
> I lick grout and luscious cunt
> When I birth new cannon fodder
> I relive the sacred slaughter
> Oh lonesome swine
> Oh one-eyed blunder
> Why can't you forget?

As he sang, the combat medic bared dazzlingly white and even teeth. Ludivina was mesmerized and repulsed by their perfection, but his music was stronger than her will, it carried her sweetly over a landscape of dry, red craters where thousands of tiny motionless figures, ants or human, were burning, decapitating, eviscerating, gouging each other. Floating above them, Ludivina felt an expansive happiness.

The old man opened his watery eyes. "Go away, you demon!" he spat. Ludivina carefully placed his head on the ground. As she left with the shiny, purple thing in her hands, she thought she heard him gurgle "egg."

Back home, she placed the purple entity on top of her Bible. She was not religious, and she could hardly read, but Bibles were the only things that were free and plentiful in the camp. Every shack had one for show—sitting by the entrance, impeccably dusted, virginal gold lettering on its unopened cover—and several others hidden around for God's help (rolling tobacco, squashing vermin, wiping asses, wrapping food, padding clothes and shoes in winter, and the hundred other things one does with paper, it being the only paper in the camp). The old man boasted about owning twenty-six Bibles. Ludivina only had this one. She kept that a secret, along with the reason why. She'd known since she was seven that anything that departed from the ordinary was dangerous. Voice didn't have to warn her. When her mother was taken away, her grandmother whispered in Ludivina's ear that it was because her daughter swept the dirt toward the center of the room, away from the door. Ludivina giggled. When her grandmother was taken away, months later, Voice, which had just manifested itself for the first time, told Ludivina that it was also due to perverse sweeping. "Not too smart, our granny," said Voice, making a tongue-clicking noise. Ludivina was torn between giggling and crying, so she did both. "Cut it out, child," Voice snarled. "Who fucking cares which way the dirt flies?" Ludivina, until then a cheerful, gregarious child who sang and danced for strangers on her doorstep every evening but hardly spoke a word, uttered, then, her first long sentence with many commas, thanking Voice for its advice, which she would follow, except for one detail: like her mother and her grandmother, she'd sweep from the door toward the center of the room, but with the window and the door closed, so no one could see her; then, when there was not a speck of dust left on the floor, she'd open the window and the door and sweep toward the outside like everyone else. Voice was silent. The shack suddenly got wintry. Ludivina, frightened, slowly peed her tiny panties. Finally, Voice laughed with a warm, melodious laughter. Ludivina curled up in the bed that still smelled of her grandmother and slept soundly, clenching her little fists.

Looking at the purple, elongated creature resting on her Bible, Ludivina wondered why she couldn't rip out the book's pages and turn them into God's help, like everyone else did. She did not think this book was the word of God. Neither did her neighbors. In fact, the existence of God himself was highly dubious, and even if he existed, he couldn't have written this or any other book. Wasn't God a pure spirit? How could he write if he had no hands? "God wrote nothing. The Okhrana, that's who cooked it up. Two hundred years ago," the combat medic drawled with the lethargic certitude of someone saying that the earth is flat. He feigned sleep when Ludivina asked for the meaning of Okhrana ("He don't know shit," Voice said, but it, too, declined to explain). "Bah! Camp chatter. What a vile, incoherent patchwork!" the old man spat. "The old imperial tax code, now that's the golden book! The breath of angels is in those pages." But he added, "Camp chatter is what keeps us in the pink." When Ludivina asked what "pink" had to do with anything, he winked: "It means don't bite the hand that feeds you."

Language at the camp was to be simple and clear. "Five hundred words!" the creaky loudspeaker voice intoned every Saturday as the sun was setting. And Wednesday at sunrise, "Mothers: learn from your babies!" This led not to silence, but to constant chatter. Shrill and repetitive, all well within the acceptable five hundred words and the decreed simplicity and clarity. The women and girls that populated the camp vomited words from sunrise to sunset, and often well into the night. They were virtuosos of the petty and melodramatic. Ludivina's taciturn nature was considered abnormal. Yet no one ratted on her. Solidarity was unknown in the camp, but fear of drawing attention to oneself was a powerful snitch deterrent. The combat medic compared the camp with Constantinople's parakeet market before the fall. The old man taught Ludivina the word "pandemonium." Voice said that under the bestial cackle there was meaning to be found: "There always is. Listen carefully. Their chatter is clear as mud."

The old man's great-grandpa could recite every line of the great tax code, which weighed as much as a grown man and could be used as a doorstop if need be. Could the old man still have the imperial tax code? "Swallow your tongue," he hissed in her ear, then coiled himself on the ground like a cobra. A sour smell hit Ludivina's nose and made her sneeze. The old cobra was frightened. Ludivina left him alone. Fear was the camp's real endemic disease. Her mother and her grandmother had had it. She had it too, though hers was not a sudden smack, like theirs, but a faint buzz constantly playing in the depth of her ear canals, a loyal and discreet insect, at times a little louder, but never unexpected. Ludivina knew that she was lucky that way. Before she fell asleep that night, she shut her eyes and imagined the imperial tax code holding open a tiny iron door through which a shaft of sunlight streamed in. The old man's great-grandpa must have been a dwarf and maybe a sun-worshipper. She ordered her right hand to open the fat book and grab a page. Her hand obeyed. The page was filled with numbers, not words, which might make desecration easier. She then commanded her right hand to tear out the page, but the hand did not move. At first, a breeze was making the pages flutter, including the one that her inert hand was still clutching. Then the picture froze, and turned to black. The mental approach having not just failed, but failed miserably, as per the often-pompous Voice, Ludivina was now on the lookout for a real, physical book other than the Bible with which to conduct her experiment. Unfortunately, except for the old man, no one in the camp, not even her mother and her grandmother, had ever seen any other book. "They're not useful," Voice had said in one of its driest moments, ordering her to stop her search.

Night was falling. Ludivina blew out the candle that lit the purple creature riding the Bible, and crawled into her cot in the dark. The possibility that God might exist in spite of all evidence to the contrary kept Ludivina awake some nights. During the day, she was sure that he did not exist. That lent days their lightness and pleasure. But nights were filled with terrifying doubts. What an evil monster he must be if he existed. She sometimes prayed to the un-God that God did not exist. The un-God is called the Devil, the old man told her once, when he was willing to open his burlap sack to show her what he was hoarding.

The sound of rain on the tin roof woke her up at dawn. The perpetually overcast sky had a yellowish, sour-milk texture. At noon, a pale sun sometimes poked tiny holes in the fouled atmosphere. Ludivina would then remove her headscarf and stand under the shafts of dirty sunlight, face upturned, hopping from one foot to the next, until her neck and her toes ached and Voice rasped, "You're not a child anymore." Voice, whose full, majestic name was Voice of Reason, was always right. Ludivina would put her headscarf back on, and lower her face to the ground, "where it belongs," Voice always said. "Mud's safer than men's eyes," Voice had intoned. It enjoyed talking in riddles, like the Bible was said to talk. That and its gloomy disposition were tiresome, but Ludivina tolerated them because Voice was her only true friend, the only one who would not betray her. Lately, Voice had been nagging her about the patriotic service: "You're almost twelve. They'll soon knock on your door. Better get ready. Or do you want to start popping out babies instead?" Ludivina wanted to stay exactly as she was. "That's not possible," Voice would say, with an executioner's finality. Ludivina would argue for hours, and sometimes stomp out of the shack, or into it, depending on where she was when the arguing had started, but Voice was unyielding on this particular point, which she called "the passage of time." It could not be stopped. Ludivina could not understand why not.

The shiny, purple, elongated being on top of the Bible had no smell or taste. Ludivina licked it at different times of the day, by surprise, hoping to catch it smelling behind her back, but it was always impenetrable, like a polished stone. As days went by, its purple sheen grew dull and wrinkles appeared on its surface. Now that the stone had turned into skin, perhaps covering edible flesh, Ludivina was dying to sink her teeth in it, but fear held her back. Every day someone would eat something bad, then clutch her throat and fall on the ground kicking and screaming, foaming at the mouth, black tongue hanging out so she seemed to be smiling. When she stopped breathing, the Hazmats would put her in their yellow body bag and carry her in their yellow hand truck to the pyre at the far end of the camp. The Hazmats were said to be two brawny ladies who lived in the government bunker near the pyre. No one had ever seen their faces, only their eyes peering from behind their goggles, and under their yellow hazmat suits, no one could really tell if they were female or male, or something in between, but they and their predecessors had always been thought to be a pair of brawny ladies. Ludivina had questioned the logic of that belief and Voice of Reason had congratulated her for her skepticism. Ludivina was flattered, as she always was on the rare occasions Voice approved of her, and immediately incorporated the word "skepticism" into her meager vocabulary. She had first heard the word spoken by the drunken combat medic, regarding his views on the patriotic service, but she only kept new words after Voice had vetted them.

Ludivina was sitting in front of the once shiny, now wrinkled, still purple thing, sucking her thumb to alleviate the hunger pains in vain, when she had a revelation: the gluttons who deserved the pyre, as Voice uncharitably described them, were always whiskery old women. Ludivina, who thought of herself as a pure spirit inhabiting a girl's body, greedily sank her teeth into the purple skin. The flesh within was smooth, with tiny seeds, slightly bitter at first, but thoroughly satisfying by the time she had eaten half of what she now suspected was a fruit, a word learned from the old man when he was friendlier to her. She burped, satiated, and felt a little guilty for having stolen the egg-fruit from him. On the other hand, he was a bearded old man, and perhaps the fruit would have killed him, too. Voice applauded her conclusion, labeling it "cynical," another of the combat medic's favorite words. "I'll return the uneaten half to the old man," Ludivina said, her belly full and her mind soaring with cynical skepticism, inflating her small, brown body to heroic heights. She took the purple half and went looking for the old man.

When she found him, he was trying to shave his beard with a rusty razor blade. "Help me," he said, handing her the razor blade with trembling hands. He was standing behind his shack, in what he called his *pissoir*. Ludivina did not want to step on the foul mud. Besides, it was too dark in there. She might cut him by mistake. When she suggested they move in front of the shack where there was more light, he put a finger over his lips and cocked his ears "like a hound dog," he said, a now extinct creature, like all other dogs, overeaten by the always-hungry humans. There was nothing to hear but the usual camp din: crying babies, squealing children playing tag, cursing, drunken grannies, screaming women and girls, fighting with each other or with their own kind. But the old man ran into his shack and hid under his bed. Ludivina sat on the Orchard Boy apple crate, the only clean surface, and lay the piece of mushy, uneaten egg-fruit on the floor, close enough to the bed for him to see it but not touch it, unless he crawled out. While waiting, Ludivina looked at the redheaded Orchard Boy and his red apples with her mind's eyes. The image was imprinted there after years of visiting the old man. It had a texture that the real object lacked. Seen with her mind's eyes, the Orchard Boy crate was always new and slightly different, velvety, lush, perfumed, even. But when seen through her physical eyes, the real object was increasingly lifeless, except for the moldy crack slashing Orchard Boy's chin, which seemed fatter at each viewing and was perhaps the only thing still anchoring it to the material sphere. Ludivina was puzzled by the mystery of the physical and mental vision, but the old man and the combat medic were uninterested, which meant they did not know the answer but were too proud to admit it, and Voice who did know, because it knew everything, pretended not to know, dismissing her question as a waste of time.

Night was falling when the old man's skinny ass began to emerge from under the bed, bit by bit, crab-like, followed by his spine, neck, head, and arms. While the old man nibbled at the purple thing, closing his eyes with delight, Ludivina sharpened his razor blade on a stone, following his instructions. "It's a volcanic stone," he said. She wondered where it had come from but did not ask.

"You can shave me now," he said, wiping his mouth. "I'm losing my beard. See the patches? The medic says it's *alopecia barbae*. So I'm allowed to shave. I'm not asking you to break the law." For the first time in her short life, Ludivina did not care if she was breaking the law or not. She could slice the old man's throat, or gouge out his eyes, or just shave his scraggly beard. The law was wildly circumstantial. The degrees of criminality were not contingent on the absolute gravity of the acts. Throat slicing of an infidel was a good deed; beard shaving, particularly by a female, an abomination punished by stoning or burning alive at the pyre. That's what the law said, but never or hardly ever carried out. "The law is make-believe. Like the Bible," Voice explained. "A tiny price to pay for peace and quiet."

The combat medic, who according to the old man was a delusional crank, like most Caliphate vets, flew into a rage at the mere mention of the law or the government. "High treason. They'll pay for it. We'll see them dragged into the streets and hung from lampposts." Once Ludivina had tried to picture a street and a lamppost, but her mind went blank. The combat medic realized it and began to weep: "This is what we have become," he said. Ludivina said she was sorry, although she couldn't figure out what she'd done to make him sad, and he said not to worry, it was not her fault. Whose fault was it? Ludivina later wondered. She was relieved when the combat medic stopped crying, blew his nose, and took her out on the trail in front of his shack. There, in the dust, he drew a street with tall buildings, a paved sidewalk, and a corner lamppost from which hung a stick figure.

PARIS
MARCH 8, 2020

PART IV

Faith Is the Substance of Things Hoped for

Corona Correspondence #25

FRANCINE PROSE

Francine Prose (Brooklyn, New York, 1947) is the author of A Changed Man *(2005), the* New York Times *bestseller* Reading Like a Writer *(2006), the acclaimed* Anne Frank: The Book, The Life, The Afterlife *(2009), and* Mister Monkey *(2016). A former president of PEN America and a member of the American Academy of Arts and Letters and the American Academy of Arts and Sciences, she wrote the introduction to the Restless Classics edition of* Frankenstein *(2015). This letter is written to Adam Ross, editor of the* Sewanee Review, *as part of their Corona Correspondence series.*

DEAR ADAM,

Our lives—like the lives of many writers and artists, I imagine—don't look, on the surface, all that different from before. My husband and I are at home in the Hudson Valley. This is our average day: coffee, breakfast, work work work, dinner, TV, bed.

Beneath the surface, bouts of terror and unease interrupt the blessed spells of relative calm and contentment. Sometimes I think the planet is fighting back, sometimes I think that this is an evil virus engineered to lower Social Security payments and the expensive health costs of the elderly, the "high-risk" group to which (it now turns out) we belong.

I panic-order peanut butter—protein! shelf life!—which I don't even like. At the rate at which we normally consume peanut butter (a jar can last us two years) we have enough for a decade. The archaeologists of the future will wonder: Was this what these people ate?

Given the widespread heartbreak and pain, I can't complain, but still: I liked the peaceful quiet better when it was voluntary, when I could see my family and friends, when I could travel. When I could leave the house.

I talk on the phone more than I used to. We FaceTime with the grand-children. Pablo, who is about to turn four, calls it "the Rona." So now we say, "Prince Charles has the Rona!" The thing that's made me happiest was that our son, who lives across the Hudson and grocery shops for us, brought us a chunk of fresh ginger even though I forgot to put it on the list. Grocery shopping was one of my favorite things in the world, and I miss it.

This morning, looking for a break from the horror dispatches from the Queens and Brooklyn emergency rooms, the New Jersey nursing homes, the statistics, the shuttered businesses, the realities of unemployment, and the parallel pandemic of uncertainty and fear, I read a piece in the *New York Times* about recently published thrillers. They all sounded sort of interesting, but what also interested me was a comment from a reader criticizing the *Times* for recommending "creepy dark works" that make people more hopeless and depressed instead of things that make them feel more cheery and hopeful. It made me think, as so many things do, What is wrong with me?

Since our house arrest started, I've been reading a lot, and until now I'd never noticed how supremely creepy and dark are so many of the books I've most loved.

Thomas Bernhard's memoir *Gathering Evidence* describes his time in a school worse than anything in Brontë or Dickens, only run by Nazis; a brilliant description of the bombing of Salzburg, which Bernhard witnessed as a boy, and which makes one's confinement at home seem like a walk in the park; and his account of the lung-disease sanitarium where a doctor was called to the phone in the middle of performing a procedure on Bernhard—and came back and punctured the wrong lung.

Darcy O'Brien's *A Way of Life, Like Any Other*, one of the great LA novels, another hellish childhood, no less dark for being so funny.

I just finished the recollections of Proust's housekeeper, Celeste Albaret, an odd and intensely claustrophobic love story that ends, not unpredictably, with the beloved employer's death.

In the middle of the night, in the dark, battling insomnia with my Kindle, I've been reading *They Were Sisters*, Dorothy Whipple's harrowing 1943 novel of domestic abuse among the Downton Abbey crowd.

Do books affect me differently than they affect the guy who complained to the *Times*? Do I take them less seriously? Less personally? Do I read in another way? In fact these books make me feel better, not because their contents cheer me up, but because they are good. A friend is teaching an undergraduate course in epidemics: Thucydides, Boccaccio, Defoe, Manzoni, Sontag. Does it make us more or less happy to observe that, in every era, human beings behaved in more or less the same selfish and selfless ways?

My friends are streaming comedies and we exchange recommendations. I have always loved the films of Will Ferrell; lately I love them even more. But do I care if something's "light" or "dark" as long as it keeps my interest? As long as it keeps me awake? What I watch changes from evening to evening, from *Next in Fashion* to *Chinatown*, from *Wild Wild Country* to the films of Maren Ade and Alice Rohrwacher.

Though maybe the crisis has already changed us more than we know. Last night, for the first time in our forty-year marriage, my husband and I agreed that a film was too scary to watch. We don't normally watch that much violent or scary stuff, but when we do, when something makes me more nervous than I'd like—the Gillian Anderson series *The Fall* comes to mind—I'm perfectly happy to go into my study and fool around with my phone until the scary part is over.

But last night we were watching a 1974 Robert Altman film, *Images*, and after about twenty minutes, it just got to be too much. It's hard to describe how disturbing it was, and it would just wreck the surprises. We understood that the adrenaline would keep us awake, and we turned off the TV. Maybe we'll watch the rest sometime, maybe never. Anyway, it was a first, our wordless agreement. So maybe that's something like what the reader meant, scolding the *New York Times*; we're living with so much fear, who needs more? We're all trying to tamp the anxiety down to a level we can endure.

I always hope that crises will make me more compassionate and less irritable, but it's rarely the case. I suppose it would help if I stopped watching the evening news. It can't be healthy to yell at the TV for the entire White House press conference. And how can the newscasters keep telling us that "We're all in this together," when, in so many important ways, we have never been more alone?

I've come to hate people posting online about what they feel grateful for: boasts disguised as thanksgiving. Oh, they say, I feel so grateful that we grow our own heirloom lettuce and drink the milk from our own cows. But here's what I feel grateful for: The weather's warming up, it's sunny, the days are getting longer, sparing us that interval of darkness, cold, and gloom before the cocktail hour and dinner persuade us, as we so want to be persuaded, that the fear and disruption will end, that some solution will be found, that, if we just keep calm and stay home and hang in there, things might still work out.

Best,

Francine

THE HUDSON VALLEY, NEW YORK

APRIL 2020

My First Lockdown

MAJED ABUSALAMA

Born and raised in the Jabalia refugee camp in Gaza, Majed Abusalama is an award-winning journalist, scholar, and human rights activist. His articles are regularly featured in Middle East Eye, Mondoweiss, Deutsche Welle, BABelmed, and Al Jazeera, among others. On the board of We Are Not Numbers, co-founder of Palestine Speaks Coalition in Germany, and the Hebrew website www.border-gone.com, he lives in Berlin.

ON MARCH 23, Germany announced nationwide measures to prevent the further spread of the coronavirus. People were advised to stay at home and public gatherings were banned; restaurants and pubs were closed. Days earlier, schools were shuttered, followed by gyms, cinemas, museums, and other public places. And so life under lockdown began.

For many of my German friends, this was the first time in their lives they were experiencing such government-imposed restrictions. For me, the lockdown in Berlin, where I live now, brought back memories from the first Intifada.

I was just a baby when the uprising started in December 1987 in Jabalia refugee camp in Gaza, my birthplace. By the time it ended, I was a school-age boy. Lockdowns, curfews, and a variety of restrictions were all I knew for the first six years of my life.

The Intifada broke out after Israeli soldiers killed four Palestinians at a checkpoint at our camp. When crowds of Palestinians went out to protest against the deaths, Israeli soldiers opened fire, killing another Palestinian man.

The killings were just the spark; the real reason was the decades of brutal military occupation and apartheid my people had endured while watching our land being colonized by European and American Jewish settlers arriving from abroad.

The whole of historic Palestine erupted in protest. To Israeli tear gas and bullets, Palestinians responded with slingshots and stones. The Israeli occupation army and Israeli "civilians" killed close to 1,500 Palestinians, more than 300 of them children.

Facing a people-wide uprising that deadly repression could not put out, the Israeli government started imposing various forms of lockdowns to try to control the Palestinian population, which had launched a sustained grassroots resistance campaign.

The curfews would come and go. The Israelis would impose them for days, weeks, even months at a time. According to American scholar

Wendy Pearlman, in the first year of the Intifada, the Israeli occupation army put various Palestinian communities under round-the-clock curfews more than 1,600 times.

During those curfews, we would not be allowed to go out. Sometimes, we would run out of food, and my grandmother and aunts would risk their lives to go outside and look for supplies to buy.

Food was scarce, as farmers were not allowed to go to the fields. Many crops lay rotting, with no one to harvest them.

Universities and schools were closed, leaving a whole generation of Palestinian children and youth falling behind on their education. We had no parks, no public gardens to go to and play in. The beach, too, was "closed" by the Israelis.

But the many restrictions, the constant harassment and persistent killings did not bring down the Palestinian spirit. All across historic Palestine, popular resistance committees were established that coordinated various activities to provide for the people. My father, Ismael, was involved in organizing the committee in our camp.

Women grew food at homes and on rooftops and founded agricultural cooperatives that they called victory gardens, to create an autonomous Palestinian economy and enable the boycott of Israeli products. Trade committees organized strikes; health committees established makeshift clinics; educational committees set up underground classes. Everyone put in whatever effort they could to help their community, and no one was left without communal support.

That, of course, angered the Israelis. I clearly remember, when I was four years old, Israeli soldiers broke into our home and started destroying our belongings. It was a punishment for my father's political activities—one that so many families endured repeatedly.

My father was also often questioned and detained for weeks, sometimes months at a time. During one of these episodes, after an hours-long interrogation, an Israeli commander asked him if he had anything to say. My father answered that he wanted to get a permit to be allowed to go to his bees. The commander laughed, saying, "You might go to prison now, and you are thinking of your bees?" My father responded that he must take care of them or they would die, and those bees fed his family. My father was detained that time for a week. The bees did not survive.

We became reliant on my mother's salary. She was working as a nurse in an UNRWA clinic. She had to go to work every day even during curfew, so she had a permit to cross the Israeli checkpoints. She would treat many of the children who were beaten or injured by Israeli soldiers in our camp. According to Save the Children NGO, in the first two years of the uprising, between 23,600 and 29,900 sought medical help for injuries.

In the summer of 1991, my mother went into labor. As there were very few phones in the refugee camp at the time, we could not call an ambulance; besides, no ambulances were allowed into the camp under the curfew. As a result, my mother was forced to walk to the UNRWA clinic, a kilometer away. She made her way leaning on my grandmother, who was waving a white scarf, hoping the Israeli soldiers would not shoot at them.

Not far from our home, Israeli soldiers pointed their guns at them and made them stop. They started questioning my mother about why they were breaking the curfew, even though it was obvious she was about to give birth; she could hardly stand on her feet. "It was a frightening moment," my mother would recall later. "I was trying to protect my belly away from their guns as the painful contractions came one after the other."

The soldiers eventually let them go, and that evening my mother gave birth to my sister, Shahd. In the morning they braved the curfew again and walked back home. We were all happy to see them and my baby sister.

Life was extremely difficult for us, but my parents always recall the Intifada as a time of liberation, often saying, "We did not give up on our resistance. We did not become subdued victims." Indeed, Palestinians set an example for a grassroots struggle rarely seen at that time.

And here I am today, three decades later, again under a lockdown— but a much different one. There are no rubber bullets, live ammunition, or tear gas canisters shot at people walking in the streets; there are no checkpoints; no violent repression the way I have experienced in Palestine.

Like my German friends, I too am anxious about the situation in Germany, but most of the time, my mind is wandering toward Gaza.

My family still lives in the densely populated Jabalia refugee camp, where social distancing is impossible. Our camp has more than 113,000 people living in an area that covers a bit more than half a square kilometer.

Already seventeen people have tested positive in Gaza. The local authorities and international organizations have warned of an impending catastrophe.

I can feel my parents' worries, especially my mother, who is still working in the UNRWA clinic. She takes a big risk every time she goes to work, where she sees dozens of people every day. Gaza's health care system has been damaged by years of a suffocating siege imposed by Israel and Egypt on the strip and by multiple destructive wars waged by the Israeli military against my people. It is extremely vulnerable and a major coronavirus outbreak would spell disaster.

Unlike Germany, where the government is already relaxing lockdown measures and talking about a return to "normal" at some point in the future, in Gaza, my people are preparing for the worst. The death and suffering this epidemic could inflict on Palestinians will be yet another entry in the long list of war crimes the Israelis have committed against us, and it will weigh heavily on the conscience of the international community which has abandoned us.

These days I keep asking myself: Has the world forgotten us, having accepted our life in inhumane conditions? Or will it do something this time to hold Israel accountable?

BERLIN
MAY 9, 2020

248

Coronapocalypse: Reflections from Lockdown

PEDRO ÁNGEL PALOU

Translated from the Spanish by Hebe Powell

Pedro Ángel Palou (Puebla, Mexico, 1966) is a novelist and essayist. He is the author of nearly sixty books including his most recent novel Todos los miedos *(2018) about violence against journalists in Mexico. He has been an anchorman on the History Channel and Canal 22 and the chancellor emeritus of Universidad de las Américas de Puebla. Palou is the Fletcher Professor of Oratory and Chair of Romance Languages at Tufts University.*

OUR PROBLEMS will not end with these days of vigilance, nor with the "flattening" of the exponential growth curve of the epidemic. If all goes to plan, in a few months our situation with respect to the virus will have altered, but so many of the things we took for granted will be gone forever. Or at the very least we will have to completely reevaluate the basis of our social interactions. One of the consequences of COVID-19 will be economic crisis, a full-blown recession. The pandemic will leave millions in poverty across the world, more than the dead. In the United States there will be a recession that will hit the poor hardest. No matter how much money the Fed injects or how many fiscal stimulus packages the government invents—it will pay a high price for its tardy response, perhaps preventing Trump's reelection—we will be marked by these months of quarantine, by economic slowdown, and the brutal unemployment that will follow as a logical consequence of the number of businesses going under: restaurants, bars, music venues, and an infinity of etceteras, such as our unfortunate bookshops.

In an article circulating at the start of the pandemic, Giorgio Agamben warned of the capacity for state coercion—biopolitics—in states of emergency. What this philosopher did not foresee was the brutal crisis in state health care systems in his own native country, Italy, and across Europe. He could not, at that moment, have imagined that so many people living in liberal democracies would opt to stay home out of a sense of responsibility, aside from state prohibitions. The era of post-sovereignty has been placed in doubt—and indeed the whole neoliberal model—with the closing of borders, sending everyone back to their country of origin and attempting to control the virus within territorial boundaries of individual nation-states.

Other consequences, in the long term, however, will be seen in new ways of socializing. Will we still go to concerts, to massive events, or will streaming and other facets of the virtual world take over forever? Will we go back to the cinema or will we watch films on our own devices, with social distancing a permanent feature? Will we order everything to be delivered to our doors so as to avoid contact with anyone on the street? Will any businesses in the hospitality industry survive? Once this is over, small groups of people will, I believe, prefer to get together in someone's home, knowing they are all healthy.

And what about education? Online education is much criticized, especially at university level. Now it is a worldwide reality and will demonstrate, in my view, how robust this system and the platforms supporting it can be. It will even provide a great deal of personal "contact" between teachers and pupils, laying to rest the age-old claim that the physical presence of an educator in a classroom is a necessary requirement.

How many of the rules we once accepted unquestioningly will be challenged? For example, at present, airlines are allowing passengers to board with huge bottles of alcohol hand sanitizer. How come? Was it not the case that a plane could be brought down with a few ounces of liquid? Who was it who decided on the appropriate amount after the terrorist plots against airlines? Knowing the absurdity of the rules about silly quantities, in the light of the coronavirus, however, will we be prepared to allow the imposition of others, just as absurd, simply because? Or will we have enough biopolitical smarts to not allow ourselves to be manipulated?

There are more questions than answers, of course. Indeed, in these days under quarantine, the whole of our life is one massive question. In Mexico we had the H1N1 virus and fifteen days of isolation, but this time it looks to be months. We will learn to work from home—and many businesses will start to do this as a matter of course after quarantine ends. In Japan, Aurelio Asiain commented on how people there have always maintained a level of physical distance; perhaps we will learn to follow suit. We will not be the same; the world economic order will have changed substantially; we will have realized that small government is not fit for purpose, that the state is needed not only to oversee but also as a guarantor of health, education, and even the economic survival of the weakest. The social, employment, nutritional, and health insecurity in which neoliberalism engulfed us across the globe has reached rock bottom. Health systems—Italy is one painful example—will have to rebuild and strengthen themselves. In the meantime, I will leave you with something I read recently: we must redefine social distancing, thinking more of physical distancing together with social cohesion, because this is something we are going to need.

UNTAMED CAPITALISM AND DYSTOPIA

In these times of imposed isolation, many of us have been thinking about what is going to happen when it's all over (and, naturally, when it will be over). The day after will, most probably, not be one of jubilation, but rather of profound concern over the cataclysm bequeathed to us by COVID-19. With acute pain, we will note the number of restaurants and small stores where we used to do our shopping, closed forever. Many, too many, people will have lost their jobs and find themselves on the borders of crisis, even with states temporarily offering fiscal aid directed at businesses and individuals. The feeling of collective bankruptcy, despite having weathered the crisis in public health, will be overwhelming.

But why imagine only a dystopia? Perhaps, out of all this pessimism, we could begin to fight, as of now, to make those changes unimaginable before the pandemic struck. For example, instituting a universal income. This was proposed by Thomas Picketty in his book *Capital and Ideology*. The reestablishment of a modified form of welfare state that could guarantee public health and education systems, retirement pensions, and public savings. If we can gain anything from the democratic forms of solidarity emerging across the world while, at the same time, we receive orders to stay at home it's that this is, more than anything else, about physical distance together with social cohesion. If, in this situation, we can shop for essentials on behalf of an elderly neighbor, isn't it logical to offer to do so always. We'll be doing our own anyway. If we can go out onto our balconies to applaud our health workers, to cheer ourselves up with music and singing, we could live together more harmoniously once this is over.

I know, of course, that even from today we must denounce the tentative steps of many governments, including that of the United States, to renege on individual freedoms, to remove constitutional freedoms in alarming ways. The state of emergency must be temporary, and even now given strict limitations. If, as the US Department of State wishes, an accused person can be held while a judge indefinitely postpones court hearings and judgments then we are negating the principle of habeas corpus, or, as we have in Mexico, the right of protection. Forms of state control are always cruel, and we must place limits on them. Biometrics and cyber controls above all. Something that not even the KGB or the Stasi ever achieved in their communist states is now completely accessible to cyber states that watch and control their citizens twenty-four hours a day. Paul Valéry said that government cannot be achieved through coercion alone, fictitious forces must also be created. Or fictitious fears. I do not want to imply that the epidemic is not serious, nor global, I simply wish to point out that we must not allow ourselves to become accustomed to arbitrary control measures. Resist the absurd; ask for reasons. As I write this, in mid-March, there are more than 365,000 cases of COVID-19 globally, with over sixteen thousand dead. We are not in quarantine purely out of obedience to government orders, but rather of our own volition. Many organizations and individuals did, in fact, respond before the politicians, as always happens. Autocracy will never be the cure for a global epidemic of this scale. Russia and Israel want to make changes to their constitutions as a result of the pandemic, justifying major restrictions within these already flimsy liberal democracies that would otherwise be impossible. It is down to all of us not to permit this.

THERE WILL NOT BE A "NEW NORMAL"

Who would have said, a few weeks ago, that we'd be living in a science fiction film, a dystopia, or a new version of the Soderbergh film *Contagion*? Who could have predicted the world would have had to stop and that we would find moments of solace watching images of animals wandering along deserted streets, fish returning to newly clean canals in Venice? The figures are terrifying: in Mexico alone poverty has risen by 48%, in the United States, unemployment may reach 30%, and the projections for those infected or killed by COVID-19 are alarming. Apparently, one hundred thousand dead is the "best-case" scenario in the United States. For the first time, these statistics made Trump see sense, resulting in his ordering the prolongation of the stay-at-home measures which even the most reluctant states, Florida and Nevada, had finally brought in. We are at home, without schools, those who can are working from home, others are simply surviving the lockdown. To make this possible, millions of people, particularly doctors and nurses, but also public transport workers and many more must go out onto the streets and, obviously, put themselves at risk. Privilege, in Latin, meant that a law only applied to a specific individual. Now we understand privilege differently, but the pandemic has brought to our attention the terrible injustice of inequality.

In New York, we have watched events unfold only imaginable in films: the sick outside a hospital in Queens, waiting for free beds; field hospitals set up in Central Park or in parking lots. In Italy, at the worst moments of the emergency, doctors had to decide who to save and who to leave to die. With every passing day, more and more of us know someone who has caught the virus or is hospitalized, or has died. The illness has been circling us, corralling us, and is now on our doorsteps, close to our families, our friends. We are in fear, great fear.

What this pandemic has revealed too, very painfully, is the precariousness in which we all live. Employment, economic, and social. Neoliberalism has, over the last decades, dismantled much of the welfare state, where it existed, and everywhere the public has been privatized. Now, defenseless—with a smaller state incapable of solving long-term problems—we are walking a tightrope. Millions will lose their jobs; hundreds of thousands of small businesses will not be able to survive this so-called "economic hibernation," as the Spanish government euphemistically termed the economic shutdown instigated some weeks ago. Many will find no recourse in our weakened public health systems and will die waiting for treatment. In many places, in fact, the elite have jumped the lines and have been given tests; or been hospitalized far earlier than those who cannot afford to pay for either tests or treatment. The panorama is unremittingly black.

Some of us may find, if not consolation, then wisdom in certain literary works. The obvious ones would be *The Plague*, by Camus, but also Daniel Defoe and Bocaccio; García Márquez and Saramago. We could look to the Greek classics, their works of theater as much as their historical treatises. Humanity has lived through this type of thing many times, although perhaps on a smaller, less universal scale, due to the slower means of transport in the past.

We can't go home. At least not to where we used to live before we had to flee to find refuge in our tiny dwellings and apartment blocks. The planet will never be the same. We have experienced, on a global scale, what the climate change activists have long warned us about: wholesale catastrophe. Not since 1918 have we lived with a global sickness of such virulence as this. We cannot even begin to calculate the magnitude of the disaster, take stock of the damage, but it will mark us forever. We will find our place in the world again, but we must rebuild that place for the public good, reconstruct all the things we dismantled idiotically.

WHAT IF THE NORMALITY WE HAD WAS PRECISELY THE PROBLEM?

There is a proposition circulating on social media. It is daubed on a wall in the Hong Kong subway, and its declaration inspired the title of this column. To me, it is the most devastating document so far written, published, or graffitied about the pandemic. All those things we got wrong are precisely what we should be thinking about now that we are isolated, in quarantine. For starters, economic inequality, and the brutal consequences of automation in industry. Over the last decades, the gap between rich and poor has widened as a result of neoliberal policies. The 1% who control and rule over the world live off the backs of the other 99% and the wholesale exploitation of our planet. In the short space of the past days we have seen animals return: fish in crystalline Venetian canals, an increase in the bear population in Yosemite. The positive consequences in terms of lowered carbon emissions can already be felt in the environment. But I am not an optimist. When we are released from lockdown, we will go back to living in the world without any respect for our ecosystems, without any thought for the millions of workers who, through their precarious state, support the privileged lifestyles of the rich.

Much has been written recently about "essential workers," making visible all those millions of souls who facilitate life in our untamed capitalist, liberal democracies. Those who collect garbage, those who work in supermarkets, emergency services personnel, those who harvest and distribute foodstuffs to our homes (not to mention, in another context, nurses and doctors). We can applaud them, but this will not mean that when our isolation is over we will properly value their contribution or that they will get an increase in wages—even a living wage (as Podemos is fighting for in Spain). They will continue to be the undocumented, immigrants, dispensable.

Foxconn, the Chinese manufacturing giant, is responsible for producing 50% of all electronic products consumed in the world and is currently replacing its assembly line workers in Shenzhen, and other plants, with a million robots. If I read correctly. A million. Phillips has declared itself proud that within the decade it will be replacing its Asian workforce with robotic production systems. There are around three billion people who represent what might be termed the "labor force." 1.5 billion of these, half, are vulnerable and 1.3 billion earn less than five dollars a day. Across the world, two billion people of working age are not in the labor market and five hundred million young people are inactive (neither in work nor studying); meanwhile, 168,000,000 children work in sweatshop conditions.

Do we see them? Do we know of their existence? Will we protect them when we return to business as usual? I doubt it. As Marx said, the purpose of productive labor is not to benefit the worker but to produce a surplus.

All necessary labor that does not produce a surplus is superfluous and has no value in capitalism.

I do believe that, as it says in the subway graffiti, it would be absurd to return to normal knowing that it was, at root, bad.

EVERY DAY IS THE SAME DAY

Referencing Joyce's *Ulysses*, Borges claimed that a single day in the life of a man contains all the days in time. Now with the COVID-19 pandemic, we can say that this day, the one that contains all time, is the same, tiresome, repetitive day. Every day is the same day since we were confined to our homes. The daily routine is both different and, at the same time, ferociously monotonous. Waking up, making breakfast, eating with relish or not—sometimes regardless of the cook's skill—connecting to Zoom for work, or to take a class, or keep in contact with family. Lunchtime arrives, dinnertime arrives, and the intervening hours arrive and are filled with whatever is available: yoga, jumping rope, walking the dog, watching videos on YouTube, dying of weariness. This is what medieval monks called acedia, the Noonday or Meridian Demon. It is the heavy weight of boredom. Later on, perhaps a drink, or another Zoom session, or possibly just watching a TV series, reading, until sleep overtakes us. And the following morning, the same. There is no Monday, or Sunday, we don't even know what day of the month it is. This is lockdown; quarantine.

The summer weather in many parts of the United States is another factor playing havoc with the little sanity we have left. People have gone to the beaches in herds—could this be an unconscious search for herd immunity? In Florida as in California, many are opposed to the lockdown. Out of hysteria or arrogance, in several state capitals people have taken to the streets in protest against the stay-at-home measures. By far the most atrocious case, in my opinion, or at least the craziest, occurred in Michigan. Men armed to the teeth attempted to enter the Capitol building in order to "liberate" their state. What would have happened if, instead of being white, these people had been African Americans?

Or Asians? Or Hispanics? The protest would have ended badly, that's for sure. Probably with shots fired by the police, hiding behind claims of threatening behavior. Those phony rednecks playing Robocop or Rambo did, however, achieve their goal, shouting insults, scrawling swastikas. It is a shame. Jorge Ibargüengoitia, the great humorist, asks where people learn to think so poorly. In school? In church? From Fox News? Listening to their president? From their families? Down the bar? This is the key question I ask myself in these ill-fated times, locked down, killing time while I watch the news, read the world's press online, and I am astounded by human idiocy. Where do people learn to think so poorly?

This is, as a result, a time of melancholy. The Covarrubias dictionary from the seventeenth century is clear: "we say that a person is melancholic when he is sad, lost in sorrowful thought," but adds a second definition: "well-known *sickness* and vulgar passion where there is little happiness or pleasure. *Melancholia est mentis alenatio*." In *Don Quixote*, the canon of Toledo defends comedy: "the principal object of a well-run republic, when allowing public performances of comedy, is to entertain the population with some harmless form of recreation and distract it, occasionally, from the evil humors which indolence is like to engender, that is to say, divert people from melancholy." Don Quixote asserts the same to the canon concerning books about chivalry: "read these books and you will see how they banish the melancholy you suffer." Could this be our solution? Levity?

Or irony, which only appears to make light of serious topics? This is why Ibargüengoitia was always so irritated when people called him a humorist. He wanted to deal in irony, to break the rules of society through stark literary portraiture. The pandemic has revealed us in all our vulnerability, but above all, in our infinite polarization. The protests in Michigan—or the case of Staten Island before them, where people brought their children to the parks bearing placards with the words: *My faith is my vaccine*, or *Jesus will protect me*—paint a picture of a population of anti-vaxxers, flat-earthers, radical evangelicals, right-wing libertarians who believe that the state must not interfere with any private decisions, who, due to their ignorance, cause outbreaks of measles or, in this instance, widespread contagion. The same sort of people, like the governor of Texas, would ask older folk to go out to work, even if they die, to save the economy, or, like the previous governor of New Jersey, Chris Christie, would claim a massive death toll is a price worth paying if it saves the economic system from collapse.

I have to ask myself if it is really true that we are all in this together.

THE CRISIS OF OUR LIVES

This will be, undoubtedly, the crisis of our lives. Better we understand that now and act accordingly, before leaving lockdown. For the largest economy in the world, for example, the data is brutal. The United States will suffer almost total collapse. We will be looking at something similar to the Great Depression of 1929. Just look at the data; as an example, one marker in particular, gross domestic product, perhaps the most generalized measure of economic health, fell by 48% in the first quarter of this year. It has not dropped since 2014. But this is also the most brutal contraction since 2008, when people openly used that word, terrifying to us all: recession. This is just the beginning. Nearly thirty million people have already filed unemployment claims and the total rate of unemployment may well reach 30% by the time we are allowed back to work. Many of the brands and shops we knew will have disappeared, the urban landscape, "Main Street America," will become a desert of billboards announcing closure or declaring bankruptcy. Even according to the most conservative economists, GDP is almost certainly going to shrink by 30%. Not since after the war have we lived through something like this. Consumer spending, on the rise for a decade, has already fallen by 7.6% (perhaps only Amazon will survive). The tertiary, or service, sector (for instance, restaurants) is logically going to be worst hit by coronavirus. Airlines, hotels, stadia, sports, concert halls. There, losses are around 10.2%, and this is only in the first quarter. It will exceed 30% by the end of 2020.

And paranoia? Even the right amount of fear? If the government gave the order tomorrow for all of us to get out onto the streets and live our lives as before, many people would not comply out of fear, because they're not sure this thing is under control. In Texas, the governor announced the reopening of cinemas at the beginning of May. The industry responded, categorically, that they would not open. It's not safe. There is a great deal of fear and no one is providing enough tests, nor antibody tests, nor is the curve sufficiently flattened to give any hope of getting out and about as if all were normal. Caution is logical and perhaps even an ancestral response to foil the virus. After becoming a near-terminally ill patient and ultimately a survivor, Boris Johnson has reformulated his strategy in the United Kingdom. In the United States new data has also changed perspectives. The *New York Times* investigated the atypical increase in deaths state by state. Many deaths due to COVID-19 have not been reported as such. Even so, the figures are chilling. Taking the total death toll from the virus as 200,000, consider that 60,000 (a quarter) of these deaths occurred in the United States, despite there being 178 countries, at least, where cases have been reported. How can these appalling numbers be explained except as the result of abysmal management of public health systems and the epidemic on the part of government? It is a consequence of ignoring the role of science and data.

In China, if you want to go out on the streets in Wuhan, you have to get a code on your cell. Biopolitics dominates everything. In a state of emergency like the one brought on by this pandemic it is appropriate to watch and punish citizens. Out of fear we are disposed to accept the power of the state to intervene in our private lives and control our activities. It is not a novelty, however, that governments are willing to enact states of emergency in which they can—and declare that they must—violate those individual liberties upon which they themselves are built. What is the point of democracy, we must ask ourselves with a heavy heart, if the very things it guarantees are undermined by the powers of a government seeking to spy, control, and manipulate. When we do finally get back out on the streets, I can only hope it is not to live in a state of siege forever.

NEAR BOSTON
APRIL–MAY 2020

The Measure of a Distance

CHLOE ARIDJIS

Chloe Aridjis (New York, New York, 1971) is the author of three novels, Book of Clouds *(2009), which won the Prix du premier roman etranger in France,* Asunder *(2013), set in London's National Gallery, and* Sea Monsters *(2019), recently awarded the PEN/Faulkner Award for Fiction. She was awarded a Guggenheim Fellowship in 2014 and the Eccles Centre & Hay Festival Writer's Award for 2020. A member of XR Writers Rebel, a group of writers who focus on addressing the climate emergency, Aridjis lives in London.*

OUR HEADS are now fitted with imaginary rulers with which we take imprecise measurements and run calculations.

I stand two meters away from the tall woman being pulled down the street by her restless Alsatian.

Two meters from my seventy-eight-year-old poet friend who lives around the corner and hasn't left his house in six weeks.

Two meters from the imprint of the local junkie who usually haunts the entrances of Tesco and Pret A Manger.

Two meters from my neighbor sitting on her steps having tea and a cigarette in her pajamas at midday.

Two meters from the empty ghost buses at Angel station, where now only essential workers and celestial beings alight.

Two meters from the closed chocolatier, whose window arrangements serve as reminders of the futility of human endeavor.

Two meters from my local pub, where the menu from its last night open is still visible on the blackboard near the window.

Two meters from the aging goth in a leather jacket standing in front of me in the queue outside the supermarket.

Two meters from the desire to destroy the mental ruler and overcome the two meters.

LONDON
MAY 4, 2020

The Descent

WU MING-YI

Translated from the Mandarin by Jenna Tang

An artist, designer, photographer, literary scholar, and environmental activist, Wu Ming-Yi (Taipei City, Taiwan, 1971) is a prolific author of novels, essays, and short stories. The Man with the Compound Eyes *(2013), his first novel in English, earned him international recognition.* Le Magicien sur la passerelle *(2017) was shortlisted for the Prix Emile Guimet de littérature asiatique and* The Stolen Bicycle *(2015) was longlisted for the Man Booker International Prize in 2018.*

AS A-LE OPENS THE DOOR, the house is brightly lit, as if someone were waiting for her with open arms. This is A-le's favorite homecoming. Each aquarium illuminates the room with blocks of interlaced light and shadow.

Inside, the simulated mudflats, gravel beaches, and creek beds look like a series of ecological photos. She doesn't indulge in the sight for long, though. She takes off her jacket and pulls up her sleeves as she enters the studio. She then takes out a pack of frozen brine shrimp, a bucket, water pipes, and a few brushes, as well as water-quality stabilizers.

Having been away for almost two months, she must clean each tank as soon as possible, engaging in the slow process of feeding the crabs, changing the water, and collecting the corpses.

As she does so, various memories float up in A-le's heart. When she was a child, what she looked forward to the most was to have her A-ba drive his Mitsubishi Savrin to the beach. Once parked, they would sit together in the back to put their rain boots on. Then they would take their shovels and the collection box to look for heaps on the mudflat.

Sometimes they would hunt for crabs on the side of the creek while tracing the stream. When they flipped the rocks over, the sawa crabs got scared, and she and A-ba would giggle at their fast escape. When A-ba hugged her and kissed her cheek, she experienced a trance of sweetness and anxiety. That's how she thought of it after reading about a character in a book sharing the same feeling.

A-ba collected samples he could breed at home. Soon the tanks started to accumulate, so many that they started putting them in the bathroom and basement. When he was at home, A-ba took the time to sort them. Like a laborer, not like a God.

A-ba moved some of the crabs to school. Only he knew how many "windows" he had; that's how A-ba always referred to his fish tanks. Occasionally, he brought his students home and the house became an ecology classroom.

A-le recalls a strange feeling watching A-ba giving lectures. When she was still very young, all his students seemed like older brothers and sisters to her; gradually, she grew to be their age, and then she became the older sister. Now, all of A-ba's students seem like children in her memory. If she had gotten pregnant young, her kids might be that same age.

After his retirement, A-ba began pursuing crabs, birds, and fish all over the world. Before the quarantine, he went to Wasur National Park, Kakadu Wetlands, and Okavango. He also went to the Everglades, and after that he visited a friend in New York.

But she hasn't heard about his father's New York friend in a long time. When young, A-ba followed a girlfriend all the way to New York, where he ended up finishing graduate school, found a job, and settled down. Their friendship lasted for more than forty years before A-le was born.

A-le's name doesn't really represent happiness; it is the Taiwanese pronunciation of a spinning top: *kan-lók*.

After A-le had just learned to walk, she would dance to music as her body spun up and down. At first, she would fall to the ground before turning a full circle. As time went by, A-le fell in love with such dizziness, entering a wonderful state of excitement. "Ah, *kan-lók*! Ah, A-le!" A-ba would call her. "You're as busy as a top!" A-le's grandmother would say.

A-ba once asked A-le which kind of crab she liked the best. Without hesitating, she answered: "monk crabs."

From a very young age, A-le could recall the names of different types of crabs as well as their general classification, just as she did with Pokémon. Whenever A-ba saw a crab, he would repeatedly read out the name so A-le could remember it.

To make A-le happy, A-ba kept a tank of monk crabs at home. A-ba failed several times before slowly mastering the tricks to take care of them. He placed them in the biggest water tank in the basement, near the spiral staircase. On one end of the tank was a tiny wave generator, and every once in a while, A-ba would bring fresh sand from the beach. "Natural sand is crucial," he would say.

When A-le was home, she would walk down to the basement to watch her monk crabs. Sometimes she would stay there all day. As she approached, the crabs would perform a dexterous earth-drilling technique they used to avoid their enemies, shrinking their legs and claws, just like a sapphire ring.

Their walking legs and claws are both slender and white; the spot where the walking leg connects with the head and breast is red. They form their own family and have only five pairs of gills. The claws are symmetrical and all of the same size, curving inward. In English, they are known as soldier crabs.

Soldier crabs can walk "straight," and when there are tens of thousands of them, they form a truly spectacular scene. A-le always feels they aren't quite like soldiers. What do they look like then?

Her friend Sophie once described walking the St. Jacob Pilgrimage Path before coming to Taiwan. There were many people following their own rhythms, walking in one direction with seemingly individual goals, when in truth, they formed a collective.

A-le thought that perhaps soldier crabs walk as in a pilgrimage. Especially with that name in Chinese, "monk crab"—it sounds as if they are always engaged in meditation.

A-ba told her a few things about the monk crabs. She remembers the story of how A-ba bought his first monk crab on an overpass in Taipei when he was little.

A-ma took A-ba's hand as they went to a mall to purchase clothes. He became fascinated by a monk crab vendor on a bridge and asked A-ma to let him stay there. "I won't run around," he promised.

The vendor, a man of somber expression, had an aluminum basin filled with crabs. Their feet made an annoying scraping sound that made A-ba feel edgy. He didn't know monk crabs could make that sound. "It's very loud. You feel like thousands of troops on horses are coming your way."

With a slight shift of the basin, the monk crabs would make a commotion. And when they felt safe, they simply shrank back into their shells. A-ma certainly didn't prefer going on without him. After a hard slap to make A-ba follow her proved useless, A-ma bought a monk crab for him.

The next day, A-ba learned that many children from the nearby elementary school bought monk crabs from the same vendor. But in a matter of days those crabs would die. A particularly naughty kid used a fishing line to tighten his crab to his index finger. He said it was like a ring. A-ba felt pained when he saw that, and he thought of punching the boy so he would let the crab go. But since the boy was big and tall, A-ba didn't dare challenge him.

A few days later, A-ba's own monk crab died too. He thought that if he had ended up fighting with the big boy, it all would have been meaningless since the monk crabs were destined to die in different homes.

The corpse of the monk crab looks like all other dead crabs. The tightening walking legs loosen up, giving the impression of expansion. The plastron, the most vulnerable part of the crab, begins to stink.

A-ba said he proposed to Ma with a sapphire ring he had bought, the kind that wasn't very expensive, and the color resembled the blue of the monk crab. In the photo, Ma looks petite and delicate, with her naturally wavy hair and dreamy eyes. A-le misses her, although she doesn't really have any solid feelings about it. It's like a person from the tropics looking at a snowy scene in a photograph: we perceive the beauty but can't feel the coldness from it. They're separable.

A-le still can't recover from her father's death. The father who used to take her to different beaches to collect crabs. The dark, non-smoking father who was always cleaning the fish tanks was coughing unceasingly in the video chat, as if he were about to drown.

"Don't be afraid," he said. "If we can't meet again, do me a favor: let the crabs go. . . ."

A-ba always lowered his head when he was looking for crabs, and he became slightly hunched and later became shorter than her. But in her childhood memories, A-ba was very tall. He would lift her up and put her on his shoulders, and A-le would see something she had never seen before:

moth larvae hanging down from silk lines in the summer park; dust on a bookshelf; a cloud she could almost touch; the white roots of A-ba's hair; a swallow nest in a low arcade near their gate. She never had the courage to tell A-ba she had seen a tiny swallow die in the nest. The swallow was naked, with its head tilted, as if it were asleep. A-le knew they were dead, although her grandmother used words like "absent," "gone," and "not there" to avoid directly mentioning death.

In the final video call, A-le didn't dare tell A-ba she is also isolated. Although she wanted to joke about it, saying, "Sometimes we also isolated the crabs! Most of them are born to wield their claws, and few are as collective as monk crabs; usually they stay inside their caves. You're probably feeling the same as they do, right?"

As A-le cleans the tanks, she sees that as expected, many crabs are dead, including her favorite tank of monk crabs. When descending, A-le had to walk down the staircase she feared most as a child. The lights in the basement are managed by a controller that disguises sunrise and sunset. Sometimes light comes from under the stairs, and other times the space is consumed in complete darkness. Though the lights are on now, the basement is filled with a highly salt-saturated stench.

A-le wonders if the whole tank is doomed. But from the corner of her eye, she sees a pair of claws slowly appearing. From a tiny hole, a monk crab exposes its faintly blue claw, then walks up expressionlessly. A-le looks closely. She sees that each claw is unusual: one large, the other small.

A-ba once told her that when all his classmates' monk crabs had died, he returned to the vendor on the overpass. The vendor took out a basin of new monk crabs, which were again making annoying scraping sounds. A-ba stared at them for a long time, then found the courage to ask the vendor how to raise them properly.

The vendor didn't really respond. He simply said that monk crabs die easily, and that one of them costs nothing but five *cuai*. "I will tell you a secret, though," he said. "If you find a monk crab with claws of different sizes, tie a string to its larger claw. That way, no matter where you take it, the crab will always lead you back to the sea."

A-le takes the monk crab from the basement to the street. They're walking together so slowly it's as if they're moving in slow motion. Most passersby don't even see that she is being led by a little monk crab. These days, people keep a distance between each other, and the distance is wide enough that no one notices a tiny sapphire rock a meter ahead of her, and the fishing line tied from its claw to her ring finger. A-le stops people when they almost step on the crab. She hopes nobody will change the crab's direction.

Occasionally, the monk crab stays still for a long time, as if listening. But the city is too rowdy, and it probably won't be able to hear anything. Other times, it walks straight forward, determined, as if it were familiar with the cityscape.

When the monk crab starts to claw and dig the ground with its walking legs or claws, A-le takes out a fish tank from her luggage she drags along with her, puts a drop of salt water containing brine shrimp larvae into it, adds a centimeter of seawater, and places the monk crab inside it. The crab uses its mouth to filter these tiny life forms.

A-le repeats this action every day. At the end of each day, she looks for a nearby hotel (most of them are generally unoccupied now), marks the spot on the street with chalk, and they resume their journey the next day.

Not knowing how many days have gone by, they reach the border between the city and the suburb, where A-le sets up a tent at night. By now she and the crab have crossed over a mountain into the suburb around the basin city. The mountain is full of echoing birdsong at this season. As they walk on, A-le battles with the fear of losing the crab in the weeds. But the crab seems to continue walking casually, just as a land crab would.

Having walked for so long, A-le watches time pass like turning pages. And that reminds her of a space-age flip clock A-ba bought in the seventies. Pala, palalala, palalalalala.

One morning, time stops turning. The sight of the faraway sea is lost in the forest and then reappears. As they continue the journey, the ocean becomes wider and clearer. Finally, she realizes that the monk crab has led her to the beach.

On the sand there are piles of rocks. The waves roar as they crash against their surface, then recede, only to come back a few seconds later. She feels as if the breaking waves are about to touch her. She is familiar with the ocean on the northeastern side of Taiwan's main island, where A-ba used to take her to collect sea creatures. But between the rocks, there is a mudflat that she and A-ba had never gone to. There, a group of monk crabs glitters like a rolling sapphire. They walk in a collectively formed living body.

A-le stares for a while before thinking of the fishing line on her fingertip. She squats as she unties the line on the monk crab with one larger claw. The monk crab starts moving forward, merging into the team indiscriminately. As A-le follows the crab with a sense of attachment—they have spent a long time together—the group of monk crabs begins to drill and dig the sand.

Each of them digs a tiny hole in the soft, wet mudflat with their claws, using their second foot as a fulcrum, plunging half of their body into the soil; with another foot they rapidly dig out the underlying soil and continue drilling with their body in a spiral shape. It's as if the mudflat were hiding countless spiral staircases heading downward.

The crabs have sealed their caves with small pieces of mud. A-le can no longer tell which tiny mound is left by her monk crab.

The sea breeze blows toward her. Wait, she thinks. Maybe tomorrow the sun will regain control, warming up the mudflat. By then, when the crabs feel the familiar vibration, they will reopen their mounds again. She will recognize the crab that belonged to her once. But when that time comes, she might no longer be able to see.

HUALIEN, TAIWAN
APRIL 28, 2020

Quarantine Chronicle

EKO

Eko (Mexico City, Mexico, 1958) is an engraver and painter. His wood etchings, often erotic in nature and the focus of controversial discussion, are part of a broader tradition in Mexican folk art popularized by José Guadalupe Posada. A frequent contributor to the New York Times, Frankfurter Allgemeine Zeitung, *and Spain's* El País, *his books in English include* The Return of Carvajal: A Mystery *(2019) and, forthcoming in 2020,* A Pre-Columbian Bestiary: Fantastic Creatures of Indigenous Latin America.

The birds have returned to Mexico City's trees. Without the whining cars' din the birds' songs are an anomaly that wakes me and the
Eye
opens.

Stumble
out of bed, a water splash on my
face and
hit the
yoga mat
to break a
sweat.

To burn the anxiety (the easy part of the practice) and meditation (not possible)

Get a ginger juice, a coffee and I'm ready to grab the ever thinning newspaper where I still work. The morning ritual is over.

Time to fire up the bright electric screens and face the straining relationships, depressed friends, unemployed colleagues and missed deadlines

By the end of the day I'm reading The Overstory and getting some trees' perspective on the quarantine...

My first impression stepping out, was nothing: everything is as it always has been. There are no eerie empty streets like NYC, London or the cardboard coffins on Guayaquil's sidewalks.

424 MUERTOS POR COVID EN SOLO DÍA

en un día 424 muer

Here the bored and the unemployed search for the best street tacos that have sprung up in every corner since the City mayor shutdown all the formal businesses, restaurants, and cantinas.
But, there are rumors, behind the official statistics...

The sick that can still walk and the ambulances are being turned away from the overrun hospitals.

EEEEEEEE

AMBULANCIA

Funeral homes can't cope with the

INCREASED DEMAND

In México, mariachis sing to our dead their favorite songs in a farewell serenade, but now the mariachis are silent. And the dead souls go without a song to their final destination.

277

Now the Catrina is wearing a facemask and she's not laughing anymore.

MEXICO CITY
MAY 26, 2020

Two Poems

ANDRÉ NAFFIS-SAHELY

André Naffis-Sahely (Venice, Italy, 1985) is the author of the collection The Promised Land: Poems from Itinerant Life *(2017) and the editor of* The Heart of a Stranger: An Anthology of Exile Literature *(2020). His most recent translation is* Aulò, Aulò, Aulò: Poems by Ribka Sibhatu, *which received a PEN Translates award from English PEN in 2020. He is the 2020 Author in Residence at UCLA.*

WILDFIRES

Early in the spring,
hiking along the coast,
we spot the charred remains
of a giant oak tree,

its hollowed trunk roomier
than most apartments. It is illegal
to sleep here, it is illegal
to be homeless here,

and so the poor reside
in rusty RVs at the foot
of this billion-dollar view.
The headline in the newspaper insists:

"America will never be socialist,"
as if that had ever been in doubt. . . .
Everywhere the rapacious harvesting of resources,
but scarcity reigns supreme. Everywhere a resurgent

love for one's country, but no faith
in the meaning of government. Everywhere a newfound
love of God, but a concurrent deadening of the soul.
All day, I read about the Gracchi,

Cato, Casca, Cassius and all night,
I dream of Brutus' final letter to Cicero
before falling on his sword at Philippi.
"Did we wage war to destroy despotism,

or to negotiate the terms of our bondage?"
We have recorded the sound
the wind makes on Mars, but we cannot
listen to one another. . . . All year we binge-watch

an endless rerun of the past. Eighty years
after Guernica, another coup in Catalonia and for
the first time in history, the brightest objects in the sky
are all artificial. A year after Woolsey,

wild mustard returns to carpet the hills,
its fire-resistant flowers bursting out of their sooty stasis.
Here will be no hibernation for us,
no sleep except our final slumber.

SPANISH FLU

The final gift of a futile war,
a second chance for death
to make a mockery of prayers
long whispered in the dark.

The first plane-borne virus, the first
headline disease, that century's only
cross-sectional culling, fatal to prince
and pauper alike—its legacy?

Hospitals: the threat of extinction
our only lever for civic reform.
Today, we live in the wake
of its innumerable grandchildren,

each one a contender for the Great
Khan's crown, each individual bristle
a village torched by sickness. Remember:
wash your hands while whistling "Happy Birthday."

LOS ANGELES
MARCH 2019

The Day after
the Plague

YISHAI SARID

Translated from the Hebrew by Ronnie Hope

Yishai Sarid (Tel Aviv, Israel, 1965) is the son of the late Israeli politician and journalist Yossi Sarid. He practices civil and administrative law in Tel Aviv. The author of five novels, his works in English include Limassol (2010) *and* The Memory Monster, *to be published by Restless Books in 2020.*

THE SKY ABOVE US is very clear nowadays, almost as clear as it was in the seven days of genesis. For a brief moment we have—like it or not—gone back to being the humble, quiet creatures that we were meant to be in the beginning. But as soon it is over, we'll ignite our chariots again and will rush from one end of the land to the other, across continents and oceans, revving up our engines until the sky grows murky again with smog.

The day after the plague it will be summer, and finally we'll be able to have a coffee at the corner café, go to the beach, and for a brief moment we'll value our restored liberty. Just for a moment, because the war for survival will resume right away, and we'll be worried about how to feed our families. Many people will be looking desperately for work, asking what has happened to all the taxes they paid the government and why it doesn't help them in their time of need. The schemers will go back to being schemers, and price gougers will go on gouging, and those close to the throne will fully exploit their closeness.

Even when we are allowed to leave our homes, we'll remain incarcerated in the prison of fear and of hatred. Those malevolent propaganda billboards will still loom over us, and politicians will use our distress to spout incitement and racism, like mosquitoes buzzing over a swamp. We'll ask ourselves, what really binds us together, apart from the primeval fear of the next calamity?

The day after, we won't throw our smartphones away, and we'll still depend upon them like addicts with their drugs. Truly, I beg your forgiveness, but I must say that in thousands of gigabytes of jabbering on social media, and in hundreds of hours of stupefying TV viewing, I never found a trace of the wisdom there is in one line of Albert Camus, Natalia Ginzburg, or Dahlia Ravikovitch, the great Israeli poet.

When all of this is over, the kids will go back to school. Please, dear parents, when you drop them off at the gate, give the teachers a smile, say a few nice words. After all, they are senior partners in our children's wondrous voyage, not merely underpaid babysitters. And senior citizens will also come back to life and mingle with other folks. Say to them, Welcome back, dear friends; without you the world is a sad and dull place.

When the pandemic is over, death will be a private matter once again. The Angel of Death will resume his routine, unseen activity. He'll use the old diseases and the well-known disasters, and will get off the headlines for the time being. Someone who lives with an ER doctor, as I do, hears about death every day. It determines the course of our lives—her coming home late in the evening, and sometimes not at all, and the busy on-call weekends. There are moments of joy and fulfillment, after she has saved someone from its claws, and hours of bitter disappointment and frustration after death wins.

They are tough folks, these doctors, and they do not need medals—this is their duty, and what they have sworn to do. But nevertheless, at this time, we can tell them thank you.

Dedicated, with love, to Racheli

TEL AVIV
APRIL 2020

In Hiatus

CLAIRE MESSUD

*Claire Messud (Greenwich, Connecticut, 1966) is the author of numerous novels,
including* The Emperor's Children *(2006),* The Woman Upstairs *(2013),
and, most recently,* The Burning Girl *(2017). Her collection of essays,* Kant's
Little Prussian Head and Other Reasons Why I Write: An Autobiography
in Essays, *will be published in 2020. A frequent contributor to the* New York
Review of Books *and the* New York Times Book Review, *Messud teaches
creative writing at Harvard University. She lives with her family in Cambridge,
Massachusetts.*

LAST WEEK I saw the groundhog for the first time. He lumbered across the patch of lawn at the bottom of our garden, looking much like a muskrat or a beaver but for his tail—the muskrat has a tail, unsurprisingly, like a rat; the beaver of course has his paddle; whereas the groundhog's tail is closer to a squirrel's. By his tail, I knew him. I don't know how long he's lived alongside us; only now does he break cover.

He waddled through the rhododendrons and slipped beneath the chain-link fence that separates us from the sports field. An hour later, he returned, bucktoothed, wide-bottomed, almost jaunty. In the meantime, a tiny rabbit, the size of a fist, nibbled at the early shoots and cast a wary eye upon the prancing blue jay that hopped in the new mulch of the garden bed, scanning for lunch. For a while, they seemed to be in silent conversation, as overhead the cardinal sang his familiar song, and the newly arrived woodpecker plucked, at zany speed, at the bark of the Norwegian maples.

Life has a different tenor, in lockdown. We watch the moon rise, the sun set; we monitor the buds' unfolding on the trees, their sudden pastel flowering; we marvel when a rare plane breaks the sky's vast silence. The beautiful minutiae of life are returned to us, lost for a decade or more in the pointless race toward self-destruction. The reminder of Death brings reminders of Life.

My grandparents lived on a cliff above the sea. Lying in bed at night, as a child, those long-ago summers, I heard the waves against the shore in the darkness, incessant, the earth breathing. The sound of eternity. My grandmother, in her last years amiably demented and immobile, sat in an armchair by the window and watched for hours the play of light upon the water, the scudding clouds, the shifting colors, the intermittently discernible line between water and air at the horizon. Occasionally, a sailboat passed, a white gnat; a submarine surfaced; or an aircraft carrier slid by on its way to port, a child's toy in the vast ocean before her. She knew—we all knew—in front of the sea and sky it was impossible not to know—the scale of our relative importance. That's to say, our lack thereof. She sat for hours, hands folded in her lap, a half-smile on her lips, and when I came to offer her a snack, a shawl, she would whisper, politely but sincerely, *"Elle est belle, la mer, n'est ce pas?"* A generic observation, not the less true for that.

Though they had moved often, my grandparents lived almost all their lives in sight of the Mediterranean. My grandfather, a Navy man, loved the sea, and feared it appropriately. They were devoutly Catholic, people for whom God's teaching—or the Pope's—gave shape and reason to their lives and to their days. They slept beneath a crucifix draped with a rosary. They accepted even painful lessons with patience and in a humble effort to understand. They appreciated beauty, although they lived modestly; when they died, they left us great spiritual wealth and not a single item of monetary value.

My father, stifled by their antique mores, had escaped eagerly to the New World, married my Canadian mother, and lived the rest of his life an expatriate. After a number of years in Australia, they raised my sister and me ultimately as North American children: I grew up wanting things, restless for worldly engagement and recognition, avid for a place in the society our family had, albeit skeptically, adopted as our own. I wanted to belong in this world, to be acknowledged and respected by its measures.

But this American society, which scorns patience and humility, which celebrates individual agency and material success, must, in order to do so, forget about Death. And in order successfully to forget about Death, you must also ignore Nature, because Death is at the heart of Nature's rhythms. Science and technology have helped to hasten that forgetfulness: we can make our bodies look younger, last longer; we can cure many ills; we can master information; we can distract ourselves and lie to ourselves with extraordinary commitment and efficiency.

Yet just as the sea beneath my grandparents' house still breaks endlessly against the shore, just as the sun repeats its diurnal journey across the sky to plummet into the ocean at the western horizon, so too Death will come, and come, and come, inexorably, for each of us in our time.

We have no control over it. What is unfolding now is above all a painful reminder of this truth. From Nature's long perspective, the pandemic is a small correction. My grandparents would have understood it as the will of God; but one need not be religious to see its greater natural logic. In practical terms, it frightens chiefly those of us who fall particularly within its purview—I am over fifty, and Nature is ready to dispense with me—but the broader metaphysical alarm that it induces arises from the fact that we are humbled, our human limitations and inadequacies revealed. We have long wanted to believe that we've killed God, superseded Nature; but wanting to believe it does not make it so. Being adaptable and resilient, we might well be able in time to resurrect that illusion, but would do so at our peril.

When my mother had breast cancer, treatable, in her late fifties, we discussed the fact that she had been granted the opportunity to take stock of her life—she considered herself unhappy—and to make changes, if she chose. In the event she changed nothing, and continued unhappy for twenty more years, until eventually dementia, surprisingly, cheered her, and her last years were filled with unexpected if quickly forgotten joys. This pandemic seems to me not unlike my mother's cancer: a threat, a warning, a reminder for society. Whether, like my mother, we ignore its import, is up to each one of us.

I am grateful to the groundhog for breaking cover; grateful for the silence that has allowed it. The devastating ongoing human suffering scars and shapes us; let it not be in vain. We humans, in our race to the future, in our faith in science and our own power, have forgotten much wisdom. We have so much to learn. Might we listen, in the unexpected quiet? The earth breathes around us.

CAMBRIDGE, MASSACHUSETTS
MAY 5, 2020

Poem for Hikmet

MATTHEW ZAPRUDER

Matthew Zapruder is the author of five collections of poetry, including Come On All You Ghosts *(2010) and* Father's Day *(2019), as well as* Why Poetry *(2017), a book of prose. The recipient of a Guggenheim Fellowship, a William Carlos Williams Award, and a Lannan Foundation Residency Fellowship in Marfa, TX, he is editor at large at Wave Books. From 2016 to 2017, Zapruder held the annually rotating position of Editor of the poetry column for the* New York Times Magazine. *He teaches in the MFA program at Saint Mary's College of California.*

I WAS REREADING one of my favorite poems, by the Turkish poet Nazim Hikmet, "Things I Didn't Know I Loved." It's one of those poems that uses memory to continually expand the circumference of a present moment of consciousness. Which is a kind of freedom, usable at any moment, especially when one is trapped, figuratively and/or literally. For obvious reasons this potential for liberation appealed to me. Here's the first stanza (translated by Randy and Mutlu Konuk Blasing):

> it's 1962 March 28th
> I'm sitting by the window on the Prague–Berlin train
> night is falling
> I never knew I liked
> night descending like a tired bird on a smoky wet plain
> I don't like
> comparing nightfall to a tired bird

The poem oscillates between more general and poetic observations, and specific memories of the life that led up to that moment on the train:

> I didn't know I loved the sky
> cloudy or clear
> the blue vault Andrei studied on his back at Borodino
> in prison I translated both volumes of *War and Peace* into Turkish
> I hear voices
> not from the blue vault but from the yard
> the guards are beating someone again
> I didn't know I loved trees
> bare beeches near Moscow in Peredelkino
> they come upon me in winter noble and modest
> beeches are Russian the way poplars are Turkish

I really like also how the book is about reading, which is of course another portal out of the present reality, as well as a deepening of it.

I wanted to write a poem that measured up, if only in aspiration, to the intense honesty of Hikmet's poem. I've also been thinking (as I often do) about Neruda's *Odas elementales*, his *Odes to Common Things*. His love of household objects in particular appeals to me immensely, as does the way that he is able, like Hikmet, to effortlessly move from detailed description to the most extravagant metaphors.

When my eye lit upon the unassuming but very beautiful object that appears at the end of this poem, I tried to channel a bit of Neruda's spirit, as well as his cheerful courage to make grand statements.

For me, right now especially, poems are a way of staying engaged with things outside my immediate sphere. They are a way of staying alive in relation to language. And a way of remembering all the things that still matter.

POEM FOR HIKMET

I want to write just one in my whole life
as true as Nazim Hikmet talking

about riding a train
the year after I was born

the year no one could listen
to rain falling without thinking

about the long war

I keep staring at my shelves
and trying to remember

where I was when I first
touched each spine

each one almost reminds me

long ago
summer meant something

the wind made that amazing sound

we laughed about through the grasses
on some island
surrounded by time

those days I loved without knowing
exactly where we were

I keep taking those books off my shelf
and making towers

that later bedevil me

the ones I didn't choose
they surely know the exact answers I need

but only if I don't disturb their sleep

I would like to be sad about childhood
one last time then forget

but first I have to know
I can make just one thing

I could hand to god and say
here's your light back

yes I agree it really would be better
if men did nothing more

but there are still many odes left to be written
to ordinary things

I keep staring at that nail clipper
its perfect silver surface

its immensely pleasing curve and tiny bevels

it should have cost the fortune
of a thousand emperors

but we bought it without even saying

marvelous one
like a poem
you are exactly

as useful as you need to be

PIEDMONT, CALIFORNIA
APRIL 2020

PART V

Love Insists the Loved Loves Back

Coronavirus Blues

GÁBOR T. SZÁNTÓ

Translated from the Hungarian by Paul Olchváry

Hungarian novelist and essayist Gábor T. Szántó (Budapest, Hungary, 1966) is editor-in-chief of the magazine Szombat. He is the author of several novels and collections of short stories published in Germany, Russia, Turkey, Italy, China, and the Czech Republic. His story "Homecoming, 1945," was developed into the feature film 1945, for which Szántó was one of the screenwriters; it received numerous international prizes.

WE WASH OUR HANDS, our food, our IDs, our credit cards, and our fucking iPhones, and we're anxious that the phones will get soaked and we'll be cut off from the outside world. And we laugh. And we are afraid.

We wave to our parents, for we can't hug them. And we wonder if we'll be able to hug them ever again; and they surely wonder this too, perhaps even more often, though we don't talk with them about it.

We can't give our grown-up children kisses and we can't give them hugs, for even though hugs in particular have often been a godsend to them in those moments when life's challenges have brought them to their knees, and even though they might be inclined to fall to their knees now, too, if they could, they can't. We must stand firm, for we don't know how long the pandemic will last, how long social distancing will last, just how much we should be saving up our psychological energies.

When we meet up with our children or our parents and accept or hand over a bag full of groceries or clothes, afterward we go home and sanitize our hands, though we begot our children, and our parents begot us.

And together we laugh, or try to laugh, at the situation while consoling them and consoling ourselves. Meanwhile ambulances come and go, sirens blaring. We count the dead and the ill, and we gauge our prospects: only those elderly who are chronically ill. Only the elderly. Only the chronically ill. And we fall silent on getting news about those among the dead who were healthy and young.

We greet our friends from afar and we wear masks even when out for a walk. At least in Budapest we can still go jogging once a day. And though we can't always exercise at our usual places—for safety reasons Margaret Island and other parks around the city are closed on holidays, when they'd get too crowded—we are grateful that so far there's no total lockdown, that so far the restrictions are just partial.

And we laugh on Zoom when we hold Seder or welcome Shabbat in the company of friends or family. But if we turn off our computers, we're in distress. How long will this state of affairs last? How long can we take it? When can we hug each other again? Slap each other on the back? Will the virus return? If it does, when will the life we once knew resume? It's already being said that we've got to say goodbye to handshakes forever, and there are already lots of people, not just our parents, but older friends of ours too, who are scared of going out onto the street, scared of taking a walk together even six feet apart and with everyone wearing face masks, and who won't meet with us even on the outskirts of the city, in nature.

And anxiously we behold measures by governments all over the world that sometimes contradict each other and here and there are authoritarian and corrupt. We shop and hoard and cook and freeze. And we guffaw. And meanwhile we are afraid: when will the stores be empty?

And we brood: why is all this happening? What went wrong and where did it go wrong, if indeed something did? One or two shortcomings in hygiene? A chain reaction stemming from regional idiosyncrasies? A series of chance cause-and-effect occurrences that, in the space of two months, toppled, like a house of cards, the front gates, bastions, and castle walls of the modern Western and Eastern civilizations many had deemed invulnerable—and that are now banging on the rear gates as well? For our part, we'd gladly close the gates of our own homes in on ourselves, except that the virus can't be locked out. No, it sneaks in through the cracks; it's there in our every thought, our every sentence, our every dream, sure to either kill us or to become part of our lives, so we must accept living with it amid our changed circumstances in a civilization organized to an even higher degree, a civilization more self-aware, more alienated, and more bleak, one in which every new lover's kiss and embrace holds the risk of the virus. And we weep that our children and grandchildren can't go on dates, or if, God forbid, they should break up now, that they'll stay alone, and in alarm we murmur lines such as these, by Rilke: "*Whoever has no house now, will never have one. / Whoever is alone will stay alone.*" And we weep. And we interpret, reflect, and contextualize. Was the trouble caused by the limits of civilization? Would it be better to apply public health norms more and more widely, no, globally, and to do so methodically, in an enforceable manner? Or does the very opposite hold true? Is this nature's answer to its plundering by civilization? Is nature bringing the world's attention to the lack of human restraint, to the urgency of protecting the environment? Or is this all a divine message, one that can cause believers to tremble, to be overcome by fear and dread, for one message or affliction by God may be followed by more messages and afflictions?

And we can brood over a solution: More globalization? Deeper, systematic cooperation in the interest of prevention, since the world's coming economic, social, and public health challenges will be manageable only thus? Or does the solution lie in the recognition that operative approaches to crisis management, while they must embrace global scientific achievements, cannot exceed the bounds of individual nation-states, just as the present pandemic can be managed for the time being only on this level? If so, must we acknowledge that international cooperation can work only in peacetime, that when global crises take hold we can count on only those government institutions and administrative bodies that operate on a relatively transparent, territorial basis?

And we shudder at the thought that the pandemic will not end; that each day's new scientific assessment is flawed and fake; that some researchers out there are issuing pronouncements only in the spirit of the usual scientific and market competition, that, at best, they can stir in us but a fleeting hope; for all this is something other than what came before, this is not simply a virus, no, but a particularly virulent group of viruses capable of regenerating and mutating ceaselessly, viruses before which even science stands speechless; that this is not simply the start of a new, unpredictable world era, not simply an alarm bell ringing for our civilization, but the end of human civilization as we know it. Two entire generations will no longer feel secure in theaters and at the movies; in opera houses and in concert halls; on trains, planes, streetcars, and buses; and in museums. No longer will they have the courage to shop in stores as before, whether for groceries or clothes, and no longer will they sit down in fashionable restaurants and cafés where others are sitting too, for those others will be the subject of their fear. And if this is how it will be, numerous sectors of the economy may regress and economic recession may sweep the globe, conjuring up seismic shifts in life as we've known it.

And sooner or later governments will ease up on the lockdowns, since economic concerns will override strict measures to safeguard public health. People will be let back to work not because the pandemic's dangers have passed once and for all, but because if there is no production and consumption, it will be impossible to ensure that social order, which rests on the smoothly turning wheels of the free market. Governments, with wartime logic, would rather plan a strategic loss in battle—a temporary new rise in the number of infections and deaths—so they can win the war by maintaining the workings of their nations' economies.

And we still don't know how far the pandemic might expand, and we console ourselves with such expressions as "herd immunity," even though we don't exactly know what we're up against.

And others—people who, at the start, in the first months of the pandemic, we still regard as sharing our lot; people we still try to help as the pandemic casts its net wider and wider and reaches ever greater masses and stirs ever more chaos in the so far still heroically struggling health care sector and elsewhere too—these others might, after a while, no longer seem to be fellow humans sharing our lot, but potential carriers of the virus, menacing adversaries; and, indeed, in the event of shortages and a need to flee, life-threatening foes.

May God or our good fate ensure that all this won't come to pass.

May our scientists find a solution. May medications that ease symptoms and a vaccine become available to us all. May there be protection for all societies, for the whole of the globe. May we be freed from the menace soon, still in our time.

BUDAPEST
APRIL 2020

Birthday

SAYED KASHUA

Translated from the Hebrew by Mitch Ginsburg

Palestinian-Israeli writer Sayed Kashua (Tira, Israel, 1975) is the author of the novels Dancing Arabs *(2002),* Let It Be Morning *(2006),* Second Person Singular *(2013), and* Track Changes *(2020) as well as the essay collection:* Native *(2017). In 2014, he moved with his family from Jerusalem to the United States, and they now live in St. Louis, Missouri.*

ON HIS FORTY-FIFTH birthday, the history teacher decided to stay in bed. With his eyes open and a dainty and devilish grin on his lips, he remained there, on his back, on the right side of the queen-size bed, gazing at the motionless ceiling fan. Perhaps he wouldn't go in to school today, he thought. After all, he'd been a teacher for twenty years and had never once taken off a day or called in sick. He did not like to deviate from routine and for the past fifteen years he'd stuck to his lesson plans, teaching ten classes and two high school grades from a rigid, neatly parceled-out curriculum. That day the twelfth graders were to be taught about the Bolshevik Revolution and the eleventh graders about the White Paper and the Peel Commission. The students, he thought, would surely be happy for a free period, while the school administration would be surprised to the point of concern by the absence of a teacher who had never in all his days been absent from a single day of school.

Even after his wife had stepped out of the bathroom and walked into the bedroom, he kept his gaze locked on the immobile fan. She asked if he'd decided to cut himself some slack on his birthday, and he didn't respond. She smiled and sat on the edge of the bed, looked at her husband's delicate grin. She wished him a happy birthday and planted a kiss on his forehead and was briefly frightened by his eyes, which didn't blink and didn't shut. She was familiar with her husband's weird sense of humor and acknowledged that he had a knack for making her laugh. She slipped a hand beneath the blanket and caressed between his legs. She promised him that there'd be special presents for the birthday boy after work and was surprised by the lack of a response. The teacher did not stir and did not speak. His wife withdrew her hand and stood alongside the bed. At first, she smiled to hide her concern. Then she told her husband to stop playing games. He was starting to scare her. Her voice carried a note of alarm. She said it wasn't funny. She shook him, asked if he was okay, placed a palm over his chest to make sure his heart was beating,

303

and then squeezed his shoulder with two hands and jostled him, telling him he was being an idiot, freaking her out.

The teacher wanted to hug his wife, to apologize for giving her a scare. He didn't mean it, he wanted to say, he'd just gotten carried away with a bit of a birthday prank. But he opted to prolong the charade, to see what would happen if he clung to his silence a bit more, staring up at the ceiling and remaining unresponsive for just another minute.

His heart sank at the sound of his wife's sobs, as she pleaded with him to give her a sign, to make some sort of signal, to stop already, it wasn't funny, not in the slightest, and c'mon, don't be an idiot. He was scaring her and she was going to call an ambulance. She started dialing, sure she'd be stopped before she finished punching in the three-digit code. But she didn't make the call. Instead she shoved him again, punched him in the shoulder and told him to quit it. She called her son and said she wasn't sure what was happening and that she was sorry about waking him and didn't mean to scare him but his father was not getting out of bed. No, everything's fine, I know, it must be a joke, yes, it is his birthday today, she said. She apologized to their son, who was in college, and promised to call him as soon as his idiotic father stopped with the charade. The teacher regretted that his wife had called their son and hoped he wasn't worried. When his phone vibrated on the bedside table, he knew right away who it was. The teacher's wife snatched up the phone and instructed him to answer it, to spare their son the unnecessary worry. But the teacher decided to wait; after all, it was still early and he could still make it to school on time. One more moment in bed, he thought, just to see what else might happen.

His wife said she was going to work. She was sick and tired of his games. His stupid prank had drained any desire she might have had to go out to eat later that night, as they usually did on their birthdays. I am so sorry, he wanted to say, I don't know what came over me, I'm really sorry and I was way out of line, I know, I just wanted to put a smile on your face, and somehow, I'm not sure how, I got carried away and made you worry. But he remained on his back, eyes open, staring at the ceiling fan, even though he knew it was time for him to get up and go to the bathroom, because he could hardly bear the pressure in his bladder. His wife said she was off to work, see you, I'm leaving now, as though parenting a small child. She opened the bedroom door and looked back at her husband, still frozen in place, and then slumped to her knees as she absorbed the meaning of the dark stain spreading slowly across their floral bedspread.

He'd gone overboard, he knew that. The whole sad little joke had gotten out of control. Even he hadn't imagined that he'd dare to wet his own bed. Maybe he should just get up? Soon, a few more minutes, he told himself, and he listened to his wife trying to assert control over her voice as she dialed emergency services and told whoever it was on the other end of the line that he was breathing, yes, and there was a strong pulse. He simply wasn't moving. His face was mask-like, eyes open. She shoved him and he didn't respond: no, his body was not rigid; on the contrary, it was soft and warm. Yes, warm. While waiting for the ambulance, she squeezed the muscle between his neck and shoulder, as she'd been instructed, and felt no response. He's forty-five, he heard her say over the phone, her voice cracking as she added that it was his birthday today, and no, there is no history of medical illness. Never been hospitalized, no allergies that she knows of, doesn't smoke, doesn't do drugs, doesn't drink, I mean maybe a glass or two of wine on special occasions.

When the paramedics come, he'll get out of bed, he thought, and he'll tell them that he doesn't know what came over him, that he felt a sort of dizziness when he opened his eyes and that he can't remember anything that happened after that, and that he must have passed out or lost consciousness. In the meantime, his wife removed the blanket and pulled off his wet underpants. With unsteady hands she battled his uncooperative body and dressed him in a fresh pair. When the doorbell rang, she ran to the door and the history teacher considered getting to his feet, but decided to wait a bit longer, curious to know what might happen if he remained there, lying on his back, and to see what the EMTs might do.

He heard them speaking with his wife and tracked the approach of their quick steps as a series of beeps and murmurs poured out of their two-way radios. Three men in white uniforms stood around the bed. One of them asked the teacher's wife for her husband's name. She responded. He addressed her husband directly, asked him how he was doing and if he could hear him; the teacher should signal with his eyes if he could. But the history teacher just gazed up at the ceiling with the same devilish birthday grin. The paramedic wrapped the blood-pressure cuff around the teacher's arm, fastened it in place, and waited for results as he asked about the teacher's medical history, exposure to certain illnesses, something her husband may have mentioned in the morning or before going to sleep, pains of any sort?

Blood pressure and pulse were normal, the paramedic said before loosening the cuff. The second EMT attached four electrodes to the teacher's bare chest and pronounced the ECG results to be standard as well. The teacher was surprised that he'd managed to pull it off, that he hadn't squirmed or shuddered, hadn't stopped them in the middle and apologized. He was surprised and quite nearly proud of his ability to remain detached, his gaze fixed on the ceiling, his lips sealed, practically in a smile, his limp body responding to the paramedics' touch without resistance, without tightness, as they took hold of him and on the count of three moved him from the bed to the gurney. He lay there and pictured himself on soft beach sands. He'd never experienced that sort of supine beach relaxation but could imagine it from the scenes he'd seen on TV and read about in books. He imagined the sun stroking his eyelids and bringing a tranquil smile to his lips. His wife climbed into the ambulance, the EMT placed an oxygen mask on the teacher's face, and the driver activated the siren.

It's too late now, he thought to himself as the EMTs wheeled the gurney into the hospital and he watched the passing of the white plasterboard ceiling panels and the changing light and color of the ER. Even if he popped up now and told them that it was all a prank that had spiraled out of control or said he didn't know what had come over him, they still would not let him go right away; it was too late, and he started to regret having missed a day of work. And what would he do the next day when he came back to class, where would he start from? The White Paper and Stalin's Five-Year Plan? Makeup classes, he thought to himself, he'll have to ask for makeup classes to get back on schedule. He'll have to ask for a double period the following day, or better yet he'll ask the school administration to give him the homeroom period first thing in the morning and he'll use that hour to close the gap and teach them the lesson they missed. Surely not all the kids will make it, but that's not a real problem, the crucial thing is to get back on schedule, to deliver the material even if only one kid attends, even if the lesson's given to an empty classroom.

He was surrounded by talk of a forty-five-year-old man with no medical history and no history of note. Healthy, generally healthy. He heard his wife on the phone, almost surely talking to their son. Why would she do that? He practically blamed her for doing so. He was taken off the gurney and placed on a hospital bed. A curtain was snapped shut and then he felt a piercing sensation in his right arm. Doctors and nurses addressed him, spoke with his wife, exchanged murmurs across his body: coma treatment, the three-part cocktail, the presentation of hypoglycemia. They asked about alcohol and drug use and issued orders about blood and urine testing and stated the dosages of thiamine and naloxone. He heard the doctor repeat the phrase *we must rule out*: must rule out cardiac disorders, must rule out syphilis, must rule out herpes and a drug overdose. Administer atropine, 10 mg morphine, connect electrodes, closely monitor, trauma, catheter, an IV drip.

The beeping of the medical machinery reverberated in his ears when he awoke, eyes open, lips spread in a smile, staring at the hospital ceiling and at a dark stain on the edge of one of the plasterboard rectangles. He wondered whether he'd fallen asleep with his eyes open, because no one approached him and no one paid any mind to his reawakening. The hubbub that had greeted him upon arrival had waned. He heard his wife sniffle and figured that she must be seated in a chair beside his bed. He wondered how much time had passed since he'd fallen asleep. Or whatever state it was that he had sunken into. The curtain divider moved gently and his wife cried at the sight of their son and he imagined them hugging and he wanted to get up and embrace his son and yell *surprise!* and put this whole story behind him. How pleasant was the touch of his son's palm when he cupped his hand in his. He tried not to let his grin grow when he thought to himself that the ordeal has been worth it just for the touch of his son's hand. Dad, his son whispered, what's going on, Dad? And he wanted to answer that everything was okay, totally fine, because all he'd really wanted was to see what it might be like to stay in bed for five more minutes, that's it. His wife relayed to their son that the doctors didn't yet have a clue; that the tests so far indicated that everything was in order, except for maybe a slightly high cholesterol level. They had also done an EEG and an ECG test and were waiting for the results of the cultures and the lumbar puncture.

When the teacher's older brother walked in, the son released his father's hand. Oh boy, he thought, this really has spiraled out of control. His brother kissed him on the forehead and asked him, what's going on? You decided to pull a fast one on everyone? You'll be good as new, my brother, I'm sure everything's fine. Then he told everyone in the room that when they were little, he used to play dead, lying completely still and not moving until the brother would tickle his waist and armpits and then he would crack up. And the firstborn brother sobbed and then tried nonetheless to tickle the history teacher, hoping that it was yet another prank, and the teacher, who knew this was coming, thought about the sea and imagined himself on a little boat, tossed in the swell, trying to recall the sensation of riding on a small fishing vessel of the sort he'd never once boarded. He didn't know the time and he worried that the school day had ended without him having had the chance to tell the administration about the homeroom hour planned for the following day. He felt his brother's fingers grazing his waist again and he once again fell asleep at sea, his eyes either open or closed, and he didn't laugh as he wanted to, as he once had.

He woke up every now and again to the hospital-room beeping, the squish of the nurses' sneakers, the sound of his son telling his mother to go home and rest for a bit, as he, their son, would spend the night by his father's side. What had his students done? What had the other teachers thought? Had the school administration called and asked about him? What had his wife told them in response? In the morning they changed his diaper, and the doctors stood by the head of the bed and said that there was nothing to report and that all of the physical and neurological tests had come back normal. On that day he was to have taught the seniors about the rise of fascism and Nazism and the juniors about the war. Now what would he do? How could he deliver that day's lesson without having delivered the previous one? It was impossible. His wife had arrived in the morning, what time was it now? And why wasn't she going to work? And what about him? Hadn't he taken this far enough? The idea that he might have to teach the previous day's lesson today was very confusing to him and his heart was filled with guilt. Years of diligence and self-discipline were being flushed down the drain because of a silly, childish birthday prank. When an orderly pushed his bed out of the room, he heard his wife tell their son that he should go home and get some sleep. The son said he would go soon, but that first he wanted to hear what the doctors in the new department had to say. And the two of them, the mother and the son, didn't want to call the department—the psychiatric ward—by its name.

The doors buzzed before they were pushed open and he could guess their weight by the sound of the orderly's breathing. The new department was quieter and the plasterboard ceiling was whiter. He could see the orderly's chin and a strip of his forehead as he wheeled him along. He tried with no luck to think of the clothes that his wife had worn that day. What did it matter what she was wearing, he thought as he considered the light blue shirt he would have worn were he on his way to school. What day was it anyway? He considered the question for a moment and had a fright, but then realized that only a day had passed since his birthday. Under ordinary circumstances he was at times bothered by the fact that he had ten different work shirts, concerned that some of his colleagues might have noted the rigid rotation of his wardrobe. But as opposed to what people sometimes think, he said to himself, no one notices your clothes, just as he'd never noticed what his colleagues wore. People, he thought, as he was wheeled into the new ward, always look the same.

He continued smiling that same little smile, a smile that was devoid of expression and maybe wasn't interpreted as a smile at all by his visitors?

Maybe a smile was just one interpretation of the expression that he'd donned the moment he'd decided to spend just five more minutes in bed. A doctor came into the room and talked about a catatonic state, about antidepressants and electroconvulsive therapy, and he heard his wife sob and protest, as though the doctor had blamed her for her husband's condition.

And now, with him in the psychiatric ward, he wondered what would happen if he suddenly got up and told the truth, namely that he had just wanted to stay in bed for a few more minutes, and to play a lame birthday prank. And what sort of sane person, the experts would surely have said, would do a thing like that? His explanation could prove more dangerous than the depression or the catatonic state the doctors had discussed earlier. A nurse arranged the tubes dangling from a metal post by his bed. His son went home, and his wife talked on the phone and said that there was nothing new, no change at all, and that she's fine, doesn't need a thing, no sense going out of your way, and thank you very much. And again the same boat swayed beneath him, deep at sea, and when he woke up without opening his eyes he didn't know if there was anyone else in the room. Was it possible that his wife had left? He sunk into a slumber again and woke up and wasn't sure if it was dark out and was frightened for a moment when he realized he didn't know what day it was, and whether another day had passed. And in the morning, was it even morning? His wife and son arrived and the teacher was once again taken to the treatment room, and he heard the doctors promise that the patient would not feel any pain at all, and that it was nothing like the scenes in the movies, and that the patients are put under anesthesia, one-two-and thr. . . . When he woke up, he was back in the room that he'd been in before, frightened that he didn't know what day it was or what time it was. His wife continued to come every evening, which surely meant she was back at work, which was a good thing, because prior to that she had just sat there in silence or spoken on the phone for hours, and then simply stayed by his side for the better part of an hour, or was it less? He counted six days and then on the seventh day his wife did not come at all. His son was probably immersed in his schoolwork, which was a good thing too, because really there was no need, it wasn't worth the hassle. He tried to glean information, to listen in on the nurses' conversations and to find out, at the very least, what day of the week it was. He thought that if only he knew how much time had passed, if only he knew the date, then he would somehow find a way to get back to the classroom, to history lessons and to routine, somehow, he had to.

He had no way of knowing precisely how much time had elapsed, around a week? And the attending physician, whose voice the teacher recognized, ruled that there was no notable change in the patient's condition and said, by way of a diagnosis, that he suffered from an unspecified psychotic disorder. And again the bed was moved and again he was shifted onto a gurney, and from there to an ambulance, this time without the accompaniment of a family member and without the driver flipping on his siren and speeding toward a medical center. And in this new room he was not alone, and every now and again he heard yelling and fragments of crying, and people whose voices he did not recognize and whose words he did not follow would come into the room and converse with him in shouted sentences and in foreign languages, some of which were known to him and some of which were not. The nurses changed his diapers, gave him sponge baths, administered medicines, and three times a day they poured the feed into the machine that delivered liquid nourishment directly into his stomach. He was shaved once a week, his wife came twice a week, his son came once a week, and occasionally he cried. In vain the history teacher hoped that his son would once again take his hand in his. His brother came to visit twice, and didn't bother trying to tickle his little brother. How much time had passed? And what day was it? And what time was it? Maybe a month, maybe a little less, and once again a doctor determined that there was no notable change and that the rehabilitative efforts were having no apparent impact, and when his wife protested and cried, she was told that they needed the room for patients with better rehabilitation potential. Orderlies wheeled the bed out of the building and he saw the sky and the feathery clouds floating above, and he didn't know if it was hot or cold, and he couldn't tell what season it was. One-two-and-thr. . . .

He was very happy to be back home. His wife and son were waiting for him along with a caretaker, who transported the teacher from the gurney to a wheelchair with armrests and a seat belt. Soon, he thought, when it was just he and his wife in the house, he'd get up and apologize to her from the depths of his heart and try to find a way to get their lives back on course. He'd ask her what day it was, what time it was, what season it was. He'd inquire what lesson he should teach the following day? Whether the war had started, whether the state had already been founded? He hoped that it was the weekend or a holiday vacation, so that his wife wasn't missing work and his son wasn't missing college classes. He was placed on their queen-size bed, on the right side, his side, and he gazed at the ceiling fan. The caretaker fixed tubes to the metal posts and spoke of three meals a day and gave operating instructions and said he would be in every morning and that it was very important to shift the patient occasionally so that he wouldn't get bed sores. The caretaker left the bedroom and the history teacher waited for his wife to come in, to sit down on the bed they shared, but she only popped in along with their son. And the son looked at his father and said goodbye from afar, and asked his mother to call and let him know if there were any developments and asked before leaving if she was sure that she was okay. Occasionally, she cracked open the door and looked in on her husband but didn't enter. She cried on the phone and said she was scared, that she couldn't handle it, just couldn't deal. His brother came over a little while later and without a word started operating the feeding pump. But his wife did not come in toward evening and the third of the three meals mentioned by the care-taker was not given to him on that day, though he did not feel hunger. At night, his wife locked the bedroom door, flipped the lock twice in its cylinder. Later he heard her locking their son's door too. She did not fall asleep that night, her eyes open and her ears attuned to each and every rustle. She was afraid of the thing that was once her husband, lying there immobile and possibly, in the face of all the doctors' assurances, waking up as a violent man, a large sick man, whose behavior she couldn't possibly predict. If he got up now, he thought, she would definitely lose her mind. Oh God, how messed up was he, and what had he been thinking? And what day was it? And what should he be teaching tomorrow? Was the war over? Which nation-states were founded and which were flattened? They'd surely hired a substitute teacher, a thought that disturbed him greatly, or had they hired a permanent replacement? And how would that teacher convey the material, and would he or she know as well as he how to prepare them for the matriculation exams? How they trusted him, the teachers and students, knowing that no one was as well-equipped as he was to prepare the students for their final exams.

With the ring of the doorbell his wife flipped the lock twice and opened the bedroom door before opening the front door and welcoming the caretaker. She must have felt safe now that she was no longer alone with this thing that was once her husband. Did she leave for work? The caretaker walked into his room, said good morning, and did not wait for a response. He changed the teacher's diaper and cursed as he did so. Afterward, he pulled him violently out of bed and placed him into a wheelchair and into the bath, where he turned on the hot and cold water and waited five minutes before placing a towel around the history teacher's body. Then he threw him back in bed, gave him a new diaper, put in the feeding tube, and flipped on the feeding machine. The caretaker sat down on a chair in the room and started talking on his cell. He said he was taking care of a guy in a vegetative state, relatively young, and that he'd be more than happy to fuck the dude's wife, total MILF he said, in need of a seriously good dicking, man. The caretaker finished the conversation and the teacher could hear female moaning from the man's cell phone and male groaning that the teacher tried to smother. What day was it? He had to find some sort of hint about the day and the date, he had to find some sort of crutch, something that would give him the strength to stand on his own two feet.

The following day the caretaker moved the teacher's bed into the son's room. After work his wife came home and locked the bedroom door behind her and unlocked it only in the morning, when the caretaker rang the bell. His son came once a week. At first, he would ask: how you doing, Dad? And he would wait a moment for a response. Later on, the teacher only heard his son walk into the house and noted that at times he peeked in on him and at times he refrained. The third meal was something he got only on the days that his brother came to visit, and on the other days he made do with the two meals provided by the caretaker. At first his brother came once a week. Soon enough that became once a month; at least that seemed to be the case, according to the history teacher's inexact calculations. He hoped that his brother would tickle his waist at least once more, because that would give him a good reason to get out of bed. A few months passed. He heard his wife leave the house at night, at times returning with a strange man. The man moved into his house and the teacher imagined him sleeping on the right side of the bed, the ceiling fan above his head. Every once in a while, his door was opened at night and the teacher wasn't sure who was looking in on him. Eventually, his son's visits stopped entirely. Perhaps a year had passed? And during one of his brother's visits he heard him say to his wife, through the open door, that he understands, that no one could possibly question her conduct, that they had to figure out some sort of arrangement, that he'll check with the authorities and see, and that she's right, she really is still young and there's no reason for this tragedy to end her life too. How long had it been? Was it summer now? Had the matriculation exams already been given? And how had his students done? He returned to the boat, swaying in the heart of the ocean rocking beneath him as he stared up at the ceiling in his son's room with that same smile fixed on his face, the one he had thought was cute and devilish and was now surely seen as the deranged and scary expression of a monster in the midst of a long hibernation. Was it winter now? And how was it that he didn't hear the patter of the rain or the thunder and the lightning that he loved and feared? Was she going to leave him now? He deserved it, he certainly couldn't blame her. What an idiot he had been, he thought to himself and for a moment he decided to forgo the crutch, forgo the option of knowing the day, the date, the time, and to stay there in his son's bed, or whatever bed he might be transferred to, smiling and gazing up at the ceiling. Dad, his son's voice carried toward him as the door opened, how are you, Dad? And his son's warm palm cradled his own, bringing the history teacher nearly to the point of tears. And his son wept in silence and said he was so sorry, and then hushed and tried to contain his weeping, as he had done as a child. His wife came into the room and her heart ached at the sight of her son. They hugged, and she said that tomorrow was the teacher's forty-sixth birthday, and that in one year all had been trampled, all had been ruined. She was sorry, she told her son, and asked him to stop crying, because he was breaking her heart and she had more than enough heartbreak already these days. Happy Birthday, Dad, the son said before leaving the room and shutting the door behind him. Tomorrow, he figured, he was supposed to teach the seniors about the Bolshevik Revolution and the juniors about the White Paper and the Peel Commission. In the morning he got out of bed, brushed his teeth, put on the black shirt, kissed his wife, and headed off to work.

ST. LOUIS, MISSOURI
2020

Living with My Younger Self

ARSHIA SATTAR

A scholar of classical Indian literature, Arshia Sattar (Bombay, India, 1960) translated Somadeva's Tales from the Kathāsaritsāgara *(1994) and Vālmīki's* The Rāmāyaṇa *(2000) from Sanskrit, both published by Penguin Classics. She has also written books for children, including* Adventures with Hanuman *(2014), and, most recently,* Ramayana: An Illustrated Retelling *(2018), released by Restless Books.*

ONE EVENING, about a month ago, I was sitting on my balcony in Bangalore, far from my mother, who lives in Pune. As the rumble of lockdown rumors in India started to grow louder, a lightning flash of clarity in my head told me that I needed to get to her immediately. I was fortunate to get a late-night flight that I could afford. I threw things I thought I would need into a suitcase and raced to the airport.

My mother will be ninety-one years old soon and I was advised to isolate myself from her for a few days after reaching her home. For about five days, I kept to one side of the house and she to the other. It struck me how odd it was to isolate oneself from the most intimate body of all—the one that birthed you, the one inside which you grew and whose blood gave you sustenance, the one whose genetic makeup is coded within you to make you who you are. My mother was impatient with my caution, but I was sure that I was doing the right thing and spent days and nights at a distance from her.

The room I was confined to is "my" room in that it has my books and other random bits and pieces from my past. My parents and I have both moved house many times, so what "my" room contains is not a coherent or continuous record of my life, but there's enough in here to give me glimpses of the person I used to be. As the lockdown days have grown longer and more empty and the nights hotter, differentiated from one another only by the light of the moon as it waxes and wanes at my window, I have been thrown upon my younger self for company. I didn't know it before, but that younger woman does haunt this room. Perhaps it is the silence and the stillness that has drawn her out, perhaps the newly padded paws of time and space have let me notice her presence and, as I surrendered to an unglamorous ennui, I recognized her.

I met this young woman first at the bookcases in our room. The cases contain an odd assortment of our reading life. There are fairy tales, Chinese, Japanese, Persian, Indonesian, German, Celtic, from Assam, from Madhya Pradesh. Some of these are part of a lushly produced

317

Hamlyn series with glorious, complex illustrations, others are more plebeian and now a little ragged. There's a lot of Kerouac and Spike Milligan, the Durrells are there with Ian McEwan and so are Atwood, Drabble, and Fay Weldon. I notice a lot of dead men but many, many living women. There are heavily marked-up school texts—Eliot (beloved and wept over) and Hardy (resisted but never forgotten) and Lawrence (cautiously accepted). There's an attempt to read poetry, it's sincere but unadventurous.

As much as these books reveal a history of a young woman finding herself in the world, they also chart a geography of place and person. There are books soft with age, with split spines and yellowed pages acquired from the pavements of Bombay, each one precious for the carefully saved rupees that were paid for it. These were books that were bought together with the man I eventually married. There are books that are in better shape, from well-kept and organized secondhand stores in the UK and the US, there's an occasional glittering hardback from a remaindered pile. If we put our minds to it, the girl and I can probably remember where we got each of those books. She remembers more clearly than I, of course, because she bought so many of them. My contributions to these shelves are fewer. I am disdainful of some of what she chose, but equally, I hide a blush when she sniggers at what I have added to the shelves.

With that girl and her books, I reentered the world that had once been mine. Together, we reach for Fanon's *Pedagogy of the Oppressed* and nod in agreement that a change was gonna come. We are shoulder to shoulder at Germaine Greer's *The Female Eunuch*, humming along at *The Complete Beatles Songbook*, and squinting a bit at John Berger's *Ways of Seeing*. She leads me back to a time when The Future meant hope, it meant progress and promised that change was always for the better and for the greater good. The hippies and their vision of a world united in a republic of flowers were but one lyrical memory away from her, the Age of Aquarius had but recently dawned, and the possibility of infinite good was within her grasp. Life was getting easier, it was likely that the world would produce enough food for every human mouth, diseases were being rapidly eradicated, technology was her friend and helpmeet, the women's movement was growing wider and deeper and fighting for the rights of more than one half of humanity. The Vietnam War had ended and the last dominoes of the colonial period were falling. Democracy held out the promise that it was the best of all political systems and voices from the Left could still rise in a clarion call that would be heeded by many.

My generation inherited every capacity—wealth, education, potential solidarity—to make the world a better and brighter place. But now, we are faced with dysfunctional political and economic systems, a planet in deep distress, the disappearance of plant and animal species, perhaps the death of life as we know it. The young woman who stands beside me at the bookcase remains eternally poised on the cusp of a radiant tomorrow, but thirty-five years later, I stand on the verge of crippling despair. The books that she read as paranoid dystopias (Orwell, Kafka, Huxley, Zamyatin) have become the gross and brutal reality of my time.

I feel judged by my younger self. Should we sit and talk, one of us so immaculate at the brink of a full life, the other shaped and worn by experience, by loss and grief? What should I say to her? Should I say, "Hello, I know you, but it's been a while . . . remind me when we last met. . . ." Should I offer an awkward embrace that acknowledges the time that has passed between us? Should I look away as I recall all the things I could have done and didn't? Should I feel a spasm of remorse for not being the person she thought I might be, should I apologize for promises unfulfilled and dreams woken from too early? Will she have words of comfort, solace, inspiration? Does my life make sense to her? Does my life make sense to me when I tell it to her?

The books that mark us, each from the other, become flagstones along the path of our hesitant conversation. With her by my side, I can revisit, if not regain, the idealism of my younger days. I'm not sure yet what it is that I offer her—perhaps my disappointments will show her that she has to make the world she wants for herself rather than expect it to be given to her. Perhaps she will understand that a universal republic of flowers needs a garden that is tended, weeded, and watered, that our highest ideals are the most delicate of all plants, that our best selves need to be nurtured, trimmed, and pruned regularly.

Now, after a month of shared space, we have a tentative friendship, this dimly remembered girl from so long ago and me. But as I grow accustomed to her presence and renew my acquaintance with her, I realize that the other person who lives in the house—my mother—has always known and cherished the young woman who inhabits "my" room. After all, she gave birth to her and to me.

PUNE, INDIA
MAY 1, 2020

Empty Days

CARLOS FONSECA

Carlos Fonseca (San José, Costa Rica, 1987) spent half of his childhood and adolescence in Puerto Rico. He is the author of the novels Colonel Lágrimas, published by Restless Books in 2016, as well as Natural History (2020). In 2018, he won the National Prize for Literature in Costa Rica for his book of essays La lucidez del miope. He teaches at Trinity College, Cambridge, and lives in London.

I

LIKE SO MANY, I have suffered insomnia for the last two months. I wake up at three when the baby begins to cry, I feed him his pacifier and then, back in bed, I simply find myself incapable of going back to sleep. I wander around the house for a bit, settle on the living room's couch and read. I have always liked reading in the early hours, with the house finally silent and peaceful, but now it is different: something about the night's stillness, the empty streets and the silence make the catastrophe more apparent. Its strange unreality is underlined; its absurdity becomes more visible.

"The disaster ruins everything, all the while leaving everything intact," says Maurice Blanchot in the opening line of *The Writing of Disaster*.

We are left looking out the window in the middle of the night, figuring out what has changed and what remains intact. The sense of unreality of the catastrophe becomes strangely tangible at those hours. Everything is happening—death, unemployment, solitude, grief—but I can only see the empty streets.

In Hollywood, catastrophe always comes enveloped in melodrama. It has a soundtrack. It floods us with a river of emotion. At three in the morning, what becomes apparent is that this is a catastrophe without a soundtrack.

II

No matter how busy things get—the baby, online classes, writing, Zoom calls, family online meetings—I have the feeling that the days are empty. Perhaps to remedy that feeling, at night, incapable of sleeping, I have taken to reading writers' diaries. Never having kept a diary myself, I suddenly find myself stealing the experiences of others. I begin with Ricardo

Piglia's diaries, and to my surprise I find, in *A Day in the Life*, the third volume of the *Diaries of Emilio Renzi*, a subtitle I had forgotten: *The Plague Years*. In the case of Piglia it was the years of the Argentine dictatorship that were at stake: "The plague, then, is the result of a crime that befalls the populace, and the plague years are the dark years during which the defenseless suffer a social evil, or rather, a state evil, descending from power onto the innocent citizens." I underline the sentence, thinking about the irony. I then move to Kafka's diaries. Also there, the sense of an invisible enemy whose presence we can feel but never grasp, the feeling of a disaster that retreats.

III

During those nights, incapable of writing myself, I begin to collect quotes. I build a small inventory of quotations that somehow explain my feelings. Quotes that balance themselves somewhere between a sense of catastrophe and a sense of stillness, like a tightrope walker about to fall.

In that inventory of quotes, I place the following:

"Something is not quite in balance, and a person pressed forward, like a tightrope walker, in order not to sway and fall."

ROBERT MUSIL

"Some of our guests were leaving, and the rest of us began to lower our voices in the fading light. No one had lit a lamp. I was one of the last to go, stumbling over the furniture. In the entrance hall the niece stopped me and said:

"Will you do something for me?"

But then she just leaned her head back against the wall, holding on to my jacket sleeve."

FELISBERT HERNÁNDEZ IN
"NO ONE HAD LIT A LAMP"

"My twilight hours are haunted by all kinds of specters, and after a certain point these specters acquire a physicality that's too voluminous to push to the back of the mind. What was kept successfully at bay during the day washes in a noisy, powerful tide."

CHLOE ARIDJIS, "KOPFKINO"

The shadowy tempest that sweeps the space,
A whirling ocean that fills the wall
Of the crystal heaven, and buries all.
And I, cut off from the world, remain
Alone with the terrible hurricane.

JOSÉ MARÍA DE HEREDIA, "THE HURRICANE"

"Boredom is the dream bird that hatches the egg of experience."

WALTER BENJAMIN

How can I reconcile the fact that these events are both boring and tragic, that they are marked both by tedium and disaster?

IV

A good friend tells me the story of two foxes that usually frequent her backyard and for whom she always leaves food. One of them was found dead two weeks ago in a nearby alley, and the other has not reappeared to eat the food in three days. She is sad about them, and in her voice I can sense that the sadness condenses something else, something I can't quite understand. Three days later, feeling empathic, I write back asking about the missing fox. The fox has eaten, yet it is nowhere to be seen. Something about it finally touches me, as if it condensed the pain of what is happening.

V

What is the style of catastrophe?

I think about my friend's fox anecdote, about its simplicity, about its brevity. I always thought that catastrophe, and epidemics in particular, demanded a baroque style. A style that paralleled the promiscuity with which the virus proliferates and reproduces. Instead, I find myself these days attracted to the frailty of certain minimalist narratives. I read diaries, fragments, poems, short stories.

I look for that style that becomes evident at night. I think of Francis Ponge's quote: "Man is a heavy ship, a heavy bird, on the edge of an abyss. We feel it." Perhaps the style of catastrophe would be able to conjure this heaviness in its battle with lightness. Heavy birds, man reduced to a thread, like in the sculptures of Giacometti.

VI

Halfway through the crisis the editors at Bloomsbury write to me: my book, *The Literature of Catastrophe*, is ready. The finished copies, they say, will be sent to me very soon. I think about the sad irony and a certain disgust comes over me: it seems senseless to publish that book now, when the nightmare is a reality. The writing of disaster should always come either the day after, as an act of mourning, or long before, as a warning. To write about the catastrophe in real time is impossible. It reduces it to journalism.

The true contemporaries of this catastrophe, I tell myself, are: Joris-Karl Huysmans, Xavier de Maistre, Samuel Beckett, Marguerite Duras, Juan Carlos Onetti, Felisberto Hernández, Maurice Blanchot, Alejandra Pizarnik. And then, of course, Boccaccio, Defoe, García Márquez, the usual suspects.

My thoughts then go back to the book and I tell myself I would have to rewrite every single page of it for it to make sense. Next to me, the baby smiles. He is the only one who seems to be unaffected by what is going on.

VII

Sometimes, I feel that the paradox behind this pandemic is that it has made evident the world in which we were already living: a world of isolation, of frontiers and walls, a world where the elderly are secluded and forgotten, a xenophobic world, where death is something invisible that happens always behind closed doors and against which we prove incapable of mourning. A world that mixes the possibilities of technological globalization—Zoom, Skype, FaceTime—with the tightening of borders and the rise of contemporary nationalisms.

If, as Michelet once said, each epoch dreams the one to come, perhaps we are only now waking up from the political nightmare of the past few years.

Sometimes I feel that the logic of the virus, which is that of repetition and difference, is precisely the logic of rumor and of the media. Tweet and retweet. The logic of post-truth. Perhaps the uncanny sense of unreality that pervades this crisis comes from the fact that now, more than ever, we are living through a catastrophe that is experienced online. Sometimes, at night, I succumb to the temptation and I finally decide to close the book and read the news. It is then that my insomnia becomes worse. I lie there on the couch, browsing through the numbers and statistics the news has to offer, incapable of reconciling the sense of tragedy with the silly unreality of the iPhone screen.

VIII

Occasionally, having lost track of time, I am surprised by the wave of applause that traverses London. A thank-you clap for the NHS workers who have risked their lives for us. In those moments, the isolation becomes simultaneously more real and more bearable. A sense of community emerges behind that applause and with it comes a sense of presence. I am reminded, in those instances, of what my former professor Hans Ulrich Gumbrecht would say: in a society that eagerly moves toward the digital and the immaterial, it is those moments of presence that bring us back to our bodies, grounding any true sense of community. The applause makes the situation more real, forcing us to think there is a joint future beyond the plague.

What is the style of catastrophe? Perhaps something choral like that joint applause. At least it helps us bear those solitary shouts that I sometimes hear after dark, which traverse the empty night as calls for help.

IX

I push myself to write these words. I am exhausted. I am tired of the pandemic and of hearing about it. But I guess that is precisely what defines a catastrophe: its capacity to swallow everything it encounters, its ability to sweep through meaning. Like a hurricane or a black hole, catastrophe is totalitarian: it forces us to speak of it and only of it. Everything becomes a metaphor of the pandemic, every book an allegory of the times we live in.

I am tired of the pandemic. I miss the days when we could speak and read about other things.

X

Spring has arrived in London. It is just as glorious as always, by far the best season here. The days are getting longer and the nights shorter. The baby sleeps the whole night and I begin to sleep as well.

In the small notebook where I store my inventory of quotes, I add another one from Walter Benjamin: "A generation that had gone to school on a horse-drawn streetcar now stood under the open sky in a countryside in which nothing remained unchanged but the clouds. . . ." Some things don't change. And after the catastrophe one hopes to recognize the face of the old world one left behind.

LONDON
MAY 9, 2020

Quarantine

EAVAN BOLAND

Eavan Boland (Dublin, Ireland, 1944–2020) was the author of more than a dozen volumes of poetry, including Outside History *(1990), and several volumes of nonfiction, and was co-editor of the anthology* The Making of a Poem *(2000). She is considered one of the foremost female voices in Irish literature. She received a Lannan Foundation Award and an American Ireland Fund Literary Award, among other honors. She taught at Trinity College Dublin, University College Dublin, Bowdoin College, and at Stanford University, where she was the director of the Creative Writing program.*

In the worst hour of the worst season
   of the worst year of a whole people
a man set out from the workhouse with his wife.
He was walking—they were both walking—north.

She was sick with famine fever and could not keep up.
   He lifted her and put her on his back.
He walked like that west and west and north.
Until at nightfall under freezing stars they arrived.

In the morning they were both found dead.
   Of cold. Of hunger. Of the toxins of a whole history.
But her feet were held against his breastbone.
The last heat of his flesh was his last gift to her.

Let no love poem ever come to this threshold.
   There is no place here for the inexact
praise of the easy graces and sensuality of the body.
There is only time for this merciless inventory:

Their death together in the winter of 1847.
   Also what they suffered. How they lived.
And what there is between a man and woman.
And in which darkness it can best be proved.

2008

Wounda

EDUARDO HALFON

Eduardo Halfon (Guatemala, 1971) is the author of fourteen books of fiction published in Spanish, three of which have been translated into English: The Polish Boxer *(2012),* Monastery *(2014), and* Mourning *(2018), which received the Edward Lewis Wallant Award (US), the Prix du meilleur livre étranger (France), and the Premio de las Librerías de Navarra (Spain). In 2018, he was awarded the Guatemalan National Prize in Literature, his country's highest literary honor. He currently lives in Paris.*

IT'S BEEN THREE WEEKS of lockdown in Paris. The street outside my window seems smaller and emptier every day, as if people were more and more afraid to venture out, whether it be for a brief walk or to forage for food. As the number of deaths continues to rise, the French government recently announced even stricter measures: only one outing allowed per day, one hour per outing, within a one-kilometer radius of home. The world outside my window is, in fact, getting smaller.

During these past three weeks I've been almost exclusively a father. I feel as if I'm no longer a writer. Writing now doesn't matter anymore, or it doesn't matter much, or it matters less than making sure that my three-year-old son sees this new reality as if it were some kind of adventure.

We go outside once a day, in the early afternoon, for a short walk or a ride on his scooter around the neighborhood, always making sure not to touch anything and to keep away from the few pedestrians and joggers. The rest of the time, at home, we make up games where there were none before: snapping off the shoots of spinach leaves, learning to pick up scraps of paper with a pair of small tweezers, creating complex designs on the floor with his collection of used metro tickets, making a family of porcupines out of Play-Doh and dry spaghetti. As I see it, my primary occupation has been keeping everything that's going on as far away from him as possible—the lockdown, the virus, the uncertainty, the overall sense of panic, the soaring number of sick and dead. And for the most part I'd succeeded. Or so I thought.

Some days ago, I showed my son the short video of a chimpanzee clinging on to Jane Goodall in what appears to be a grateful embrace. I explained to him that the chimpanzee's name was Wounda, and that Goodall and her team were releasing Wounda again into the jungle of the Congo after it had been rescued and rehabilitated. And my son, as soon as the video ended, started to sob inconsolably. At first, I was almost proud of his tears, which I interpreted as empathy or emotional intelligence. And maybe they were, at least in part. But then I couldn't help wonder how much built-up frustration he also was releasing in those tears, how much sadness he had been storing up all these weeks and hiding from his father.

At some level, and despite our best efforts, I know my son feels what's going on. He senses something in his world has been broken, perhaps permanently. The first thing he asks every morning, still in bed, is if today he finally gets to return to his school, see his teachers, go to the Jardin du Luxembourg to run and play in the sandbox and scoot around with his friends. My son, I know, is starting to miss being a kid.

A few days have passed now since he saw the video, but he still talks constantly about Dr. Goodall—he calls her Jane—and about Wounda. This afternoon, while we were lying in his bed trying to nap, I happened to record him telling Wounda's story in his own way, in his own words. And as I listened to him, I thought of a woman and her team healing a chimpanzee, and a chimpanzee healing a son, and a son healing a father.

PARIS
APRIL 11, 2020

The Arm of Mercy

GRACE TALUSAN

Grace Talusan (Manila, Philippines, 1972) is the author of The Body Papers *(2019), a* New York Times *Editors' Choice selection, a Must-Read for the Massachusetts Book Awards, and the winner of the 2017 Restless Books Prize for New Immigrant Writing. Born in the Philippines and raised in New England, Talusan teaches at the Tisch College of Civic Life at Tufts University and is the Fannie Hurst Writer-in-Residence at Brandeis University.*

MOMENTS BEFORE we closed our doors to anyone outside our household, I was traveling with my parents in Texas, a flight or two away from our homes in Massachusetts. Last minute, they had decided to join me for the first leg of my paperback tour for *The Body Papers*. Their stated reason was to visit with old friends in Dallas. These friends had also emigrated from the Philippines and became like family during our first years in America, but we had not seen each other for years. Also, my parents wanted to sightsee in San Antonio and Houston. This is what they told me, but I knew they could not bear the idea of their daughter, unaccompanied, sleeping in hotel rooms and driving hours from strange city to city through an unfamiliar state. Even though I am a middle-aged woman, well past child-abduction age, my mother imagines that if I travel alone, a maniac in a white van will offer me candy or a box of puppies and I will follow him unwittingly to my torture and death.

After their seventieth birthdays, my parents became more serious about doing things from their bucket lists and visiting with loved ones because you never knew if this was the last time. Every year, there were more funerals, and it was becoming harder for them to fill the seats around the table for their weekly mahjong games. My mother began attaching labels with our names to jewelry and other items around the house that she thought we might fight over after she was gone. She made me follow her through their living room once to the Steinway piano that no one ever played so that she could show me a Hummel figurine that was labeled *Grace*. "Fine. Thank you," I said. I put the figure down and turned to leave the room. Now, I feel guilty that I let my impatience show, but I didn't particularly want the figurine and could not imagine fighting with my siblings over it. I also didn't want to think about the inevitability facing all of us: how someday she would not be waiting for me at home and we would be left with her objects and house slippers and her papers—the cards, awards, newspaper clippings, and school photos—she kept of us as evidence of her good work as our mother.

On Sundays, when my husband and I would visit my parents for our weekly meal together, my father would warn, "You really need to spend time with your mother so she can teach you how to make her food." But that would require hours, whole days even, that I did not have. If I wanted to cook Filipino food, I would follow a recipe or a cooking video online and if I had questions, I would call my mother. I would make enough to share with my parents, but when my father would taste my version of chicken adobo or *pan de sal* or sweets such as *sans rival* or *ube halaya*, he struggled to politely inform me that there was too much of this and not enough of that. All the criticism led back to his one central complaint: *This doesn't taste as good as your mother's, and once she's gone, you will be sorry you did not take the time to learn her recipes.* I wondered if he thought she would go first and wanted one of his daughters to be able to cook her dishes exactly the way she had. He had no interest in learning these himself. The first time in her life that my mother traveled without him, I went to their house on the day she was due back, to check on him, but also to make sure that the house was clean enough to prevent an argument. In the sink, I counted nine unwashed coffee cups. One brown stained cup for each day that she had been away. As I washed each mug, I was filled with rage about the patriarchy and invisible labor, constructing arguments in my head that I was too much of a coward to have with him. Maybe if I were still in college, I would have tried to talk with my father about gender roles and personal responsibility, but at this point, really, why bother? Keeping my mouth shut was a kind of mercy.

Last year, my mother attached a sheet of paper with a magnet to my refrigerator door at eye level. This was the poem she wanted me to read at her funeral Mass. "Um, are you sick or something?" I asked. She shook her head no and answered with her favorite response, "But you never know."

Despite the awareness that death was out there and we would meet it, someday sometime, none of us wanted to talk about it. To imagine the possibility or to utter any of the "d" words—death, dying, died—in relation to our loved ones felt terrifying. To write about death feels as dangerous and unwise. Bad luck. I could tempt it to come sooner by writing it down. Our family has seen many of our clan die young; we knew that tragic diseases and fatal accidents were always possible, but now that my parents were firmly in their golden years, the thought of losing them permanently was always there in every conversation and visit, a shoe still undropped.

I write this two months since everything changed. We know more now than we did back then, but we still don't know enough. When I think back to how I made my decisions about traveling to Texas in early March, I realize that I did not have the proper information to make good decisions. But still, I had enough information to know that this was a virus that ravaged one's respiratory system, and as someone with asthma and a recent bout with pneumonia, that could be particularly bad for me.

I considered canceling my trip to Texas. The first stop was San Antonio, where earlier that week the mayor had declared a state of disaster and a public health emergency, which the online chatter assured was just a precautionary measure, a way for the mayor to extend his power and secure funding, and I wouldn't likely be in any danger. On Tuesday, March 3, the night before I was supposed to get on a flight to San Antonio, I canceled that portion of the trip, readings and panels planned a year in advance, and immediately fretted that I was being overly cautious. I called my parents to let them off the hook and told them that they should not come with me to Dallas and Houston because they belong to a vulnerable population, the elderly. They laughed because that term still doesn't fit how they feel inside. "I'm serious," I said. "You're over seventy."

I asked my brother, a physician, for advice. He works in a university research hospital and probably had better access to information. I told him that so far there were no reported cases in the cities we were going to, but I was concerned about the virus at the airports and on the airplane. He texted back, *If our parents get sick and die because they traveled with you, I will never forgive you.*

After waiting a beat, he added an emoji to show he meant this as a joke. We haven't lived in the same state since college, so my brother stays connected by texting me alarming messages, followed by a "just kidding." Every year or so, I'll receive a text from him late at night or early in the morning: *Where are you? You said you'd pick me up at the airport.* Or, *It's too bad my sons don't remember you, but that's what you get for not visiting more.*

We were still several days away from everyone using the phrase "global pandemic." We didn't know how contagious the virus was. We didn't know that asymptomatic people could spread the virus unwittingly. We didn't fully appreciate what exponential growth was. We did not yet know that before the month was over, my parents would lose their lifelong friend to COVID-19.

The event organizers in Dallas and Houston confirmed that all the events, months in the planning, were still on. At the first stop, Interabang Books in Dallas on Saturday, March 7, I came across my mother's friend in an aisle. Over thirty years had passed since I had last seen her, but I recognized her right away, almost unchanged except for her silvery white hair, shaped along her jawline in a youthful bob. Without thinking, I stepped forward to hug this woman who I had thought of as a long-lost aunt. She took a step back and crossed her arms in front of her, pressing her hands together in prayer position. I felt my face redden with shame and I excused myself. "I need a minute before the reading." My mother's friend was right to keep her distance, but I was embarrassed by my faux pas.

A day later, in Houston, people would mention that they probably shouldn't hug or shake hands a moment before doing so anyway. I looked up from signing books at an event for a Filipino group to see my mother saying goodbye to people, strangers only a few hours before, with a cheek kiss, a common way we might greet our *kababayan*, especially those we feel close to or warmly toward. I admonished my mother in the car. "You can't let strangers get that close," I told her. She said, "I know, but I couldn't help it. They were all so sweet." I realized that my mother rarely spends time around young, vibrant Filipino Americans, and who was I to keep her from our community's embrace?

Monday, March 9. Only twenty-four hours later, we were teetering on the cusp of change, though we didn't know it yet. The university where I was supposed to visit had suspended classes and my event was canceled. The next week's events in New York were also canceled, and I began to receive emails from later stops on the tour, postponing events one by one. Now, no one apologized for not shaking hands. I signed the book of a woman in scrubs and she gifted me with portable hand sanitizer, now a valuable item as stores were reporting shortages. We didn't know yet about the virus spreading in droplets, so no one wore masks, and when we took pictures, we pressed close together.

Wednesday, March 11. Every hour that ticked by that day, I felt more anxious. By then, I had a strong feeling that we were on the precipice of something big. That evening, the NBA suspended the season indefinitely after a Utah Jazz player tested positive for the virus. At my reading, I announced, "This will be the last event of my book tour, so I will enjoy being together and I hope you do, too." I savored every minute of that evening, which was the last time I could pretend things were normal.

As I signed books, I was constantly aware of my parents. I cringed as I watched them thanking the audience personally, mostly people from Houston's Filipino community, who supported my book with so much enthusiasm. Earlier that day, a young woman invited us to her family's Filipino restaurant, and as he piled another plate with the stews and meats and noodles of the food he always longed for, the food from home, I had never seen my father happier, except when his grandchildren were born.

A new immigrant from the Philippines joined us, and on his phone he played a clip of himself from his recent appearance on *The Ellen DeGeneres Show*. "Ellen?" my mother said. "I sent her your book. You should go on that show. She likes Filipinos." I shook my head at my mother: *Stop*. The young man and his friend, bored, hung a poster of themselves, in the style of the other posters, on the wall of a Texas McDonald's and no one noticed. My father was impressed by the giant checks for $25,000 each that Ellen gave them.

"That's good," my father said, looking at me. I've seen this look my whole life and can read it instantly. *You should get Ellen to cut you a giant check, too.*

After brunch, they took us to see a bust of José Rizal, Filipino national hero, at Hermann Park in Houston. Our hosts dropped whatever they had planned that day and spent it with us. I was touched, but also understood the gesture. I had done this myself when a visitor from the Philippines suddenly appeared and I had to clear my schedule with only hours' notice. Another woman squeezed in time between getting off from work, feeding her children dinner, and fighting her way through the notorious Houston traffic to bring a fitting, special dessert to the event at Brazos Bookstore: *brazo de Mercedes*, translated as "the arm of mercy," referencing the arm of Our Lady of Mercy. The sweet meringue and custard rolled cake is supposed to evoke the warmth of a mother's embrace. To me, eating *brazo de Mercedes* is like eating a dense cloud. My father ate two plates and told me later that he still thought my mother's recipe was best. That night, he had listened through my entire talk, which was a first for him. When he attended my book events, he would leave and sit in the car once I began to speak. I don't blame him for not wanting to be in the room. It is, after all, a book about the most painful times in our family. Plus, my father cannot sit still, even for a forty-minute Catholic Mass, leaving three quarters of the way through the service after taking Communion. After the bookstore closed, we took the leftover slices of *brazo de Mercedes* to the hotel. It had been a great night, but I felt guilty. What if someone got the virus by attending my book event? Would their suffering, even their death, be my fault? About a week later on Facebook, through her status updates, we would find out that the woman who so generously fed us the *brazo* had a high fever and then was coughing a lot and then was swabbed for a test from her car and then it was confirmed, she had the virus. I remembered my brother's warning about exposing our elderly parents to the virus. It was only in hindsight that I could see that my last book event in Houston was the evening before everything changed.

I was happy to get on the plane the next morning. My mother handed me a pack of disinfectant wipes so I could wipe down my seat and tray table on the plane. I felt self-conscious about the sharp odor and worried that my seatmates would think I was being paranoid. To distract myself, I caught up on email and saw a long message from a lifelong friend in Spain. José lived in a small coastal city in the northwest corner of the country. My family had visited his family a few summers ago, where we enjoyed a leisurely seaside lunch that was so delicious that we cried for joy. We did not know that bread and fish and wine could taste like that.

In the email, José apologized for his poor English skills, the length, and tone of the email, but he was desperate for us to take him seriously. He was a time traveler, a few weeks ahead of the United States, and warned about the storm that was coming our way. We needed to heed his warning: "Stay inside." We probably could not imagine what he was describing, but we needed to believe him. Where he lived, they had not acted fast enough against the virus. We still had time to change what was about to happen. He loved all of us very much, he wrote, and as I finished his email, I was weighted down with sinking, cold terror. Was José sick? Was I sick? Was this the last time we would ever communicate with each other? "Death is all around us here," José wrote. "And this is what is to come for you."

Death was always with us, but like the two funeral homes near my apartment that I drove past all the time, I didn't notice until the virus forced me to.

After my mother's friend who worked at the grocery store died so quickly and unexpectedly of the virus—isolated and alone—my mother sprang into action. Instead of planning for a death sometime in the future, she wrote down her account passwords and packed a bag that should go with her to the ICU. There wasn't much in this bag, only holy water from Lourdes and a rosary, a reversal of preparations from those other times she packed a hospital bag, when she was about to deliver us, her babies. Things had happened so fast and her friend was not able to have a priest by her bedside to administer the Sacrament of Extreme Unction, and if it came to this, would I promise to contact Father Cyriac in Atlanta to administer Last Rites over the phone, but preferably on a video call? And since none of us would be able to visit if she were hospitalized and she might not be able to communicate anymore, could we relay her wishes to the nurse? This was important to my mother as it was the last sacrament in her life as a Catholic. "Yes," I assured my mother. "Of course." I could offer her this one mercy.

There is so much uncertainty about the virus. Two months in, we still don't know. We might have mild symptoms, or we might need a ventilator. Our immune system might overreact and kill us. We might recover easily and experience no lasting medical issues, or we might recover enough to leave the hospital only to drop dead a day later from a blood clot or heart attack or stroke.

I've always coped with anxiety and the unknown by reading. As an immigrant girl, I read shelves of children's books at the library to learn how to be an American. Since returning home from Texas, I've read and read until I feel sharp stabs behind my eyes. I can't get enough: Thousands and thousands have died. Thousands more will die. Because of one dinner party with an infected guest, in one New Jersey family, seven members get the virus and three die. My sister lives in a city with the second highest infection rate in the state. There are accounts of people getting the virus from pressing an elevator button or choir practice or in the case of our friend who died, being in the wrong place at the wrong time when someone shed the virus onto her. One fifth of California nurses are Filipino and have been disproportionately impacted by COVID-19. My brothers work in hospitals and many of my cousins are nurses. My father can't stop himself from going out in the world for unnecessary errands. Our life for the foreseeable future is a result of multiple failures of leadership and policies such as testing. The virus has laid bare our country's structural inequalities, such as economic and health disparities, and emerging data shows that Black and African American people in the United States contract and die from the virus at a disproportionate rate. My husband is Black American.

Besides losing someone I love to the virus, what scares me is how quickly I've become adjusted to what once would have seemed intolerable. After two weeks of sheltering in place, I stopped taking my temperature every night and feeling phantom symptoms. After three weeks, I don't wake up and fall asleep in tears. Two months in and my entire life is inside my apartment and online, and yet, when people ask how I'm doing, I say I'm fine. And it's true, but it's also a lie, what I tell myself in order to get through the day. I am doing exactly what humans evolved to do; to make a life amid whatever hand you're dealt. This is a kind of mercy.

GREATER BOSTON
MAY 19, 2020

More Was Lost in the War

DANIEL ALARCÓN

Translated from the Spanish by Ilan Stavans

Daniel Alarcón (Lima, Peru, 1977) is a novelist and radio producer whose books include War by Candlelight *(2005)*, Lost City Radio *(2007)*, At Night We Walk in Circles *(2014)*, *and* The King is Always Above the People *(2017)*. *The executive producer of Radio Ambulante, a Spanish-language narrative journalism podcast, Alarcón is an assistant professor of broadcast journalism at Columbia University. His honors include a Whiting Award in fiction, a Guggenheim Fellowship, and a Lannan Literary Fellowship.*

FIVE YEARS AGO, when I was being shown the apartment where I now live with my family, the agent reached the last room at the end of the hallway, approached the window, and apologized. On the other side of the avenue there was—is—an immense and incomplete construction. That summer day in 2015, one could see, in the middle of an empty lot full of holes and tunnels and giant mounds of soil, the unfinished skeletons of a pair of half-assembled buildings. It was enough to make out, if not the details, at least the scope of the project's dizzying ambition. It was ten in the morning and hundreds of construction workers scurried among the enormous machines. "It's loud, I'm not going to lie to you," the woman said with an uncomfortable smile. "But someday they'll finish."

The truth is I wasn't bothered. I'd left New York in 2002 and had always wanted to come back. I thought of my younger son, just two years old. He'll be a New Yorker, I thought, one of those who measure their age by the size of the buildings that spring up around them. I imagined he'd spend hours looking out at the cranes from his window, the trucks, the construction workers moving amid the chaos, and that it would be a privilege for him to grow up in this forest of steel and cement and then be able to say, as a grown-up, that he remembered when none of this was existed. This, in the end, is what it means to belong to a place: to carry its history with you always, intuitively. I always wanted to be a New Yorker; at times, not being one has felt like a personal defeat. I thought: my son will be a New Yorker without even giving it a second thought.

He's six years old now, with only vague memories of having lived any-where else, and he doesn't even notice the details of the city that felt so special to me when I moved here in 1995. Like a true resident of Manhattan, he thinks that all cities are islands. His favorite breakfast is a bagel with lox. He knows uptown from downtown. He has favorites among the many bridges that connect the boroughs to each other and to the world. When we share the elevator with neighbors, my son, polite and well-behaved, asks which is their stop—not which is their floor—as if he were a conductor on a subway train.

And on more than a few occasions, I've found him looking out the window, basking in the sun while contemplating the massive construction and its constant movement. In four years, four buildings have appeared, open to the public now, and there are three more in progress. They don't stop building. They never stop. That's New York, I used to tell my son proudly, when we'd look out the window together in wonder as the construction workers prepared for another day of work under a merciless rain or heavy snow. It doesn't matter how cold it is, I'd say. The winds blowing furiously from the river can't stop them. Nor the oppressive heat of summer. They never stop. Never.

Until last month, of course, when everything stopped.

2

I spent my first few years here in a kind of invented nostalgia, tormented by the idea that the truest version of New York had existed five, ten, or twenty years before I arrived. I walked a lot, wanting to see every street, each building, and each neighborhood and record the details, to talk to everyone I found on the way and collect their stories; sometimes I'd take the subway to the last stop, as if I needed to confirm that the city actually ended. I have a collection of memories of those early years I wouldn't dare share with anyone. Not because they're compromising or scandalous but because they are precisely the opposite. They're ordinary: first loves and broken hearts, small successes and defeats that somehow felt enormous. I remember readings and concerts and works of art that transformed me, but not more than my friends' smiles, which gave me life. I came to New York at eighteen, immature, insecure, curious, long-haired. I shaved my head a few weeks after arriving, thinking I might look less out of place that way. The memories I have of those years are those of any adolescent who comes to a strange new place and tries to invent a version of himself he doesn't hate. I'm so moved by these ordinary memories that I'm ashamed to present them as special.

Maybe the only thing special about them is their background, New York. I realize now I arrived in a moment of transition: Rudy Giuliani was mayor and police violence was on the rise, along with an economic expansion that erased entire communities. I came to the city before 9/11, when we were all less afraid, or perhaps when we understood fear differently. Little by little I came to realize I hadn't arrived late, but right on time, that we all arrive right on time to this place, that city that never stops changing always makes space for the new arrival who wants to become someone else. I fell in love with the city, a love with precise points on the map and on the calendar. Astor Place, November 17, 1995. The West End, March 9, 1997. Yankee Stadium, June 4, 2001. Now that the pandemic has cut history in half, I think a lot about the version of New York we might find on the other side, how it will transform the geography of my memory. To think of an *after* that isn't devastating requires a great deal of imagination, perhaps more than I have, and I want to protect my memories at all costs, though I know it's impossible.

Before all this, I used to look out my window in the morning and watch the passersby on their way to the subway. I'd note how they were dressed in order to decide what I needed to wear or how to dress my youngest son. With or without boots. With or without a raincoat. With or without a scarf. Even for something so basic I relied on my neighbors. Now that I see hardly anyone out the window, I don't know what to wear. It hardly matters, I suppose, because I don't have anywhere to go.

New York without New Yorkers makes no sense. It's late April now and we've become accustomed to the sirens. More than once, on the short walks I take with my dog, I've come across an ambulance parked in front of a building, just in time to see first responders dressed like astronauts rush in to pick up a sick neighbor. Faced with a scene like this, it's normal to wonder if the patient will come home someday or die alone in a crowded, overwhelmed hospital. It's normal to ask these questions, just as it's normal to weep from anger and helplessness.

3

More was lost in the war.

I liked that phrase a lot when I was a child, although it took me years to understand. My mother often used it to minimize or dismiss a child-hood grievance. For example, if I said I wanted some toy all my American friends had, my mother, always calm, would swat my complaints with a simple "more was lost in the war." It was brutal and bulletproof, no way around it. It was years before I finally dared to ask her what I always wondered: which war?

Any war, she said. All of them.

Despite what was happening in Peru, where I was born, war for me was something exotic, distant. I grew up in a peaceful suburb of a peace-ful city in the American South. Everything happened on the other side of the world. You'd see it on TV, mixed in and blurred with commercials and sitcoms and sporting events. As a gringo, I knew our wars were constant, but they were fought in faraway countries, where death and destruction were distributed among the unlucky ones who had decided to live in the line of fire. We in the United States didn't even keep a tally of what they lost, since it wasn't our problem. No one taught me this. Like all national-ist myths, I learned it on my own.

By now, we've become accustomed to losing, of course, and not only in war. As I write this, the number of deaths from coronavirus in the United States has reached 50,000, with more than 11,500 in New York City alone. It's a frightening number, absurd, tragic. I'm here, in this city, and have trouble believing that thousands of my neighbors have died unnecessarily from this plague. At the same time, I know this number will only grow, and that maybe, at some not so distant point in the future, someone will read this text, will come across that number, and will find it small. Quaint. There will be so many more dead. My incredulity will seem naive.

The building where we live has emptied out, and these days, if we meet anyone in the hallways, we avoid each other. We don't even smile, as if the virus could spread with even that small gesture of kindness. It's because we're afraid. All of us. We take the elevator alone. We lock the doors and wait for the sirens that never seem far away. From the window, we see the ambulances race by on empty streets. There they go, I tell my son, who understands enough to be afraid. They never stop, I say. Never.

NEW YORK
APRIL 24, 2020

Three Poems

CHRIS ABANI

Chris Abani (Afikpo, Nigeria, 1966) is a novelist, poet, essayist, screenwriter, and playwright. The recipient of the PEN USA Freedom to Write Award, a Lannan Literary Fellowship, a California Book Award, and a Guggenheim Fellowship, among other honors, his fiction includes GraceLand *(2004),* The Virgin of Flames *(2007), and* The Secret History of Las Vegas *(2014). In 2016, Restless published his short memoir,* The Face: Cartography of the Void. *He is a Board of Trustees Professor of English at Northwestern University.*

MANHOOD

And that uncle with a look of regret
for what was to come, sang softly, jujuwua.
The shuddering moan of blood,
a song to calm the sacrificial,
the loss across the river.
The way a dying animal will look at you
is seared into me.
We die together and all over again.
And the snaking cane he brought down,
like Baal's priests, drew blood,
the prayer is the pause between each lash,
that breathily sung word: jujuwua.
You were Elijah gone to heaven to fetch a fire,
but what of the witness who cannot turn away?

TERMINUS

The true epiphany is that beauty happens
whether we seek it or not.
A boy may become entranced by his shadow
with the dark, with the incessant. Maybe
we carry death with us. It sits behind the eyes
like a shadow on a lake. Sorrow comes to us
like this at the edge of a sea: an immensity.
I chase my brother across continents, devoutly
following in his footsteps trying to find
the one who cannot be found, the lost boy
who haunts me, almost as if he said:
I will fashion you from your relentless darkness.
Yes, we walk everywhere with our shadows
the way Aracelis Girmay's voice hovers
between song and sob as she peels
the lines of poetry from the page.
There is no small measure of pyromania
in this, a self-immolation. Sometimes
we are blessed with the night sky,
a leopard, starred and spotted.

FRAGRANCE

Sometimes grief is acceptance
that love has always been inadequate.
Sometimes it's just another day
and the light comes in through the window.
And my brother calls about ahunji.
A herb somewhere between thyme and clove,
the smell of hunger and satiation at once.
I think of that endless summer of fragrance—
smoke from burning bible pages, the smell
of burned rice sticking to the pan
lifted into elegy by the smell of crushed ahunji.
And blood, coppery and hot, leaking
from the cane welts on our bodies.
And I make a joke and, he laughs, but
it hurts, and he says, stop my ribs—
But he uses the Igbo, egara, a word that
opens and closes like a fish's gills,
life and death pulling and pushing.

CHICAGO
2020

This, Too, Shall Pass

YOSS

Translated from the Spanish by David Frye

Yoss (Havana, Cuba, 1969) is internationally considered one of the most important science fiction writers in the Spanish language. A teacher of literary workshops and lead singer of the heavy metal band Tenaz, his novels in English include A Planet for Rent *(2015),* Super Extra Grande *(2016),* Condomnauts *(2018), and* Red Dust *(2020), all translated by David Frye and published by Restless Books.*

AS I BEGIN to write these lines, it is Monday, April 20, 2020.

A while back last year, when my wife Dania and I first realized that 2020 would be the Year of the Rat by the Chinese zodiac, she complained it was going to be one of the tough ones. I joked that I didn't believe in bad luck and that we could call it the Year of Good Eyesight instead. You know, twenty-twenty vision.

But yesterday, Sunday, April 19, we passed a milestone: 1,000 patients have tested positive for the coronavirus here in Cuba. And finished our first month of quarantine. Yet we presumably still haven't even reached the peak of the epidemic, the point at which new cases start to decline.

Looks like Dania was right and I was wrong. But it's not like being superstitious brings bad luck; good and bad luck aside, we're apparently all in for rough times. I'm afraid that lots of people will end up calling 2020 after the name of the old film—our Year of Living Dangerously.

*

The first news of the new virus arrived as far back as October or November, I don't remember exactly when. The danger didn't seem real. It was far away, in China, some city called Wuhan. How many people in the West had even heard of it before last year?

As a disease, it didn't seem as scary as an outbreak of Ebola or AIDS or that mad cow disease from the '90s. It wasn't even dengue or Zika or chikungunya: not necessarily fatal or neurodegenerative, didn't seem to leave any sequelae. Not much more than some new type of flu. So what?

In Cuba, the prevailing attitude in early February was still the comfortable and carefree one of "maybe the neighbor's son will die, but not me." A false feeling of latitudinal security: this couldn't happen to us.

People do die here in the tropics, but from dengue, yellow fever, exotic diseases, even cholera. Not from a cold. That's something to fear in cold countries, poor people.

There was even a rumor—the umpteenth bit of fake news—that the virus couldn't survive temperatures above 27° C (80° F). It always gets hotter than that in Cuba, even in the winter.

Besides, aren't we always bragging that we have one of the best health care systems in the world? Completely free, with an emphasis on prevention. No need to worry at all.

So we didn't worry. Detergent, toothpaste, and other items did begin to disappear from the shelves—but, you know, what hasn't there been a shortage of in Cuba at some point over the past few years?

*

Our friends abroad, however, painted almost Dantesque scenarios for us in their messages. My friend and Italian translator, Danilo Manera, a writer and professor of Iberian Studies in Milan, wrote to tell me about how empty the streets were there, as if they were under curfew, as he expressed his regrets for having to cancel his plans to visit me in Cuba again in the fall. I felt he must be exaggerating: surely everything would be back to normal much sooner than that.

Mauro, another Italian, a photographer and teacher from Turin and a friend of my wife, kindly sent us photos of the empty streets in that populous industrial city. Those images conveyed a terrible sense of desolation, like snapshots from the Apocalypse: the world of man devoid of man, like some pathetic stage with no actors.

Daría Synitsina, our Russian translator friend, who had visited us in Cuba in November 2019 and allowed us to reciprocate for her hospitality in Saint Petersburg the previous January, withdrew to the countryside, to her brother's dacha near the sea, with her three daughters and her husband from Ghana. Schools had been closed in Russia, and while no one was forced to stop going to work, President Putin announced that no action would be taken against anyone who preferred to stay home.

The slogan "stay home" began to go global. Everyone was living on the internet more than ever: children, taking virtual classes; adults, telecommuting.

What a terrible prospect for Cuba, where connectivity is scarce and slow. As a writer I have an email account from Cubarte, the corporation that provides digital access to artists, with a maximum bandwidth of 42 KB per second, for which I pay just 50 Cuban pesos (the equivalent of about $2) a month, making me one of the privileged. But many millennials go without eating before losing their presence on social media—Facebook, Instagram, Twitter, or their Cuban equivalents.

*

As the situation rapidly deteriorated around the world, and as the TV news spoke only of the escalating crisis, in Cuba everything was business as usual. At least, that was the impression they gave.

*

My mother, Zandra, is eighty-two; she's had operations on one hip, a knee, a breast, cataracts. She uses a cane, even around the house, and she hardly ever goes outside anymore; but her eyes still sparkle, since she used to be an actress, whenever she sees an announcement for an upcoming literary discussion or variety show on TV. Especially if it's coming up soon.

In addition to her acting, my mother always worked as a dentist. She was the first person I heard use the medical term "respirator," instead of the more common "face mask," in my childhood, when she was always heading off to her workplace, the Dental Clinic at H Street and 21st.

I remember that the director, Sardiñas, whose daughter Alina is still a very good friend of mine many years later, was always telling all the dentists to put on their masks. My mother, for her part, hardly ever took hers off. I learned from her that it wasn't some sort of magic mask to protect the user from contagion, but mainly a courtesy that doctors showed their patients, to avoid infecting them with their own germs. Which our mouths are swarming with. Which is why a bite from another human is so likely to cause an infection.

And it's also why—now that using a face mask has become first common, then obligatory, in Cuba due to the pandemic, so much so that if you walk down the street without a mask the police will reprimand you, and they constantly air TV tutorials on how to make masks, how put them on and take them off, even how to wash them—I remain quite skeptical about their effectiveness.

Yes, I cover my face when I'm out and about, just in case I'm an asymptomatic carrier of the coronavirus; there's no call for me to infect healthy people. I'm not that selfish or unconscious. I've never drunk alcohol or coffee, never smoked, never suffered from any respiratory disease, and I've practiced sports regularly and intensely; so the virus might not affect me much, but it could make someone else seriously ill.

But I still don't wear a conventional face mask, just a cloth tied across my face from my nose down: a black scarf with a white design that looks like the lower jaw of a skull. A souvenir from my visit to Amherst, Massachusetts in 2014.

Maybe it's macabre, but after all, aren't I the danger here? Why not put people on notice? Don't come near me, or I'll breathe all over you.

*

The first cases of COVID-19 in Cuba, from mid-March, were detected among foreign tourists. Italians, to be specific. With almost embarrassingly low last-minute sale prices on travel to Cuba, visitors from all over the world had rushed here to take advantage of their forced vacations: isn't it better to go swimming, sunbathe on the beach, and drink mojitos than stay locked up at home?

Many Cubans now think that not shutting off the flow of travelers into the country as soon as the first case was confirmed was a major blunder, but the mistake was understandable; international tourism is currently Cuba's main source of foreign exchange. So if declaring a quarantine, closing the border, and imposing isolation is like killing the goose that lays the golden eggs, why not take maximum advantage of it first and force it to lay more than an egg a day?

It is true that, in the long run, this policy of squeezing out the last drop didn't turn out well. Cuba has had to take financial responsibility for caring for the nearly one thousand tourists trapped here when their own countries closed their borders.

I don't envy them. They aren't on vacation anymore. They aren't allowed to leave their hotels or use the pools. Forget about going to the beach or sightseeing by taxi, much less on foot. They're practically under house arrest, though without the ankle monitor bracelets associated with such sentences in the first world. I suppose we don't have enough of them to go around.

Being a film buff, I can't help but compare their situation with that of the Tom Hanks character in Steven Spielberg's 2004 film *The Terminal*: a citizen from a former Soviet republic is trapped in a New York airport, unable either to enter the country or return to his own, which no longer exists following the breakup of the USSR. Similarly, the character of Serguei, one of the protagonists in the Cuban film by Ernesto Daranas, *Sergio and Serguei*: a Soviet cosmonaut, played by the great actor Héctor Noas, likewise trapped while his country disintegrates, but in orbit, while it's unclear who's to be in charge of getting him back to Earth.

Of course, neither character was in danger of catching a deadly illness.

*

The same Monday afternoon that I found the gym closed and told my wife about it by phone, March 23, she came home a few hours later from the Belarusian embassy with the tough news that all the Cuban workers there had been given compulsory vacations. Laid off, that is, until further notice. To avoid infecting the Belorussian staff.

Dania is a sensible and prudent woman. Unlike me, with my tendency to blow everything as soon as I'm paid, she has the healthy habit of "saving bread for May," to use the fine Cuban phrase. That is, she's set aside a little something. Even so, losing your regular income just when things might start to get more expensive is enough to worry anyone.

For now I also have a couple hundred CUC from when the Czech embassy paid me for my cultural promotion work. But with no foreign tourists coming in, I don't see when I'll be getting any more money. Time to scrimp and save, for sure.

Dania's son Alain came home from school that Monday telling us that it looked like classes were still on. But the TV news panel Mesa Redonda made the official announcement that night: all teaching activities were suspended until at least Monday, April 20. He jumped for joy.

From now on, we'll be spending almost all our time in our small apartment, which some friends call The Tower, after its location high atop the tallest building in the neighborhood. Before, we would only coincide at night. With Dania at work and Alain at school, I was the only one who spent most of the day at home.

Let's just hope that more contact doesn't make things too awkward.

*

The pandemic report is broadcast every morning at eleven. Sometimes it's the prime minister, sometimes the Minister of Health, most often it's Dr. Durán, national chief of epidemiology. Whoever it is, they always have their face mask on as they drone to the cameras about the numbers of confirmed cases, hospitalizations, and deaths, updated as of the night before.

Many of the positive cases are foreigners in isolation. At first, there are few or no Cubans aside from those who've recently traveled abroad or had contact with tourists.

Is this true? Well if it is, such an idyllic situation won't last long.

Almost every afternoon the journalist Randy Alonso and his guests on the TV news panel, all wearing the obligatory masks, also focus on the progress of the epidemic.

The country finally shuts down to tourists, and all or almost all those already on the island proceed to be sent home. Probably a little late, but better late than never, right?

My wife also follows world developments of the situation over the internet, using her smartphone. Through her I learn that President Lukashenko of Belarus has declared that the whole business of quarantines and airport closings is paranoia and exaggerated hysteria from the West; he won't decree anything of the sort in his country, won't even use a face mask.

Same with Brazil's president, Jair Bolsonaro. In one of the former Soviet republics in Central Asia—one of the stans—the president declares the epidemic a fake and sets punishments for anyone who talks about it or even appears in public wearing a mask. He's going full ostrich.

Sweden, for its part, decides to play by other rules: declare no lockdown, let as many citizens as possible become infected, then treat them.

Which method will prove more effective? As I see it, some are sacrificing the economy in the name of health; others, health in the name of the economy. But in truth, it's impossible to imagine modern society without a compromise between the two.

But above all, the show must go on. If, as the saying goes, a stopped boat earns no freightage, a stopped economy starves its citizens.

What will be left of the already struggling Cuban economy when it's deprived of its main source of income, tourism? How many months can we take it? Not many, I'm afraid.

*

Regardless of the "stay at home" campaign, Dania, who goes out every morning to buy whatever food she can find, especially vegetables, says the streets are still full of people and the stores still have endless lines.

My wife is very worried. She inevitably recalls the Special Period of the 1990s, and the shortages in the USSR in the late 1980s, which she also lived through, a time when people got in line first and asked what they were lined up to buy after, because whatever the store had for sale, it was sure to be something you needed.

Dania says that she's not sure she can take any more hard times like this.

There are still street vendors, but the private farmers' markets and butcher shops are closing one after the other. People are afraid of catching the disease, and with good reason. In the few places that are still open, the vegetables and other foods aren't exactly being handled in the most hygienic way.

They're starting to talk about asymptomatic patients, people who transmit the virus without showing symptoms themselves. Healthy, highly dangerous carriers. But how can they be detected? Will every citizen have to be tested? The country doesn't have the resources for such an undertaking.

In general, though Cuba has only limited resources, they always appeal for solidarity and putting a brave face on things. They send brigades of Cuban doctors, with plenty of media publicity, to Italy and other countries affected by the pandemic, even though there's already talk about the high risk of infection run by health workers who treat patients.

Well, you know, Cuba has to keep up its image of solidarity at all costs. We don't have much else left, beyond that symbolic heritage.

*

They loudly hype the case of the British cruise ship with several COVID-19 patients aboard, which after being rejected by several other Caribbean ports is finally allowed to dock in Cuba, where national health personnel attend to the sick while the other stressed passengers are gradually sent home on charter flights.

Very humanitarian, to be sure. Though they say little about the considerable sum Her British Majesty's government has paid the Cuban state for those services. There is some mention of $2 million in financial compensation, though. Very handy in these difficult times, when the blockade or embargo, tightened during these last months of Trump's first presidential term, has made it hard for Cuba to acquire many medical supplies—beginning with the famous artificial ventilators, the ones they say there are never enough of in the countries worst hit by the pandemic, to prevent the most severe coronavirus patients from suffocating when their lungs fill with fluid and they can no longer breathe on their own.

In this internet era, everything comes out, even without Julian Assange and his WikiLeaks.

The Cuban government, of course, denies everything; journalistic transparency has never been a distinguished feature of the supposed dictatorships of the proletariat.

*

There have been some sad and absurd cases of contagion in Cuba. People who put on a Santeria feast despite all the warnings against it; the more than fifty seniors in a nursing home in Santa Clara who got infected, nobody knows how. We're starting to see cases, especially the asymptomatic positives, in people about whom it is impossible to figure out how they contracted it.

In the United States, President Donald Trump does what he does best when things are going bad: divert attention from what is not in his interests, and accuse others. Through his spokesman Mike Pompeo he tries to blame China: according to them, the current pandemic is a man-made virus that escaped from a biological warfare lab.

A pretty theory, if not for the fact that it is precisely China that until a few days ago had the highest number of cases. Brilliant weapon, one that starts off by decimating your own population.

Well, the record for the most cases is now held by the United States, hands down.

So Trump, after first downplaying the new coronavirus, is complaining that the World Health Organization tricked him and that they're protecting China. And he's threatening to take away all their funding.

Why does this remind me of when he ordered the closing of the US embassy in Havana in 2017, with the fantastical excuse that several Yankee diplomats had suffered neurological damage from some mysterious sort of "sonic attacks," obviously caused by the Cuban government?

Throw mud, see if anything sticks—and that's how you divert attention. Must be a golden rule in international politics.

*

On Thursday, April 9, they officially announce through the TV news panel that, beginning on Saturday, April 11, all stores except those that sell basic food and medical supplies will be closed and that public transportation will also cease. Apparently the much anticipated reduction in traffic expected from the lockdown was not enough, so they've imposed this more drastic measure.

Now the country is really going to be paralyzed.

With an ugly premonition, the next day I call Almendares Optics; no answer. Have they also decided to close? So I've wasted more than a week of visual inconvenience for . . . nothing?

Sad but true. Apparently, that's the way it is. On Monday, after calling and calling and again getting no answer, I resign myself to the inevitable—and put my contact lenses back in. I've gone without them for eleven days, and seeing this well again is a huge relief. It doesn't even bother me to know that, sometime later, when the situation returns to normal, I'll have to go through the whole ordeal again.

At least I've tested my strength, and I know I can manage it.

*

They say that they are going to try the doctor and nurse responsible for infecting the seniors at Santa Clara for criminal negligence; they felt sick and feverish, yet they continued to care for their patients without worrying about the harm they might cause.

363

Some of the first COVID-19 patients have already recovered, and now they're helping those who are still ill by donating blood to supply them with immune plasma. Admirable.

A biologist friend tells me, in a long phone conversation, that although he doesn't believe the pandemic is a government stunt, he does think they've been taking advantage of it to reinforce their control over a populace that had been slipping out of their grip recently, given the internet and information transparency.

Could be. After all, like many who have some medical and/or epidemiological knowledge, I don't think the quarantine and the face mask obsession do much good; they only give the illusion that something is being done to control the pandemic—when it already seems inevitable that lots of people are going to get sick. Really, in the modern world it's impossible to keep up the strict sort of isolation that they're calling for.

But what totalitarian government can admit, just like that, that it's powerless against something?

*

Even with half my face covered by my skull-jaw scarf, apparently I'm still a pretty recognizable figure. I've appeared on TV several times in the past year, especially on a very popular science program, *Pasaje a lo Desconocido*, as a biologist and science fiction writer. So several people on the street have stopped me, brimming with the trust in strangers so typical of Latinos, to ask me what I think about the pandemic.

One very serious fellow even questions me about the likelihood that the new coronavirus came from space—maybe in the tail of some comet? Under the circumstances I don't feel like engaging in a long discussion, so I quickly tell him about Arrhenius, the Swedish Nobel laureate in chemistry, and his theory of panspermia as the origin of life on earth, which Fred Hoyle and Chandra Wickramasinghe later subscribed to. And I tell him, it could be; it's not probable, but still possible, and maybe that's why completely new flu strains appear every few years. From outer space!

We part, both satisfied.

As a writer and reader of fantasy literature, it's very curious to live through times like these. Lots of people accuse us science fiction writers of being incurable pessimists and killjoys, claiming we're always prophesying the end of human civilization and even the planet. Whether by giant meteorite impacts, nuclear wars, alien invasions, the appearance of artificial intelligence in computers, or epidemics that destroy the whole population of Earth.

There's always been a very fertile streak of alarmism in fantasy literature. And in this moment it's impossible not to think of Stephen King's classic novel *The Stand*, known in Spanish as *The Dance of Death*. Though in the novel, the near disappearance of humanity, falling victim to the terrible flu nicknamed Captain Trips, is only the opening premise for a confrontation between the forces of light and darkness, which try to recruit their soldiers among the few survivors.

There've been plenty of books and films about the end of humanity from illness. *28 Days Later*; *The Walking Dead*. I suppose we writers try to exorcise our worst fears by writing them out. Or do we hope that those who can prevent these apocalyptic futures from coming true will wake up after reading our works and take action in time?

To be sure, the coronavirus is no Captain Trips. Its case fatality rate does not even reach 7%, no matter how contagious it is, due to its pneumatic means of transmission. But if these months have proved anything, it is that the modern world is not ready to face a large-scale epidemic. It wasn't ready at the end of World War I, when it was decimated by the Spanish flu, and it's less so now that we're more than seven billion people living in the global village.

Let's consider them both mere warnings. Wake-up calls. Because it appears that human culture isn't going to end this time either.

So, then? Is anyone going to do something about it? The next pandemic could be much worse. . . .

*

China seems to be over the worst of it. After eleven weeks of lockdown, you can now enter and leave Wuhan again. Some optimists in Europe are already talking about returning to normal, too, but others fear a second, more deadly wave of the pandemic after summer passes and the worst season for respiratory diseases arrives.

For the moment, the end of the tunnel still isn't in sight—much as you want to hope that it's there, right around the next bend.

*

A legend tells of an Arab monarch from antiquity who summoned his wise men to ask them for something he thought would challenge their knowledge to the limits: he wanted a miraculous spell, a magic formula, that would cause sadness in the midst of the greatest joys but would give a glimmer of hope in the depths of the greatest sorrows.

For a long time the sages whispered together until at last one of them approached the impulsive king and handed him a piece of parchment on which was written a unique, beautiful, terrible phrase:

THIS, TOO, SHALL PASS.

All we can do, then, is remain optimistic and patient, stay at home, and, thinking of the coronavirus, the quarantine, and all our discomforts, whisper to each other by way of consolation:

This, too, shall pass.

And later on, will we ever have a good time remembering and recounting to those who did not experience through it, how challenging these times were.

HAVANA
APRIL 22, 2020

My Seclusion

GIACOMO SARTORI

Translated from the Italian by Frederika Randall

Poet, novelist, and dramatist Giacomo Sartori (Trento, Italy, 1958) is an agronomist specializing in soil who has worked abroad with international development agencies in a number of countries and has taught at the Università di Trento. An editor of the literary collective Nazione Indiana, he is the author of two novels translated into English by Frederika Randall: I Am God (2019) and Bug (2021), both published by Restless Books. He divides his time between Paris and Trento.

I MUST ADMIT that now that this forced seclusion is about to end, I'm almost afraid it will. Partly because my ordinary life is not really all that different from this, and so it's all intrinsically familiar. I'm no cloistered monk, but in my life I've found myself isolated at times, and I've suffered, but I've also learned to endure it. The long days of solitude, concentrating on my writing or scientific studies, sitting at the wobbly table I use as a desk, calm me. The business of living, gestures repeated with tiny but bold variations—making something to eat, tidying up, running a load of washing—is gratifying.

My relationship with the immodest delights that the metropolis I live in flaunts so casually is one of shy and tormented frustration. It's inebriating to walk by outdoor tables where groups of regulars are drinking and ostentatiously enjoying themselves, maybe there's even a counter offering oysters (I adore the savage simplicity of oysters, despite the ethical complications) and I'm transported peering in restaurant windows, thinking how much I'd like to enter and take advantage of those inviting pleasures. It's exciting to feel desire, and to feed it with promises I won't keep. In fact I've always been disappointed in those rare times when I put my money where my mouth is, so to speak: everything was very expensive, and not all that delicious, perhaps spoiled by some trivial thing, or how boring the people were. In short, I had no desire at all to go back to that place that had so attracted me.

So I'm infinitely more at ease now that all those lethal desire traps are closed. I walk—you write out your own permit, valid for one hour, but I cheat a little as any self-respecting Italian would—studying the shutters drawn down, which give me a feeling of order and peace. But privately I know this is something truly unusual: not even during the ineffable Revolution, not even during the heroic Commune, not to mention the German Occupation, when the Parisians were in fact circulating in numbers to rival the Nazi Party, did anything like this happen.

Those magnificent long-legged girls and beautiful women Paris has always been quite generous with have disappeared from circulation, and this too gives me peace. They have probably been evacuated to their second homes, or transferred to a heaven designed by Botticelli, or maybe they're merely sequestered in their apartments, I couldn't say, but in any case, you don't see them on the streets anymore. Not one. The few people around are not beautiful, they're like me (and they keep their distance; when they see me, they cross the street, for fear of contagion). If you observe them—this was especially true during the early weeks—they are very badly dressed, shabby as prison inmates. In short, it's calming not to be troubled by any gorgeous beauty queens, equipped with those handbags dangling from an arm with the elbow bent at a right angle (a manner I privately call "a la parisienne"), staring straight ahead like a Sphinx, pretending not to be aware of their lethal charm. As I've aged, I've simmered down considerably, but this sudden extinction certainly aids my spiritual inclinations.

My walk is more relaxed, and I'm happy to say there are very few cars, and the air is cleaner. I walk by people's houses and dream of other eras and other lives, what I've always loved doing most. I'm supposed to limit myself to a one-kilometer radius, but here too, my Italian side kicks in, and while I stick to the poorer part of town, I go quite a bit further. When the mood strikes me, I snap some photos with my phone. A human shipwreck lying in his or her own filth, sickly delivery persons of goods and food purchased on the Web, precarious writings on the wall, stupefied people just sitting on a bench, tiny doorways to crummy little filthy hotels that, unlike the large luxury hotels, have remained open. Sometimes I post one of these on a social network I'm on, and receive some sparse likes. More than ever I'm conscious of the tyrannical rose-colored glasses conformism of that site meant for photos, more than ever I see it as the showcase of a tarted-up West adrift with its cats and dogs, its photos of flowers and luxuriant vegetation (it is spring, yes) selfies, book covers, photos of vacations before the virus.

If there aren't any pretty girls there are loads of animals to make up for them, and I have an instinctive bond with animals. They don't bother me, they amaze me and they move me. Outside the window of my study, it looks like an aviary; I've never seen such a coming and going of birds. A multitude of cats have appeared on the streets, and the rats dart between your legs, and on the canal not far from home, a pair of swans has built their enormous nest right beside the street, and they take turns sitting on it. The fish in the canal are jumping like dolphins, so pleased that nobody's giving them a hard time.

To be sure, apart from my daily walk, I remain conscientiously confined to my very small apartment, where many other people would surely suffer. However, I'm the son of a mountain climber, and when I was a boy I loved the books my father read about the mountains, where the challenge was to endure extreme conditions and minuscule tents, and indeed this was a way to confront your own limits and improve yourself. And I also loved the accounts my mother read of Sir Francis Chichester's solitary ocean crossings, there too were tiny cramped spaces and metaphysical wildernesses. Paradoxically, even in books about the war—and my father, who was a committed ex-Fascist, had a slew of these—I found this same tension between suffering and satisfaction.

If it was a sailboat, my apartment would be a nine-meter. Though it is small, it has everything I need, and I think I'd be worse off in a larger space. In the tiny kitchen, the dish cupboard is inside a chest suspended in midair out the window. You have to open the window to reach inside. I like to play my own ship's steward, it's fun to calculate how long I can hold out. Even though I eat mostly rice and lentils, and with a few kilos extra can survive for a long time. I rarely go to the supermarket, the way I'd dock at some port to take water and flour on board, and then I can hold out for weeks. I don't have to cross the ocean, I have to traverse these times when quite a few people are in the hospital dying.

And let's not exaggerate, the solitude of these days is quite relative, there's the cacophonic accompaniment of the social networks, overwhelmed with the photos and the words of other solitudes, and the steady downpour of news and interpretations analyzing and reanalyzing the present, and graphics and numbers, not to mention the hundreds of online substitutes for live events, the cheerful surrogates of social reality, books being presented, thousands of videos and concerts, the Web's immensity.

And above all there are video calls, which do away with my uneasiness on the telephone, showing me eyes and the words that bodies I love speak (bodies never stop speaking).

I have experienced real solitude, and it is quite another thing. Many years ago I was living in an African city, headquarters of the foreign legion and other armies, a place that was really an immense whorehouse. The streets were whorehouses, the cafés sordid whorehouses, and even worse the restaurants and the port: there was nowhere I could go. It was too hot to walk, even supposing I wanted to walk. There were no streets with sidewalks, no parks, past the shanty town that marked the edge of that Gomorrah, there were no crops (although theoretically I was here for that), no nature, only a scorching hot rocky landscape. I was getting a salary, I was here to work, but I had no work. Work was always about to begin, and it never began.

I had a house all to myself, and even a large jeep I could use to go wherever I wanted, if only there had been someplace to go. I couldn't telephone, apart from a few minutes once in a while, because the cost was prohibitive. The internet didn't exist, and I had no television. I had a small radio but I was never able to get it to work. Weeks passed, and months, and there was only that void that was destroying me, that survival without purpose and without sense, without contact with other people.

The solitude of today has nothing in common with that angst that had me by the throat; it's merely the condition of a person who needs to be alone to write books, who's chosen to spend his life that way.

Now certainly I interpret it this way partly because, all things considered, this is one of my good periods. I've settled some problems that had caused me to suffer for a long time, I met a person I consider a gift from some god: and we talk every day, and I'll join her when they allow us to travel again. My latest novel came out in the fall, and got a lot of notice; I was lucky because many books published recently simply sank into oblivion. I'm not even doing so badly economically, I have a few months of grace and a contract already signed for several months' more scientific work. Many have financial worries at present, dramatic ones, and worries about their relationships, and I too, in other less opulent times, would be struggling.

But even I, during those first weeks, was quite upset. Rage overwhelmed me. And also angst, under which, digging deep, I found anger. Fury at the predictability—the unpredictable predictability—of what was happening. Capitalism's majestic machinery had run aground on account of its excesses and its recklessness, which I'd always condemned, and of which I was acutely aware because of my scientific preparation and my job. Now the worst was happening, and I was powerless and even felt slightly responsible. I hadn't done enough, hadn't been fully engaged, and even now I was more an onlooker than a militant. And I was angry because all around me I saw only nostalgia for the past, a haste to return to that collective madness of consumption and waste and materialism that had brought about this pandemic. That course would quickly produce even more devastating damage and bring, inevitably, conflict and death.

I must change my life completely, I thought, I must devote myself to political struggle. My harmless studies of the soil were, yes, potentially beneficial in their small way, providing knowledge about the environment, but they were not enough. My writing ran the risk of trapping me in my own solipsism. In a burst of enthusiasm recently, I wrote and published a heartfelt appeal to Italians to cut back sharply on their meat consumption, a concrete measure to begin to come to terms with so-called nature. But no one backed my petition, no one even spoke about it. People were too taken with the bookkeeping of death, the mechanisms of how this virus spreads, and the dangerous reactions of power, quite similar in my native and adoptive countries. In just a few weeks, personal freedoms and the elementary bases of democracy had been swept away. We saw that, contrary to what we'd always thought, it wasn't impossible for capitalism to face an environmental problem of its own making. But it would do so at the expense of democracy. Putting out the fire with people's blood, as it were. The preliminary stage we were living suggested that was our unequivocal future. I felt more angst and, at bottom, rage.

Then I gradually came to, and recognized I'm not the center of the world, I'm not the savior, just reacting to what's happening, like everyone else. It may be that what's happening now are the first steps that will lead us into conflict and death, but that I have no way of knowing. But I do have a small margin of maneuver. I'm afraid of death too, as is the custom in our materialistic society, but I can work on that. In my own small way I'm already doing something. In my work, I've always sought to remind people that soils are fundamental to human survival, and must be spared and protected. And even in my novels, such environmental themes are central. That's already something, although I must make more of an effort. I'll keep my eye on what's happening and aim to do my best. For the moment, I will savor my solitude—and cultivate my garden.

PARIS
MAY 5, 2020

Acknowledgments

The editor wishes to thank the staff of Restless Books for their invaluable efforts in putting this volume together in a relatively short time: Nathan Rostron, Arielle Kane, Alison Gore, Jodi Marchowsky, and Christine Pardue, along with interns Jenna Tang, Ghjulia Romiti, and Kylah Balthazar. Some material first appeared in newspapers and journals. All efforts have been made to contact copyright holders. In the case of any inadvertent omission, please contact the publisher: Restless Books, 232 3rd Street, Suite A101, Brooklyn, NY, 11215, email publisher@restlessbooks.org.

Chris Abani: "Terminus," "Fragrance," "Manhood." © 2020 by Chris Abani. Used by permission of the author.

Majed Abusalama: "My First Lockdown." © 2020 by Majed Abusalama. First published in *Al Jazeera* as "My first lockdown was during the first Intifada" (May 9, 2020). Used by permission of the author.

Daniel Alarcón: "More Was Lost in the War," translated by Ilan Stavans. © 2020 by Daniel Alarcón. © 2020 for the translation by Ilan Stavans. Used by permission of the author and translator.

Khalid Albaih: "Our Old Normal." © 2020 by Khalid Albaih. First published in *Al Jazeera* as "Your 'new normal' is our 'old normal'" (April 27, 2020). Used by permission of the author.

Jon Lee Anderson and Ilan Stavans: "The Age of Calamity." © 2020 by Jon Lee Anderson and Ilan Stavans. Used by permission of the authors.

Chloe Aridjis: "The Measure of a Distance." © 2020 by Chloe Aridjis. Used by permission of the author.

Eavan Boland: "Quarantine." © 2020 by Eavan Boland. First published in *New Collected Poems* by Eavan Boland. Reprinted by permission of W.W. Norton. Used by permission of the author.

Priyanka Champaneri: "Draupadi on the Mountaintop." © 2020 by Priyanka Champaneri. Used by permission of the author.

Nadia Christidi: "Coronarratives." © 2020 by Nadia Christidi. Used by permission of the author.

Louis-Phillippe Dalembert: "Peregrination," translated by Ghjulia Romiti. © 2020 by Louis-Phillippe Dalembert. © 2020 for the translation by Ghjulia Romiti. Used by permission of the author and translator.

Ariel Dorfman: "Confronting the Pandemic in a Time of Revolt: Voices from Chile." © 2020 by Ariel Dorfman. First published in *The Nation* (April 6, 2020). Used by permission of the author.

Eko: "Quarantine Chronicle." © 2020 by Eko. Used by permission of the author.

Carlos Fonseca: "Empty Days." © 2020 by Carlos Fonseca. Used by permission of the author.

Rivka Galchen: "The Longest Shift: A New Doctor Faces the Coronavirus in Queens." © 2020 by Rivka Galchen. First published in the *New Yorker* (April 20, 2020). Used by permission of the author.

Forrest Gander: "Not Without." © 2020 by Forrest Gander. First published in *Emergence Magazine*. Used by permission of the author.

Claire Messud: "In Hiatus." © 2020 by Claire Messud. Used by permission of the author.

Rajiv Mohabir: "An Area of Critical Concern." © 2020 by Rajiv Mohabir. Used by permission of the author.

André Naffis-Sahely: "Wildfires" and "Spanish Flu." © 2020 by André Naffis-Sahely. Used by permission of the author.

Naivo: "The Intrusion," translated by Allison M. Charette. © 2020 by Naivo. © 2020 for the translation by Allison M. Charette. Used by permission of the author and translator.

Andrés Neuman: "Genesis, COVID.19," translated by Ilan Stavans. © 2020 by Andrés Neuman. © 2020 for the translation by Ilan Stavans. Used by permission of the author and translator.

Maxim Osipov: "The Song of the Stormy Petrel: A Cautionary Tale," translated by Boris Dralyuk. © 2020 by Maxim Osipov. © 2020 for the translation by Boris Dralyuk. Used by permission of the author and translator.

Pedro Ángel Palou: "Coronapocalypse: Reflections from Lockdown," translated by Hebe Powell. © 2020 by Pedro Ángel Palou. © 2020 for the translation by Hebe Powell. Used by permission of the author and translator.

Shenaz Patel: "Our Lives as Birds," translated by Lisa Ducasse. © 2020 by Shenaz Patel. First published in Télérama.fr (April 2020). © 2020 for the translation by Lisa Ducasse. Used by permission of the author and translator.

Francine Prose: "Corona Correspondence #25." © 2020 by Francine Prose. First published in the *Sewanee Review* (April 2020). Used by permission of the author.

Frederika Randall: "Augury." © 2020 by Frederika Randall. Used by permission of the author.

Lynne Tillman: "Plague Days." © 2020 by Lynne Tillman. First published in Literary Hub as "Lynne Tillman on the Small Act of Leaving the House" (March 25, 2020). Used by permission of the author.

Mario Vargas Llosa: "A Return to the Middle Ages," translated by Samuel Rutter. First published as *"CORONAVIRUS: ¿Regreso al medievo?,"* in *El País* (March 14, 2020). © 2020 by *El País*. © 2020 for the translation by Samuel Rutter. Used by permission of the author and translator.

Juan Villoro: "The Parable of the Bread," translated by Charlotte Coombe. © 2020 by Juan Villoro. First published as *"Parábola del pan,"* in *Reforma* (April 24, 2020). © 2020 for the translation by Charlotte Coombe. Used by permission of the author and translator.

Gabriela Wiener: "Chronicle from the Vortex of a Global Tragedy," translated by Jessica Powell. © 2020 by Gabriela Wiener. First published as *"Crónica desde el vórtice de una desgracia global,"* in *El Diario* (March 25, 2020). © 2020 for the translation by Jessica Powell. Used by permission of the author.

Wu Ming-Yi: "The Descent," translated by Jenna Tang. © 2020 by Wu Ming-Yi. © 2020 for the translation by Jenna Tang. Used by permission of the author and translator.

Yoss: "This, Too, Shall Pass," translated by David Frye. © 2020 by Yoss. © 2020 for the translation by David Frye. Used by permission of the author and translator.

Matthew Zapruder: "Poem for Hikmet." © 2020 by Matthew Zapruder. First published in *Poetry Society of America* as "Matthew Zapruder on Nazim Hikmet's 'Things I Didn't Know I Loved'" (March 28, 2020). Used by permission of the author.

RESTLESS BOOKS is an independent, nonprofit publisher devoted to championing essential voices from around the world whose stories speak to us across linguistic and cultural borders. We seek extraordinary international literature for adults and young readers that feeds our restlessness: our hunger for new perspectives, passion for other cultures and languages, and eagerness to explore beyond the confines of the familiar.

Through cultural programming, we aim to celebrate immigrant writing and bring literature to underserved communities. We believe that immigrant stories are a vital component of our cultural consciousness; they help to ensure awareness of our communities, build empathy for our neighbors, and strengthen our democracy.

Visit us at restlessbooks.org